It is absolutely clear that a fundamental rethinking of our apparatus of justice is needed today, and urgently so. It must begin with deep reflection on our values and our beliefs about governing. This collection of essays offers the best starting place I have seen for the work in front of us. Read it. Use it.

Todd R. Clear, *Distinguished Professor,*
School of Criminal Justice, Rutgers University-Newark, USA

An impressive list of contributors who seek to make sense of the latest penal developments, transcending the narrow confines of the penal system, and moving beyond the habitual pessimism that invades us all.

Elena Larrauri, *Professor of Criminal Law and Criminology,*
Universitat Pompeu Fabra, Barcelona, Spain

Not since the early 1960s has a generation had a better opportunity to reshape the very premises of the penal enterprise and now on a global basis. New ways of thinking about justice are critical even more than a better empirical basis for making policy.

Jonathan S. Simon, *Adrian A. Kragen Professor of Law and Director of the Center*
for the Study of Law and Society, Berkeley Law, University of California, USA

JUSTICE AND PENAL REFORM

In the aftermath of the financial crisis of 2008, Western societies entered a climate of austerity, which has limited the penal expansion experienced in the US, UK and elsewhere over recent decades. These altered conditions have led to introspection and new thinking on punishment even among those on the political right who were previously champions of the punitive turn. This volume brings together a group of international leading scholars with a shared interest in using this opportunity to encourage new avenues of reform in the penal sphere.

Justice is a famously contested concept and this book takes a deliberately capacious approach to the question of how justice can be mobilised to inform new reform agendas. Faced with the expansive penal developments of recent decades, much research and commentary about crime control has been gloomy and dystopian. By contrast, this volume seeks to contribute to a more constructive sensibility in the social analysis of penality: one that is worldly, hopeful and actively engaged in thinking about how to create more just penal arrangements.

Justice and Penal Reform is a key resource for academics and as a supplementary text for students undertaking courses on punishment, penology, prisons, criminal justice and public policy. This book approaches penal reform from an international perspective and offers a fresh and diverse approach within an established field.

Stephen Farrall is Professor of Criminology at the School of Law, University of Sheffield.

Barry Goldson holds the Charles Booth Chair of Social Science at the Department of Sociology, Social Policy and Criminology, University of Liverpool.

Ian Loader is Professor of Criminology at the Centre for Criminology, University of Oxford.

Anita Dockley is Research Director at the Howard League for Penal Reform.

JUSTICE AND PENAL REFORM

Re-shaping the penal landscape

*Edited by Stephen Farrall, Barry Goldson,
Ian Loader and Anita Dockley*

Routledge
Taylor & Francis Group

LONDON AND NEW YORK

First published 2016
by Routledge
2 Park Square, Milton Park, Abingdon, Oxon OX14 4RN

and by Routledge
711 Third Avenue, New York, NY 10017

Routledge is an imprint of the Taylor & Francis Group, an informa business

British Library Cataloguing in Publication Data
A catalogue record for this book is available from the British Library

Library of Congress Cataloging in Publication Data
    Names: Farrall, Stephen, author.
    Title: Justice and penal reform : re-shaping the penal landscape / edited by Stephen Farrall, Barry Goldson, Ian Loader and Anita Dockley.
    Description: Abingdon, Oxon ; New York, NY : Routledge, 2016. | Includes bibliographical references and index.
    Identifiers: LCCN 2015034290| ISBN 9781138191068 (hardback) | ISBN 9781138191075 (pbk.) | ISBN 9781315640648 (ebook)
    Subjects: LCSH: Imprisonment. | Corrections. | Criminal justice, Administration of.
    Classification: LCC HV8705 .J87 2016 | DDC 365/.7–dc23 LC record available at http://lccn.loc.gov/2015034290

ISBN: 978-1-138-19106-8 (hbk)
ISBN: 978-1-138-19107-5 (pbk)
ISBN: 978-1-315-64064-8 (ebk)

Typeset in Bembo
by Taylor & Francis Books

Printed and bound in the United States of America by
Edwards Brothers Malloy on sustainably sourced paper

In memory of Nils Christie 1928–2015

CONTENTS

LIST OF ILLUSTRATIONS

Figures

Tables

LIST OF CONTRIBUTORS

Ruth Armstrong is Research Associate at the Institute of Criminology, University of Cambridge, UK.

Vanessa Barker is Docent and Associate Professor of Sociology at the Department of Sociology, University of Stockholm, Sweden.

Nils Christie was Professor of Criminology at the Department of Criminology and Sociology of Law, Faculty of Law, University of Oslo, Norway.

Anita Dockley is Research Director at the Howard League for Penal Reform, UK.

Albert W. Dzur is Professor of Political Science at the Department of Political Science, Bowling Green State University, USA.

Stephen Farrall is Professor of Criminology at the Centre for Criminological Research, University of Sheffield, UK.

Barry Goldson holds the Charles Booth Chair of Social Science at the Department of Sociology, Social Policy and Criminology, University of Liverpool, UK.

Jonathan Jacobs is Professor of Philosophy at the Department of Philosophy, John Jay College of Criminal Justice, New York, USA.

Ian Loader is Professor of Criminology at the Centre for Criminology and Professorial Fellow of All Souls College, University of Oxford, UK.

Shadd Maruna is Professor of Criminology and Dean of the School of Criminal Justice at Rutgers University–Newark, USA.

Matt Matravers is Professor of Political Philosophy at the Department of Politics, University of York, UK.

Fergus McNeill is Professor of Criminology and Social Work at the School of Social and Political Sciences, University of Glasgow, UK.

Thérèse Murphy is Professor of Law at the School of Law, Queen's University Belfast, Northern Ireland.

Ann Oakley is Professor of Sociology and Social Policy at the Social Science Research Unit, Institute of Education, University College London, UK.

Sonja Snacken is Professor of Criminology, Penology and Sociology of Law at the Department of Law and Criminology, Free University Brussels, Belgium.

Elizabeth Turner is Lecturer in Criminology and Sociology at the Department of Sociology, Social Policy and Criminology, University of Liverpool, UK.

Noel Whitty is Professor of Human Rights Law at the School of Law, University of Nottingham, UK.

INTRODUCTION

Re-shaping the penal landscape

Stephen Farrall, Barry Goldson, Ian Loader and Anita Dockley

It is a timely moment to be thinking again – and afresh – about penal reform and to consider the prospects and possibilities of creating social and penal institutions that can contribute to the realization of safer and more cohesive societies. For several decades now the prospects for creating such institutions have been bleak. Against a backdrop of rising crime, and the 'heating up' of the penal climate (Loader and Sparks, 2010), penal reform has been a slow and difficult endeavour. Energies have been expended on defending past gains or exposing penal excess rather than on imagining and creating better alternatives; in a hostile climate, decent and effective penal practice has more often than not been advanced by stealth. But are things changing? Are there reasons to believe that space is emerging for new thinking and social action in the field of penalty?

Odd though it may seem, one such ground for hope is the aftermath of the financial crash of 2008. Western societies have now entered a period of austerity, which has – crudely put – meant that the money is no longer available to support continued penal expansion of the sort experienced in the US, UK and several other western societies over recent decades (see, for example, Faulkner, 2010; Hough, 2013; Goldson, 2015). To be sure, it is not at all obvious that austerity alone will create the conditions for penal retraction, still less significant reform, as several commentators have noted (Gottschalk, 2015). Economic austerity has a close cousin called penal austerity. It can nonetheless be observed that austerity has been one important trigger for a slowing down and even retraction of the use of imprisonment in several US states (Garland et al., 2014) and for the emergence in the UK of renewed official interest in rehabilitation (Home Office and Ministry of Justice, 2015). These altered conditions have also prompted introspection and new thinking on punishment among those on the political right who were previously champions of the punitive turn. The 'Right on Crime' initiative in the USA is a prominent case in point: a conservative movement that has vowed to 'be tough on criminal justice spending' and apply principles of small government to the penal domain.[1] At the very least, there has been a marked loss of impetus and appetite for further carceral expansion.

A second reason why a window may have opened for new thinking about penality is the 'crime drop' and its social and political consequences. It is now well established that since the mid-1990s levels of volume of crime across western democracies have been falling (Roeder et al., 2015). Though the reasons for this change are debated, and it remains unclear whether crime has migrated into forms that operate below the radar of official attention and response, there is little doubt that something has changed. One notable effect has been that crime has slipped down the hierarchy of public concerns. An *Economist*/Ipsos MORI poll conducted in March 2015 found that only 12 per cent of those interviewed named 'crime/law and order' as the 'most important issue facing Britain today' – the corresponding figure when the same question was asked in 2010 was 25 per cent.[2] In her contribution to this volume, Sonja Snacken reports a cognate decline in worries about crime across Europe (as measured in recent Eurobarometer polling). We can relatedly observe the declining attention afforded to crime and justice issues in recent national elections both in the US and the UK. In the 2015 British General Election the issue barely featured at all. In sum, evidence is mounting that crime is no longer the structuring presence in social relations and political life that it plainly was during what Jonathan Simon calls 'the years of fear' (Simon, 2014: 156; the exemplar analysis of those years remains Garland, 2001).

The fact that previously heated political debates about 'law and order' have cooled of late has not yet been fully recognized by criminologists. Nor are the causes and effects of this change well understood. It is unclear at present whether we are witnessing a change in the penal climate or merely some temporarily milder weather. It may be the case that social insecurities and anxieties which were for several decades channelled through crime have been refocused on terrorism and migration. It is also implausible – sociologically – to think that the 'crime drop' will usher a return to an era when penal affairs were managed 'off-stage' by insulated elites (Loader, 2006). For all that the character of the crime question may be changing, matters of order and disorder, and compliance and transgression, are likely to remain on the political agenda and continue to be subject to bouts of outrage and scandal. While crime has slipped down the agenda of public concern and political attention in recent years, a legacy of postures, practices and sensibilities forged during 'the war on crime' remain embedded in the landscape.

Yet it may also be that a climate of opinion is emerging that makes it possible to 'get a hearing' for things that had for many decades become politically unsayable; to cast a new eye on previously taken for granted penal practices, and to advance new, more creative and socially progressive, ways of thinking about questions of crime, justice and penal reform (Green, 2015). In the USA, the Supreme Court's prioritization of 'human dignity' in its interpretation of the 8th Amendment prohibition on cruel and unusual punishment has been taken as one small sign that change is afoot (Simon, 2014). The recent publication and discussion of high-profile reports on the *problems* of mass incarceration and police racism and brutality are also indicators that the terms of debate about crime and justice may be shifting. We have in mind here the inquiry set up by the National Academy of Sciences into the causes and consequences of high rates of incarceration (Travis et al., 2014) and the President's Task Force on 21st Century Policing, the final report of which was published in May 2015. The report's opening line captures well the changing climate of public discussion: 'Trust between law enforcement agencies and the people they protect is essential in a democracy.' The hope is that we are witnessing the emergence of a 'new common sense' on crime and justice – one no longer so attached to the idea of crime control as a Manichean struggle between the law-abiding and the dangerous and disorderly, and more willing to countenance justice interventions that acknowledge associations between criminal harm and issues of, say, drug and alcohol abuse and mental health (Simon, 2014: Ch. 7).

This volume brings together a group of internationally leading scholars with a shared interest in trying to open up new avenues of reform in the penal sphere. While there are some discernible differences within and across the analytical positions and perspectives adopted by the contributing authors, what unites the collective 'project' is a concern with thinking about ways in which different conceptions of justice might inform the reshaping of the penal landscapes of western democracies.

Justice is a capacious and contested concept. It is capable of being understood both within the restricted confines of criminal justice and justifications for punishment (Brooks, 2012) and in a wider register of social justice where the issue at stake becomes the criteria used to distribute primary goods within or – increasingly today – across societies (e.g. Rawls, 1971; Walzer, 1983; Sen, 2009). The relationship between these two iterations of justice – criminal and social – has long been a thorny theoretical problem and an urgent practical question for those who think and act in the realm of penal reform. Recent theorization has supplemented the focus on substantive (criminal or social) justice with a concern with the fairness of the procedures by which social burdens or benefits are allocated: the attendant debate on procedural justice has brought into view the association between justice and concepts such as democracy, participation, consent and legitimacy. Research and theorizing on the connections between procedural fairness, legitimacy and compliance has in recent years been increasingly influential in the study of policing and prisons (Bottoms and Tankebe, 2012).

In this volume we adopt a consciously expansive approach to, first, understanding the possible points of connection between the idea of justice and questions of social ordering and penality and, second, the issue of how justice can contribute to the rethinking of penal reform strategies. What is shared across the contributions that follow is the idea that the question of how societies respond to crime, and punish law-breakers, cannot and should not be separated from wider considerations to do with the social and political arrangements of those societies. That relationship between penality and justice is, moreover, understood to be two-way. We need to think about the ways in which ideas and practices of solidarity, democracy, trust and legitimacy (and their partial application, or even absence) shape practices of crime control and punishment. But we also need to explore the reverse idea – namely that police, criminal justice and penal institutions can be civic agents, part of whose purpose is to contribute to the maintenance, repair and strengthening of social bonds and to extending and deepening processes of democratic inclusion.

Several of the contributors to this book start with the question of punishment, its purposes and justifications, which they set out to rethink in various ways. Jonathan Jacobs reminds us that punishment inescapably spills over into matters pertaining to the formation of character and the production of civil dispositions in ways that are mainly corrosive but which can in principle be remade so as to strengthen the quality of a liberal political order. Matt Matravers guides the reader through a thought experiment about the nature of punishment through which he seeks to loosen the association that is typically made between punishment and hard treatment – or suffering. Fergus McNeil, uses the ingenious metaphor of plumbing in order to rethink punishment not simply in terms of the harms to which it responds but also in terms of the goods it may seek to promote. How, he asks, can we think positively about the role that punishment can play in fostering different modes of integration without falling into the (expansionist) trap of thinking that punishment is therefore a good thing? How, in short, can we reinvent rehabilitation? In her contribution, Ann Oakley asks what would happen to our crime control and justice practices, and to 'deep-seated system(s) of control and privilege', if we did more than gesture towards the most stubborn social fact about crime and violence – its close connection to hegemonic masculinity.

The question of the relationship of punishment to concepts of trust and legitimacy is taken up by several contributors. Drawing upon the framework established by David Beetham (1991) and recently extended by Bottoms and Tankebe (2012), Sonja Snacken develops an account of legitimate punishment that accommodates both public opinion/consent and human rights, the latter of which, she argues, are a constitutive part of the basic value structure of European societies. Skilled political leadership is, Snacken contends, vital if these various – often on the surface competing – components of penal legitimacy are to be reconciled in penal practice. Vanessa Barker makes the concept of trust central to her idea of how policing and punishment can be reimagined as forms of civic repair. In so doing, she sketches an agenda for penal reform that encompasses four elements – accountability, responsiveness, participation and the idea that all parties whose lives are touched by police and penal institutions are treated in ways that cultivate practices of 'political friendship' (Allen, 2004). This analysis of the close relationship between justice and inclusive participation is also found in the chapters written by Elizabeth Turner and Albert Dzur.

A concern to make human rights more central to penal practice is a theme that runs across several contributions to the volume – Jacobs, Snacken and Barker most obviously. But that issue receives its most extended and explicit treatment in the chapter by Murphy and Whitty, who, having presented three forms of what they call 'single-mindedness' about rights, lay out a research and practical agenda for thinking through how rights actually structure the consciousness of penal actors and the inner lives of penal institutions – and may do so better in future. The question of prison is also central to the contribution by Ruth Armstrong and Shadd Maruna. Having reviewed what we know about the social effects of imprisonment, they ask: what would have to change if we were to make prisons agents of social justice, institutions designed to maximize civic inclusion? The answer, they suggest, takes us beyond current technicist practices of justice reinvestment towards what they call 'justice reinvention'. Finally, the question of democratic participation is taken up in the chapters by Turner and Dzur. Elizabeth Turner explicitly theorizes justice in terms of its association with practices of inclusive deliberation and makes such deliberation a core element of her proposal for remaking policing as an agent for addressing and repairing social harm. Following a wide-ranging analysis of how institutions organize and colonize the practice of justice and dispute resolution, Albert Dzur makes a cogent case for extending forms of what he terms 'load-bearing participation' and draws lessons from various sites – communities, schools and prisons – where such experiments in democracy have been enacted. The idea of 'democracy as a political system in which people actively attend to what is significant' (Bellah et al., 1991: 273), and of justice as an always potentially transformative face-to-face encounter, also surface as the key lessons of Nils Christie's Afterword.

Faced with the expansive, expensive and corrosive penal developments of recent decades, much research and commentary about social ordering and crime control has legitimately been oriented to critique – quite a bit of it gloom-laden and dystopian. Set against this backdrop, this volume seeks to contribute to a more forward-looking and positive sensibility in the social analysis of penality, one that is worldly, hopeful and oriented towards the creation of more just penal arrangements (Loader and Sparks, 2016). Taken as a whole, this volume aims to rethink – in the altered conditions of today – the ways in which the idea and promise of justice can inform strategies for remaking and reimagining institutions and practices of social ordering and crime control. It brings together scholars from the UK, North America and Europe and it combines the perspectives of criminologists, sociologists, philosophers, human rights lawyers, political theorists and political scientists. Our contributors differ in their analytical approaches and emphasis: some offer new ways to theorize punishment and its relation to justice and cognate concepts; some open up new avenues of empirical enquiry; others make concrete suggestions for where reform strategies might travel. Each, however, provides ideas and insights that resonate in all modern democracies in addressing vital and pressing social and governmental questions – how to combine citizen safety and security with an ethic of justice and human rights within and across various criminal justice spheres including, but not limited to, policing, courts, community interventions and prisons.

The book is the latest manifestation of a close and active collaboration that has developed over recent years between the Howard League for Penal Reform and the academic community. Such collaboration has a long and distinguished history, but it has of late been revived and deepened in various ways. The first concrete example of this was the publication of *The Penal Landscape: The Howard League Guide to Criminal Justice in England and Wales* (Dockley and Loader, 2013). That volume brought together a range of scholars who are members of the Howard League's Research Advisory Group to offer a state-of-the-art assessment of the issues and questions that confront various aspects of the criminal justice environment today. The present volume is in some ways a successor to that collection – hence its subtitle. But it is much more ambitious in scope than the earlier collection. The current book arises from the symposium on 'What is Justice?' that the Howard League for Penal Reform has been running since 2012 under the stewardship of the editors of this volume. The symposium has sought to initiate a range of public conversations about the idea of justice and how it relates to – and might transform – current penal cultures and practices.[3] This book is intended as one of those conversations. Earlier versions of the papers brought together here were first presented at an international conference run as part of the symposium at Keble College, Oxford in October 2013. The publication of this book also marks, along with a series of other events, the Howard League for Penal Reform's 150th anniversary in 2016.

In advancing the wider project, we are grateful to each and all of our contributors as well as to colleagues from the Howard League for Penal Reform, especially to Jenny Marsden for copy-editing the final manuscript. We also wish to thank Tom Sutton, Heidi Lee and other colleagues at Routledge for sharing our belief in the necessity of, and potential for, reshaping the penal landscape. We dedicate the book to our late colleague, Nils Christie, who completed his reflections on 'Justice in Modernity' shortly before his death. Nils committed a long and exemplary life's work to precisely the questions, issues, challenges and possibilities that are articulated in the pages that follow.

Notes

1 See http://rightoncrime.com.
2 www.ipsos-mori.com/researchpublications/researcharchive/3542/EconomistIpsos-MOR I-March-2015-Issues-Index.aspx.
3 These initiatives have included a series of podcasts – termed 'Ideas for Justice' – in which a diverse range of public figures and campaigners respond to the invitation to say what justice means to them and a number of 'one idea for change' workshops for practitioners, policy-makers and other stakeholders in the criminal justice system. Further details can be found at www.howardleague.org/what-is-justice/.

References

Allen, D. (2004) *Talking to Strangers: Anxieties of Citizenship since Brown v. Board of Education.* Chicago, IL: University of Chicago Press.

Beetham, D. (1991) *The Legitimation of Power: Issues in Political Theory.* London: Palgrave/ Macmillan.

Bellah, R., R. Madsen, W. Sullivan, A. Swidler and S. Tipton (1991) *The Good Society*. New York: Knopf.

Bottoms, A. and J. Tankebe (2012) 'Beyond Procedural Justice: A Dialogic Approach to Legitimacy in Criminal Justice', *The Journal of Criminal Law and Criminology*, 102/1: 101–150.

Brooks, T. (2012) *Punishment*. Abingdon: Routledge.

Dockley, A. and I. Loader (eds) (2013) *The Penal Landscape: The Howard League Guide to Criminal Justice in England and Wales*. Abingdon: Routledge.

Faulkner, D. (2010) *Criminal Justice and Government at a Time of Austerity*. London: Criminal Justice Alliance.

Garland, D. (2001) *The Culture of Control*. Oxford: Oxford University Press.

Garland, B., N. Hogan, E. Wodahl, A. Hass, M. Stohr and E. Lambert (2014) 'Decarceration and its Possible Effects on Inmates, Staff and Communities', *Punishment & Society*, 16/4: 448–473.

Goldson, B. (2015) 'The Circular Motions of Penal Politics and the Pervasive Irrationalities of Child Imprisonment', in B. Goldson and J. Muncie (eds) *Youth Crime and Justice*, 2nd edition. London: Sage.

Gottschalk, M. (2015) *Caught: The Prison State and the Lockdown of American Politics*. Princeton, NJ: Princeton University Press.

Green, D. (2015) 'US Penal-Reform Catalysts, Drivers and Prospects', *Punishment & Society*, 17/3: 271–298.

Home Office and Ministry of Justice (2015) *Policy Paper 2010 to 2015 Government Policy: Reoffending and Rehabilitation*. London: Home Office.

Hough, M. (2013) 'Procedural Justice and Professional Policing in Times of Austerity', *Criminology & Criminal Justice* 13/2: 181–197.

Loader, I. (2005) 'Fall of the "Platonic Guardians": Liberalism, Criminology and Political Responses to Crime in England and Wales', *British Journal of Criminology*, 46/4: 561–586.

Loader, I. and R. Sparks (2010) *Public Criminology?* London: Routledge.

Loader, I. and R. Sparks (2015) 'Reasonable Hopes: Social Theory, Critique and Reconstruction in Contemporary Criminology', in A. Liebling, J. Shapland and J. Tankebe (eds) *Crime, Justice and Social Order: Essays in Honour of A. E. Bottoms*. Oxford: Oxford University Press.

President's Task Force on 21st Century Policing (2015) *Final Report of the President's Task Force on 21st Century Policing*. Washington, DC: Office of Community Oriented Policing Services. Available at: www.cops.usdoj.gov/pdf/taskforce/TaskForce_FinalReport.pdf [accessed: July 2015].

Rawls, J. (1971) *A Theory of Justice*. New York: Belknap Press.

Roeder, O., Bowling, J. and Eisen, L.-B. (2015) *What Caused the Crime Decline?* New York: Brennan Centre for Justice, New York University School of Law.

Sen, A. (2009) *The Idea of Justice*. London: Allen Lane.

Simon, J. (2014) *Mass Incarceration on Trial: A Remarkable Court Decision and the Future of Prisons In America*. New York: The New Press.

Travis, J., B. Western and S. Redburn (eds) (2014) *The Growth of Incarceration in the United States: Exploring Causes and Consequences*. Washington, DC: National Academy of Sciences.

Walzer, M. (1983) *Spheres of Justice*. New York: Martin Robertson.

1

FROM BAD TO WORSE

Crime, incarceration, and the self-wounding of society

Jonathan Jacobs

This chapter discusses some of the morally most problematic features of incarceration in the forms it often takes in prisons in the United States and the United Kingdom. The main points of the analysis apply to other countries as well, though it is probably the case that, at present, the issues are most pronounced in the US and UK. That criminal sanction – and incarceration, in particular – is currently beset with numerous morally concerning features is familiar. What is meant to be new in the present approach is the way that the normative architecture of the issue is formulated.

By 'normative architecture' I mean the basic contours of the issue as a nexus of ethics, politics and moral psychology. In brief, the core elements of the view are this: while a liberal polity should not require specific virtues of its members or enforce some specific conception of how to live, it is also antithetical to the principles of a liberal polity for it to *worsen or harm* members in known, regular and avoidable ways. Current forms of incarceration often have such effects. They can be said to amount to a type of *coercive corruption* in ways that raise doubts about their legitimacy. The discussion explains the motivation for that formulation and elaborates the main content and implications of the view.

At the outset we should note that the analysis is not intended as part of an argument for abolishing incarceration as a form of criminal sanction. Nor is it meant as part of a larger argument against punishment as a criminal justice institution in a liberal polity. Parts of the view could be used in the service of such views but that is not my purpose. I would hope that, *even supposing that liberal polities can be justified in punishing and in employing incarceration as a form of punishment*, the analysis supplies strong reasons for concluding that many current practices are of doubtful legitimacy and they merit urgent reconsideration on account of the nature, scale and severity of the problem.

The discussion is divided into three sections. The first explicates a claim about the relation of mutual support between a liberal legal/political order on the one hand, and civil society on the other. That relation is important because the values and principles distinctive of a liberal polity shape the normative issues in quite specific ways. The second section examines morally objectionable features of contemporary incarceration, especially in the US and the UK. The third section considers ways in which certain features of incarceration damage civil society in general, not just prisoners.

The problems discussed are broader even than the wide scope I indicate for them. There is a growing literature studying the ways in which society overall – from the socioeconomic conditions of people's lives to issues concerning criminalization, law enforcement and legal representation – may be accountable for some of the worst aspects of contemporary incarceration. For example, Craig Haney's *Reforming Punishment: Psychological Limits to the Pains of Punishment* includes a good deal of discussion of the ways in which issues of poverty, race and education in society more broadly are criminogenic and aggravate the ills of incarceration by hugely increasing the numbers of people imprisoned (see Haney, 2006, esp. Chapters 4 and 5). The problems are not confined behind prison walls. As Alice Ristroph writes, 'an account of criminal responsibility must not rest with attributions of responsibility for individual criminal acts; it must address collective responsibility for the criminal law itself' (Ristroph, 2011: 109). Even if we do not believe that poverty and unrelieved grim prospects are sufficient excusing conditions or justifications for criminal conduct, we should acknowledge that the issues cannot be adequately understood simply in terms of individual offenders' behaviour. That much is clear whatever one's larger view of just how criminal justice should be understood in relation to justice more comprehensively understood.

The question of whether the former should be assimilated to the latter, or whether it concerns specific principles and issues that are formulable independent of a larger, broader conception of justice is a complex, important question. Also, it seems clear that for many people the opportunity to lead a law-abiding life with a real chance of being elevated out of poverty and out of criminogenic conditions is poor. Here we only gesture toward the complex question of how social conditions and the politics of criminalization and law enforcement shape crime, criminal justice and prison populations. The concerns of the present discussion merit focused attention, though it is true that they are connected in important ways with numerous other, and wider, issues.

The political/legal order as a crucial context

It is both conceptually and ethically important that we are addressing issues concerning punishment in the context of the liberal polity. It is conceptually important because extensive individual rights and liberties are crucial to the liberal polity.

Given the liberal order's preservation and protection of a wide scope for individual freedom, an individual's specific interests and concerns, and what he or she *is like*, are not a proper, direct concern of the state. The liberal state does not require virtue and does not require people to have specific states of character. Yet, a liberal order can only be sustained if people have certain attitudes and dispositions. In the absence of effective concern with certain values and principles, the liberal order will be vulnerable and weakened. The state permits considerable breadth with regard to how people come to have the relevant attitudes and dispositions but we will see the significance of them as the discussion proceeds.

In fact, the liberal polity can accommodate different ideas about why it is important to endorse that kind of political/legal order. Some persons might have a commitment to the relevant values and principles because they believe that there are no objectively justifiable conceptions of a well-lived life and, *thus*, the state should preserve freedom for people to pursue the sorts of lives they wish, as long as they do not harm other persons or violate their rights. Others might be committed to the liberal order because they believe that there *are* objectively best kinds of lives but the state should not exercise coercive power in requiring people to lead their lives in those ways. Another possible endorsement of liberalism could be the understanding of how intolerance, dogmatism and repression ruin lives and the resulting appreciation of liberalism's commitment to minimizing the role of such phenomena in politics. Still others might be committed to liberalism because they believe that the exercise of one's own rational agency is necessary for leading a life both desirable and worthwhile, a deeply gratifying and flourishing life. That commitment to liberalism is supported by the belief that a genuinely happy life requires the agent's own causality, *thus* the state should impose upon people minimally in regard to how they lead their lives.

In recent and contemporary political theorizing, diverse conceptions of what underwrites the liberal polity have been developed (Galston, 2002; Rawls, 1971; Sen, 2011; Rasmussen and Den Uyl, 2005). Moreover, it may be that one of the distinctive features of a liberal polity is that it can accommodate a measure of disagreement about exactly what *form* it should take and about the best justifying reasons *for* it. To require that there should be some single, specific basis of commitment to a political order could itself take an illiberal form. A liberal polity can tolerate a measure of disagreement over at least some matters regarding even basic institutional arrangements and policies.

There is an important relation between (i) the political/legal order and (ii) civil society. The political/legal order is a matter of formal institutional arrangements, legal requirements and permissions. This includes official institutional practices and officially defined responsibilities, roles and procedures of justice. Civil society is the complex, overall sphere of voluntary activities and associations that people undertake in contexts that are not determined by requirements issuing from the state. In the US for example, civil society comprises a great deal of economic activity, leisure and cultural life, religious life, philanthropy, education and other kinds of activity. There are laws requiring people to attend school for a certain number of years, and the state regulates significant aspects of banking, finance and commercial activity, as well as providing extensive infrastructure. However, the economy remains largely a market economy and, for instance, there are all sorts of options with regard to education, what kind to pursue, where and to what level.

There is vibrant, open civil society in the UK, too, despite the state's larger role in various departments of life (such as health care). Though the state has significant roles in various aspects of people's lives in the US and the UK, there is no question that civil society in these countries is more open, dynamic and pluralistic than it is in Saudi Arabia, North Korea and the People's Republic of China. The role of the market in the economy of China is striking, but it is clear that (i) the Chinese Communist Party exercises control over departments of life that are open in the US and UK, and (ii) even in the economic sphere mainland China practises something rather like state-capitalism rather than permitting a more genuinely open market as the basic arrangement.

What is so significant about the relation between the liberal order and civil society? It is that *the liberal order makes possible civil society* (in the institutional, formal sense) and *participation in civil society can provide people with reasons to want to preserve (or extend the freedoms of) the liberal order*. Enjoying the freedoms of participation in civil society can motivate acknowledgement of the value of the liberal rule of law. Elected representative government and democratic process are crucial elements of a liberal order. But the daily business of living occurs in the context of civil society. That is the setting in which freedoms are enjoyed in what we might call a *routine* way, many of them likely to be taken for granted by people living in a liberal polity. However, there is nothing automatic or given about them. In the absence of certain political-legal institutional arrangements, and in the absence of certain attitudes and habits, those freedoms may be neither valued nor understood.

It was noted that a liberal polity does not require people to have specific virtues. Yet the preservation of that order does depend on what I shall call a 'civil disposition'. By that I mean a reliable, durable combination of trust and trustworthiness, the absence of which renders the kinds of interactions and associations constitutive of civil society far less possible. Trust and trustworthiness make possible a complex metabolism of voluntary interactions without everyone needing to first undertake an examination of whether the persons with whom they are interacting can be expected to act in good faith. Whether the issue is making a purchase in a grocery store, organizing a sports league for neighbourhood children, raising funds for the community hospital, renting office space or one of countless other undertakings, it can be a largely routine matter because people have a more or less civil disposition. When renting office space one might have a lawyer read the fine print on the lease. When raising funds for the hospital it is prudent to be sure that someone with a record of handling other people's money responsibly has responsibility for the funds. A civil disposition does not altogether eliminate the need for checking credentials, due diligence or being legalistically fastidious. Nonetheless, the vast range of activities people undertake in civil society on a voluntary basis and with a general presumption of confidence depend upon the prevalence of a civil disposition.

A civil disposition is relevant to the present issue in a twofold way. First, the sort of harm done to many prisoners undermines or impedes a civil disposition on their part, making it more difficult to re-enter and participate in civil society successfully. Second, there is a deficit of civil disposition on the part of many members of free society. That results in additional obstacles to ex-prisoner re-entry, including the attitude that, even after completing sentence, a former prisoner is still to be regarded as a *criminal*. That can deepen ex-prisoners' demoralization and alienation, the effects of which can last beyond release from prison, complicating the effort to reintegrate into free society. There is further discussion of this matter below.

The relationship between the liberal order and civil society is important in another respect. I remarked that the liberal order is weakened by the absence of certain broadly shared values and concerns. To have genuine, extensive freedoms people need to be willing to tolerate at least some kinds of conduct and ways of life they might find objectionable or obnoxious. They need to restrain themselves from imposing their values upon others through explicit political means such as legislation or other, more informal but still powerful means (consider how a newspaper's editorial slant and radio programmes and social media can be employed with such purposes in view). The pluralism of a liberal order depends upon acknowledging a distinction between something being offensive or objectionable and it being genuinely harmful to other persons and their interests and welfare, and it requires toleration of some degree of the former.

At the same time, pluralism needs the support of some widely shared valuative commitments and concerns, many of them reflected in the criminal law. While, inevitably, there are disagreements over what is to be criminalized in a liberal polity, there will almost certainly be strong agreement on the propriety of criminalizing certain types of conduct because of how they impose upon freedoms and cause harm. The disagreements occur against a background of broad, stable agreement on many matters. As Andrew von Hirsch has commented:

> That dissensus exists in modern societies on some legal and ethical issues is undeniable: witness the ongoing debates about abortion and drug use … . However, if we turn our attention to the core areas with which the criminal law should deal – the prohibition of victimizing acts of force, theft, and fraud; and the enforcement of certain basic duties of citizenship such as the payment of taxes and the preservation of the environment – there appears to be a greater degree of agreement.
>
> (von Hirsch, 1996: 105)

In a society under a liberal rule of law it is likely that the great majority of citizens will not only be law-abiding, they will be law-abiding *because* they find many of the action types that have been criminalized abhorrent. 'Most of us comply with the law most of the time, not because we rationally weigh our fear of the consequences of detection against the benefits of the crime, but because to commit the crime is simply unthinkable to us' (Braithwaite, 1989: 81).

Regarding some conduct such as the use of certain drugs, pornography and prostitution there may be persistent disagreements (though with shifting constituencies of support and opposition) and their legal status in a particular society may be different at different times. In the US, for example, attitudes regarding same-sex marriage have changed dramatically in recent years. Attitudes regarding certain types of drug use are leading to a reconsideration of laws criminalizing possession and use of marijuana. Some people may feel as strongly about these matters as they do about murder or larceny. Still, even they are likely to recognize that there is a difference between types of conduct that must be criminalized in order for life in the society to be anything but terrifyingly precarious, and types of conduct that are not so utterly unacceptable.

Taking the liberal rule of law seriously involves recognizing that one may disagree with some matters of law but still see that such disagreement is not a basis for flouting the law or for regarding obedience to law as discretionary.

> In such instances, what the law says to those who dissent from the stand it takes is not simply and unqualifiedly that the conduct in question is wrong, but rather that this is now the community's authoritative view. Even if they dissent from its content, they have an obligation as members of the community to accept its authority—to obey the law, even if they are not persuaded by its content, unless and until they can secure a change in it through the normal political process.
>
> (Duff, 2001: 65)

Taking that obligation seriously is related in an important way to a civil disposition. It is an important form of the restraint mentioned above. We may need to accept the obligation to obey at least some laws we do not endorse; we may need to refrain from criminalizing some types of conduct we regard as unacceptable. At any given time there will be some emotionally charged, divisive issues, but the fact that those divided by them seek to get their way through the political process attests to the shared sense of the legitimacy of the state's institutions.

The border between what is regarded as clearly and always morally wrong and what is a matter of currently prevailing norms regarding right and wrong is at least somewhat porous. A society's view of where the border is to be drawn can change over time (consider slavery in the US and women's suffrage in the UK and US). In any case, one aspect of a liberal state's legitimacy is that criminalization and criminal sanction are, at least in general, recognized as morally intelligible. By 'morally intelligible' I mean that the reasons for prohibiting and punishing the conduct in question can be recognized as relevant to the well-orderedness of society and welfare of its members and in a way that is fair. If new laws were to apply retroactively or if strict liability was extended dramatically to range across many kinds of outcomes for which people clearly were not responsible, those would fail the test of moral intelligibility. It is crucial that decisions concerning criminalization are not arbitrary or dependent upon justificatory considerations that people cannot comprehend.

Requiring moral intelligibility is a way of respecting persons as *voluntary, accountable agents who act for reasons* and can understand considerations in favour of, and also against, a type of conduct. Moral intelligibility involves a broad notion of 'moral', i.e. concerning the context of action–relevant rationality. If the putative justifications of laws are inscrutable they impose upon people prohibitions and requirements that fall outside the scope of what could be rationally endorsed (even if, in fact, they do endorse them).

In seeking to loosen what, for some, may be a tight connection between criminal conduct and moral judgement Hyman Gross has argued:

> Even if all crime can confidently be said to be morally wrong, it is a serious mistake to suppose that conduct with which the criminal law concerns itself is prohibited and made punishable for the reason that it is morally wrong. Conduct is prohibited by rules with teeth only because it is thought of as some sort of peril.
>
> *(Gross, 1979: 15)*

One could argue that 'peril' constitutes a morally significant factor because it concerns harm to persons, but it would be a mistake to assert a necessary connection between moral wrongness and justified criminalization, as though it is suitable to criminalize any immoral conduct. A liberal polity should permit broader rather than narrower scope for free action, and broader scope is likely to include types of conduct over which there is moral disagreement. One mark of a healthy liberal polity could be its success at accommodating morally contested issues without those disagreements tearing the social fabric or motivating serious doubts about the legitimacy of the political order.

We will see, however, that incarceration impacts many prisoners in ways that motivate doubts about the legitimacy of criminal justice. Some of the most objectionable features of current forms of incarceration are antithetical to liberal principles, not primarily on account of the *suffering* they cause but on account of the *harm* or *damage* done by severely restricted freedom of action and movement and elimination of opportunities for exercising discretion and making decisions, aggravated by lack of privacy, overcrowding and violence (Sykes, 2007, esp. Chapter 4). That weakens the civil disposition, and the weakening not only diminishes the civility of civil society but also undermines the liberal order.

The kinds of damage done by incarceration

As a brief preliminary to the discussion of the sorts of damage done by incarceration to character and agential capacities we should indicate the chief reasons the issue is significant for a liberal polity.

We have noted that it is part of the normative architecture of a liberal state that persons are to be respected as voluntary, accountable, rational agents. The recognition of agency, of persons as capable of acting for reasons and capable of endorsing or rejecting laws, policies, practices and institutional arrangements on the basis of reasons and principles, is integral to the liberal polity. Whatever one's conception of the proper, specific institutional form of a liberal polity the notion of persons as voluntary, accountable, rational agents is fundamental to the distinctive character of a liberal order. If persons are not addressed and treated in ways that recognize and respect that status, it is a failure to accord what they are owed as members of a liberal polity. It is not as though being found guilty of a crime renders someone less than a member of a liberal polity, even if one is (justifiably) deprived of certain liberties and the normal scope of voluntary activity.

We cannot take up the general question of the justification of punishment here. Suffice it to say that it is possible to justify punishment – including the deprivation of liberty and some of the forms of suffering that accompany that deprivation – in a liberal order. In addition, given the significance of respecting persons as voluntary, accountable, rational agents in a liberal order there is a role for desert, for retributivist considerations in the justification of punishment. We find this reflected in the work of several theorists of punishment, even when they do not agree wholly on the details of the justification of punishment or its aims (Morris, 1968; Duff, 1991; Murphy, 1988). Concern with desert is closely connected with regard for persons as agents accountable in the distinctive ways made possible by rationality.

Considerations of desert can only have a justifying role in a context of rational, accountable agents. If those punished are not agents in the relevant sense, capable of understanding reasons for action and the role of norms and principles in how the state regards and treats them on account of their conduct, then desert would be out of place. Typically, persons *are* agents in the relevant sense (making allowance for excusing conditions) and that is why desert has a vital role in determinations of the proper proportionality of punishment. Moreover, desert has a more complex role than just functioning as a ceiling on proportionality, a guard against punitive excesses. It is true that the concept *desert* does not imply highly specific punitive measures. *Nothing* implies specific punitive measures in a fully non-conventional, extra-institutional way. Still, considerations of desert have an integral role in thinking about what constitutes proper proportionality. It is not as though the involvement of conventional elements means that just *any* conventions of punishment can be acceptable.

Supposing that punishment can be justified, why and how does so much current incarceration *fail* to be justified? A summary answer to that question is this: the terms and conditions of a great deal of recent and contemporary incarceration not only cause suffering (which, again, in certain measures is justifiable), they also *worsen* and *damage* prisoners, which is a way of being disproportionate. Also, the various impediments and disqualifications many ex-prisoners face are ways for punishment to exceed just desert by continuing after official completion of sentence. While the present emphasis is on desert, even in consequentialist terms current carceral practice would still be morally objectionable. If prison *worsens* prisoners, damages their characters and corrupts relevant dispositions, then it is doubtful that current practices are a cause of a net gain in overall social welfare in either the short or long term.

Among the most relevant considerations of moral psychology is that there is evidence that the length of many sentences and the conditions in which they are served demoralize many prisoners in ways that erode their capacity for moral agency and for practical rationality generally. Incarceration has an impact on a prisoner's states of character that goes deeper than boredom, negativity of mood, frustration, strongly feeling the lack of intimate associates, and so forth. The impact of prison can shape fundamental attitudes and capacities for agency. Often, the impact persists beyond release from prison. To explicate this claim we need to consider a few key points concerning character.

By *character* I mean relatively stable dispositions that guide choice, and shape reactions, attitudes and motives (Jacobs, 2001). A person's states of character are specific ways in which capacities for practical reasoning, decision and reactive sensibility come to be disposed through a combination of natural temperament, experience, habituation and one's own voluntary activity. It is almost certainly not possible to separate out, in exact 'amounts', the involvement of each of those sources of character. Still, it is clear that each of us has certain natural propensities and susceptibilities; that our own choices, actions and responses make a difference to what we are like by shaping dispositions to choose, act and react in specific ways; and that how we are habituated and otherwise influenced by others contributes to shaping our states of character.

A human being normally has capacities for deliberation, the weighing of considerations, reflecting on motives, the ordering of priorities and the formulation and pursuit of ends, interests and commitments. In addition, a human being has various affective capacities and susceptibilities and those become disposed in more or less stable ways on the basis of experience, the ways in which others are examples (for good or ill) and our own efforts to shape our reactive attitudes, desires and patterns of motivation in certain ways. Jointly, the ways in which those capacities are actuated and integrated are constitutive of states of character (Jacobs, 2001, esp. Chapters 1 and 2). Our lives would be very different if that were not so.

There are complex and important questions concerning the proper role of considerations of character in criminal justice. Moreover, it can be difficult to eliminate or minimize considerations concerning character at several important places in overall criminal procedure. States of character are often thought to be relevant to sentencing. In addition, judgements concerning someone's motives can influence beliefs about what type of action we take the person to have performed. That is, what we claim someone *did*, what action it was, can be shaped by our understanding of what the person's motives and perspective were, and by features of the person's characteristic strategies of practical reasoning. It is not as though a person's capacities for rational agency are separate from their states of character, with there being only contingent relations between capacities and character. States of character are not merely accessories to who a person is as a rational agent – they are more integral to agency than that.

In addition, thoughts concerning states of character can be important in one's self-conception, one's aspirations and regrets, one's beliefs about how others regard one's self, and in a person's narrative self-understanding, whether it is reflective, honest, detailed and thoughtful or self-deceiving, defensive and self-servingly selective. Knowledge of someone's states of character enables us to anticipate many of their reactions, understand their decisions and attain insight into their motives and emotions. We might go to certain confidants or family members with *these* issues, and go to other persons with *those* issues because our knowledge of their characters enables us to judge who is likely to be considerate of our feelings, slow to anger, interested in helping, willing to listen carefully, and so forth. Judgements and expectations based upon beliefs about people's characters inform all variety of our interactions, shaping our approaches to issues and to people.

To be sure, in many contexts we have little knowledge of people's characters and do not need such knowledge. In civil society we have a great many anonymous interactions of many kinds and we have various expectations based on people's roles and responsibilities rather than their characters. Still, even if character is not especially relevant in a particular context, the ways that people behave will reflect their characters and some people, on account of character, may be unsuited or especially well suited for specific roles and responsibilities.

'Surface' features of the way a person presents or expresses him or herself, features such as being extroverted or especially sociable, or whether someone is typically cheerful or hardly ever enthusiastic might not be related in significant ways to states of character. Both a cheerful person and a person who rarely exhibits enthusiasm or exuberance could be courageous, generous, honest and fair, for example. Or they could both be selfish liars. Someone who is cheerful could fail to be compassionate and generous. The latter two are states of character while the former is not. Character states are the basis for many judgements that have *normative significance* on account of how those states figure in deliberation, decision and in what the person regards *as reasons*, and *why*. It is not always evident whether a feature of a person is a state of character or some other element of the individual, such as an attitude, a perspective or a way of carrying and presenting oneself. In addition, these can be related to each other in various ways. For example, someone's cheerfulness might be related to her also being friendly, considerate and compassionate. Still, it is fairly clear that, for example, kindness is more than just a 'surface' feature of a person; it concerns one's motives and aims, though it also has typical modes of presentation or expression. In general, states of character are ethically relevant features of people. To be sure, socio-historical factors can influence what sorts of states of character are encouraged and praised, regarded as admirable or the opposite. In addition, the particularities of an individual's social and economic place in society can influence her values, concerns and priorities. While numerous influences shape character, we can see that one's states of character have important roles in the explanation of one's judgement, actions and responses, and that they are thickly implicated in how one's capacities for agency are disposed and exercised.

One's character is not a fully *fixed* set of dispositions if by 'fixed' we mean (i) there is no role for voluntariness in coming to have them, or (ii) that states of character are unsusceptible to change, or (iii) that a person's character states are exhibited in a completely uniform way across different contexts. Those notions of fixity fail to acknowledge several aspects of character. Those aspects include (a) the respects in which one's own voluntary activity has a role in coming to have states of character, (b) the ways that reasoning and judgement are involved in many expressions of character, and (c) the respects in which effort and aspiration can be important to how one sees one's own character and might seek to develop or change it. One is not assured of being able to change a disposition, even with sustained effort. Nonetheless, aspiration can shape motivation and the effort to alter some of one's dispositions and have certain states of character in a more efficacious and full-fledged way (Annas, 2011, esp. Chapters 2 and 3). Someone who comes to the recognition that she should be less selfish and more concerned with the welfare of others might be motivated to undertake a project of ethical reorientation.

In addition to the ways that social and cultural context can shape a person's values, aims and aspirations, character itself can be part of the explanation of why certain courses of action or reasons for acting may not even occur to a person or are dismissed when they are presented (McDowell, 1979). It may simply not occur to a firmly virtuous person that one way out of a difficult situation is to lie (Williams, 1982). That would not be a failure of imagination; it would be a sign of deeply rooted virtue. Suppose there is someone else, some innocent person, not well positioned to expose the lie, who can be blamed without much chance of the (lying) accuser being found out. An agent's virtues may render that consideration simply irrelevant. Similarly, appealing to a profoundly vicious person's sense of humanity may be utterly pointless; that person may *have* no sense of humanity or may have a highly selective one. In general, however, even firmly anchored dispositions do not mean that it would be ethically irrelevant or altogether hopeless to suggest to the person that there are reasons in favour of trying to alter aspects of one's character. We do not always know just how firmly established our dispositions are.

It would be very encouraging if, in penitentiaries and correctional institutions many prisoners undertook successful projects of ethical self-correction. However, the evidence of how incarceration affects people is not encouraging in that way. It appears that for many prisoners the experience is demoralizing and has a damaging effect on their states of character and self-conceptions (Sykes, 2007: esp. Chapter 4, and Duguid, 2000: esp. Chapter 8). Thus, '[It] is not surprising that the over-crowded conditions and anti-rehabilitation ethos that characterized the last several decades in American corrections appear to have greatly increased the criminogenic risks that persons must overcome following incarceration' (Haney, 2006: 224), and Joan Petersilia writes:

The average inmate coming home will have served a longer prison sentence than in the past, be more disconnected from family and friends, have a higher prevalence of substance abuse and mental illness, and be less educated and less employable than those in prior prison release cohorts. Each of these factors is known to predict recidivism, yet few of these needs are addressed while the inmate is in prison or on parole.

(Petersilia, 2004: 53)

While a liberal state is to be restrained with regard to requiring certain specific character states, there is a lengthy tradition of conceptualizing punishment in terms of correction and prisons as penitentiaries. The aspiration of neutrality has become more pronounced in liberal theory as societies have become more pluralistic and diverse. At the same time, there seems to be less broad and less deep support for institutionalizing reform as an aim of incarceration. This is explained in part by discouraging results of such attempts in the nineteenth and twentieth centuries and in part by the fact that in earlier times, at least in the US, there was a more generally shared set of religious and ethical views and a more widely shared conception of rightly ordered values and character than in recent decades.

It is not necessarily inconsistent with the principles of liberalism for punishment to have reformation among its aims. It depends on how that end is understood and how it is pursued. Suppose there is good evidence for believing that certain prison conditions and activities in fact tend to be helpful to repeat offenders who have a genuine interest in desistance, and suppose they encourage non-trivial numbers of prisoners to make genuine attempts at ethical self-correction. This would be a situation in which the conditions effectively encourage certain changes in dispositions but not by the imposition of a systematic, explicit project of pursuing reform. There is a growing literature on desistance and the sorts of attitudes and perspectives on the part of offenders that are effective (Laub and Sampson, 2001).

Eliminating some of the worst features of current carceral realities would surely be helpful. Those include severe overcrowding; the near-total absence of activities involving the exercise of prisoners' deliberative capacities; the extensive, and sometimes long-term use of solitary confinement; and the extremely limited opportunities for prisoners to exercise judgement, make decisions and cooperatively address issues of common concern. It is important to keep in mind that many offenders *enter* prison with poor education, low levels of literacy and histories of violence and substance abuse, and many suffer from psychological ill health. 'Like prisoners with mental illness, many of those with developmental disabilities remain officially undetected in the prison systems in which they are housed' (Haney, 2006: 253).

It appears that either there is not yet an adequate understanding of what those more salutary conditions are; or the resources or the will to reorganize imprisonment in accord with such conditions are lacking. It is clear that for many prisoners the prevailing conditions in prison, including the policies and practices governing prison life, are not conducive to incarceration achieving constructive ends, apart – perhaps – from a modest measure of incapacitation and deterrence.

Another agency-eroding feature of prison life is that prisoners are often subject to disciplinary regulations and sanctions they regard as arbitrary, and in many cases they are correct to see them that way. Rules and patterns of enforcement can be altered without warning and prisoners can find themselves having to adjust to changes in administrative culture and emphasis that are inscrutable to them. Moreover, 'correctional institutions are particularly unforgiving places. The consequences of doing things incorrectly or inadvertently violating a rule may be severe' (ibid.: 253). Sykes writes:

> The rules, the commands, the decisions which flow down to those who are controlled are not accompanied by explanations on the grounds that it is 'impractical' or 'too much trouble'. Some of the inmate population's ignorance, however, is deliberately fostered by the prison officials in that explanations are often withheld as a matter of calculated policy.
>
> *(Sykes, 2007: 74–5)*

To the extent it is possible, prisoners often formulate their own rules and regime of self-government, enforcing a certain conception of solidarity or at least cohesion with 'us against them' as its animating principle. These unofficial social systems often include many different statuses and roles, as well as sanctioning those whose behaviour is not in compliance. Some prisoners find this an important source of feeling as though they have some power. However, for others, who may be on the lower rungs of the hierarchy or lacking standing altogether, this can mean that they are exposed to a second source of power and sanction and their situation can be doubly vulnerable, liable to sanction imposed by the staff of the prison and by other prisoners (ibid., esp. chapter four).

Various associative bonds (including race-based or ethnicity-based gang affiliation) imported into prison life from outside are often bases of solidarity, protection and status in prison life. Often, there is a prison culture into which one is inducted, a culture upholding various 'traditions' of regarding offenders of certain types in specific ways. For example, sex offenders are often despised and singled out and require special protection against prisoner assaults. Homosexual prisoners are often victims of homophobic violence, and offenders who have harmed or killed children are sometimes targets of a sort of selective moral outrage on the part of other prisoners. Unfortunately, these elements of prison culture and social order tend not to encourage a civil disposition.

There is disturbing data on the frequency of sexual coercion, violence and assault in prison.

> More recent [than the 1980s] estimates suggest that over 20% of prisoners are coerced into some form of sexual conduct while incarcerated. In a mid-1990s study, researchers reported that about 22% of male prisoners had been

victimized in this way (including 13% for whom the coerced sexual activity involved intercourse) and that, once having been victimized, prisoners were targeted for an average of nine nonconsensual incidents of sexual contact.

(Haney, 2006: 182–3)

This illustrates how prison can impact prisoners' attitudes concerning what they regard as acceptable or 'manly' and how the culture of prison life shapes their conceptions of themselves and others. As Haney suggests, 'having engaged in these forms of sexual aggression – in response to the deprivations and pressures of prison life rather than preexisting preferences – may distort their sexual identity and their ability to create and maintain sexual intimacy outside of prison' (Haney, 2006: 184). Sexuality is just one issue among many through which prisoners' sensibility, valuative judgements, self-conceptions and regard of others can be powerfully influenced by some of the widespread features of prison life.

Prisoners serving very long sentences are especially likely to lead lives of tedium in which there is precious little scope for deliberation, decision, planning or cooperative undertakings involving mutual reliance and trust, except in the very limited ways that are tolerated by both administrative culture and the prisoners' culture. The sorts of habits and attitudes required for participating in civil society have almost no place in many prisoners' lives, and so the capacities for them go unexercised and undeveloped. In addition, the incidence of physical violence, near-total lack of privacy and inadequate resources for addressing mental health issues aggravate the situation. 'Whether they experience some form of PTSD [post-traumatic stress disorder] or some other diagnosable psychological disorder, many prisoners do adapt to the pains of imprisonment by developing overt psychological symptoms – clinical depression, paranoia, and psychosis' (ibid.: 185). In a study of prisoners in British prisons one ex-prisoner remarked:

> I remember being there – on the edge of a precipice. You lose all hope. Your inner self changes, You start to think, what does anything matter? It was about four years before I left [Whitemoor prison], around 2003, about eight years in … . It builds up – your efforts to be good are not being recognised. You think, "I've tried, you're not going to give me a chance." You hit a wall where nothing matters. Suddenly, you are capable of anything. You'd betray anyone … . You lose your moral compass.
>
> (Liebling, 2013: 6)

The study's author noted that '[a] lack of attention being paid to hope and identity in high security settings was identified as a major difficulty for prisoners and those managing or working in high security prisons' (ibid.: 4). It is understandable that order and security are priorities for prison officials and staff. However, in American and British prisons the form of day-to-day life that results from the overriding concern with order and security is what I call 'rule-governedness without *telos*'. The limits on prisoners' activities are so stifling that it deadens their sense of having any capacity for agency and whatever developed capacities they have are at serious risk of atrophy. The study of British prisoners concluded that prisoners came to regard relationships as 'risky' and '[t]he very word 'trust' was regarded with some alarm' (ibid.: 6). Another result, similar to what is found in US prisons, is that '[p]risoners became ever more cynical and distrusting, and their behaviour increasingly and narrowly instrumental or strategic. They were experts in manoeuvre – and yet outflanked by an unfathomable system that had all the power' (ibid.: 5).

Those conditions and experiences harden the sensibilities of many prisoners and lead to the formation of habits and attitudes antithetical to civil society. Many prisoners develop symptoms of psychological illness, or the illnesses with which they entered prison are aggravated and untreated. But even many prisoners who are not clearly candidates for psychiatric treatment or psychotherapy adjust to prison life by acquiring dispositions that are conducive to, or indicative of, vicious states of character. The overall upshot is that the conditions many prisoners endure are, in effect, what I have called *coercive corruption*, even if they are not intended that way.

The erosion of agential capacities – capacities for prudent rational self-determination and for participation in the many threads in the fabric of civil society – occurs through the damage done to character. Some prisoners' vices are aggravated. Some, as indicated in the quotation above from a prisoner, feel that they have become morally disorientated in a way that involves a real sense of loss. For some, one of the aspects of demoralization is loss of the sense of being capable of investing one's activities with any but the thinnest meaningfulness (Haney, 2006: 173–4). It is not as though one can just decide to 'wait it out' and resume a more normal, more independent, engaged form of life upon release, especially for those with lengthy sentences. The effect of incarceration can go deeper than that, resulting in lasting changes. What one 'has to do to survive' may become rooted as a set of general dispositions, impossible to tactically, *ad hoc*, discard or leave behind upon leaving prison. That is one way that such conditions of incarceration can diminish the civility of civil society, weakening the modes of agency that underlie a civil disposition and rational self-determination.

In addition, prison culture can do significant damage to trust and to prisoners' conception of the legitimacy of the rule of law and the criminal justice process that has put them in prison. Prisoners find that it is often very much in their interest to trust almost no one and, for reasons of the kinds indicated above, many come to have little respect for law and its agents of enforcement.

There are enlightened prison wardens and in some prisons there are innovative attempts at ameliorating particularly bad conditions. Such attempts would have better prospects if they did not often run up against constrained resources and a lack of broad public support. In some prisons prisoners work hard at earning benefits for good behaviour that are meaningful, such as the opportunity to take courses offered in the prisons. No doubt, some prisoners do undertake a project of reflection and manage to reorient themselves in ways that are very much to their credit. While we should be on guard against misrepresenting the reality and exaggerating its worst features, the overall picture is disquieting.

The wider impact on society and the liberal political/legal order

Even if we maintain that the state should not be directly concerned with requiring people to have specific states of character, there are good reasons to pay more attention to the effects of incarceration on character. The state does not require persons to be notably virtuous. Of course, it is an excellent thing if citizens strive to acquire and also exercise civic virtue. Civil society gains considerably and it can also be salutary with regard to political order if people are trustworthy, trusting, honest, fair and exercise other virtues. However, in a large, diverse, pluralistic society it is perhaps most important, in the political sphere, that people should (i) be restrained in regard to imposing their values on others through the political process and legislation, (ii) exhibit sufficient trust and trustworthiness to sustain the legitimacy of political institutions, and (iii) tolerate ways in which others choose to lead their lives and their different perspectives (though within limits of reasonableness), acknowledging the difference between finding something obnoxious and being harmed by it. There is no single, fixed line distinguishing those two categories but an important aspect of the civility of civil society is the willingness to share the social world with people unlike oneself and the groups with which one identifies. Habits and attitudes of certain kinds are necessary for certain general principles to actually, effectively inform political and social life. The latter are not freestanding and self-sustaining, so to speak (that is an important respect in which people's characters are strongly relevant to a liberal polity even if not a direct concern of the state).

That is one of the main reasons why the ways in which prisoners are damaged is significant. Many prisoners undergo very little preparation for release, they lack financial resources, and often there is not a stable domestic environment to which they can return. Many lack records of employment of the kind that are helpful in seeking work. In addition to deficits in education, financial resources and skills, many ex-prisoners have also endured conditions that have idled their capacities for reasoning, judgement, cooperative problem solving and formulating and pursuing ends. A long prison sentence can idle the capacities one needs for *planning* a life in contrast to simply *waiting* in a condition of enforced idleness. The result can be a withering of unexercised capacities and a loss of agential capacity, not just a suspension of the exercise of it.

Even if we believe that imprisonment should involve deprivation of liberty, it should still be possible to permit opportunities and occasions for the constructive exercise of rational capacities. Otherwise, what reason is there to think that incarceration will make a constructive difference apart, perhaps, from incapacitation and possibly deterrence? Those count, to be sure; but if they are more than offset by the damage done, the matter needs reconsideration. If there are reasons to conclude that the prison experience impedes the acquisition of a civil disposition and undermines it if it was present, it is plausible to suppose that released prisoners will not be prepared for re-entering free society, at a cost to the civility of society.

In the current state of affairs there are many persons who are law-abiding, have little or no inclination to commit crimes and exhibit a basically civil disposition, yet feel little concern for those who are incarcerated and for the difference made to society by having such large numbers of prisoners enduring what they endure. In addition to indifference to prisoners' predicament there is also 'positive' incivility, i.e. the attitude that offenders *should* suffer a great deal and that *whatever* happens to them while incarcerated is either deserved or in any case morally acceptable *because they are offenders*. Such intensely punitive views should not be interpreted as especially robust versions of retributivism; they are vengefulness unconditioned by thoughtful proportionality and a genuine concern with just desert.

It is understandable that some categories of offenders are regarded with especially strong feelings of animus and distrust, and popular anger is very easily aroused by stories of persons committing crimes while on probation or being charged for the fifth time, having been convicted of offences each of the prior four times, and the like. Yet even such cases are not justification for a general unwillingness to adopt a civil disposition toward ex-prisoners. People are willing to continue imposing punishment *beyond* completion of sentence, in the sense that they maintain hostile, unsupportive attitudes in ways that reflect a deficit of civil disposition on the part of free society, and that only aggravates the situation.

There is weakening of the civil disposition from two directions, from inside prison and from outside it. Many prisoners and ex-prisoners do not regard the institutions and practices of criminal justice as legitimate. That loss of trust can weaken support for the liberal-democratic rule of law. At the same time, many members of society are loath to accept ex-prisoners as equal participants in civil society. Rather than this being an effective way to *preserve* the liberal rule of law, it weakens it, and is indicative of a selective commitment to liberal values and principles. It is a source of incivility through accepting and endorsing the fact that large numbers of people undergo avoidable, undeserved suffering. It reflects a willingness to ascribe to prisoners a diminished status as members of the society. That is a contraction of the liberal rule of law insofar as it involves regarding some citizens as irremediably second-class.

A liberal democracy needs to be on guard against people losing interest in it. A loss of interest on the part of those who do not regard the political order as including them or as responsive to their interests and rights can put liberal values and principles at risk. Disenfranchisement and other official and unofficial barriers to participation in political life and civil society can result in a situation in which laws and policies apply to large numbers of people who are excluded from the political process through which laws and policies are formulated. That loss of interest has a counterpart on the part of law-abiding members of society when *they* conclude that persons who have been punished *should* have a fundamentally and permanently diminished status as members of society.

There are, of course, many advocates of prisoners' rights and many opponents of mandatory sentences and excessively harsh sentences, and there are many individuals and organizations helping ex-prisoners return to free society and try to lead law-abiding lives. Most prisoners do want to lead law-abiding lives. Though there are plenty of repeat offenders, most prisoners are not career criminals, and many prisoners' desires and aspirations are like those of upstanding, civil, law-abiding citizens. At the same time, it must be acknowledged that many persons enter prison with already damaged agential capacities and vicious states of character. Both they, and many who were not already damaged as agents, are worsened by their prison experience. The question of the causal role of overall social conditions in explaining criminal conduct is very complex, highly important and strongly relevant. All we can say about it here is that, whatever the causal contribution of those conditions in general, we know that prison often aggravates and reinforces dispositions of exactly the most unconstructive kinds and inhibits the acquisition and strengthening of more civil and prudential habits and attitudes. While considerations of risk and dangerousness must be taken into account, it is a distortion of just desert to assume that because someone was convicted of a crime that person should have diminished liberty, opportunity and standing indefinitely.

There are prisoners who do not succumb and are not damaged in the ways indicated. Some master their circumstances and make mastery of them a central project in ways that do not lead to despondency and agential impotence. There is some evidence that prisoners who have very firm political commitments are able to meet their circumstances with resolve and a determination not to be 'broken' (Moen, 2000). But the fact that it is possible to withstand the conditions of incarceration (when they are especially objectionable in the ways we have been considering) should not be interpreted as a reason for concluding that perhaps they are not so morally problematic.

It should be evident that there are reasons of principle and reasons concerning the public interest for a large-scale rethinking of how we punish. That rethinking should take seriously the mounting evidence of the damage being done to individuals and the wider consequences of it. How we regard and treat prisoners and ex-prisoners is not only a *sign* of the civility of society and the liberalism of the rule of law, it also makes a *causal* difference to, respectively, the civility and liberalism of the social world and political order.

Acknowledgement

I would like to thank the editors of this volume for the opportunity to contribute to it and for their helpful comments and suggestions. In addition, Routledge has granted permission for me to use material that has appeared in some earlier publications of mine, especially: 'Punishing Society: Sanctioning Others and Harming Ourselves', in *Criminal Justice Ethics*, December 2014. Also, I would like to acknowledge a grant from the National Endowment for the Humanities 'Enduring Questions' programme. That grant was for development of a course, 'Is Virtue Its Own Reward'. That study of issues concerning agency and character helped shape some of the ideas articulated in this paper.

References

Annas, J. (2011) *Intelligent Virtue*. Oxford: Oxford University Press.

Braithwaite, J. (1989) *Crime, Shame, and Reintegration*. Cambridge: Cambridge University Press.

Duff, R. A. (1991) *Trials and Punishments*. New York: Cambridge University Press.

Duff, R. A. (2001) *Punishment, Communication, and Community*. New York: Oxford University Press.

Duguid, S. (2000) *Can Prisons Work?* Toronto: University of Toronto Press.

Galston, W. (2002) *Liberal Pluralism: The Implications of Value Pluralism for Political Theory and Practice*. New York: Cambridge University Press.

Gross, H. (1979) *A Theory of Criminal Justice*. New York: Oxford University Press.

Haney, C. (2006) *Reforming Punishment: Psychological Limits to the Pains of Imprisonment*. Washington, DC: American Psychological Association.

Jacobs, J. (2001) *Choosing Character: Responsibility for Virtue and Vice*. Ithaca, NY: Cornell University Press.

Laub, J. H., and R. J. Sampson (2001) 'Understanding Desistance from Crime', *Crime and Justice: A Review of Research* 28, (ed.) Michael Tonry. Chicago, IL: University of Chicago Press, 1–69.

Liebling, A. (2013) 'Moral and Philosophical Problems of Long-Term Imprisonment', manuscript, 6. This paper is a developed version of a paper the author delivered at the 'Re-Thinking the Ethics of State Punishment: Philosophy, Theology and Penal Theory,' 3rd Annual McDonald Symposium in Theological Ethics, held at the University of Cambridge, May 13–15.

McDowell, J. (1979) *The Monist* 62(3), 331–350.

Moen, D. (2000) 'Irish Political Prisoners and Post Hunger-Strike Resistance to Criminalisation', British Criminology Conference, Selected Proceedings, vol. 3, June.

Morris, H. (1968) *The Monist* 52(4), 475–501.

Murphy, J. G. and J. Hampton (1988) *Forgiveness and Mercy*. New York: Cambridge University Press.

Petersilia, J. (2004) *When Prisoners Come Home: Parole and Prisoner Reentry*. New York: Oxford University Press.

Rasmussen, D. and D. Den Uyl (2005) *Norms of Liberty: A Perfectionist Basis for Non-Perfectionist Politics*. University Park, PA: Pennsylvania State University Press.

Rawls, J. (1971) *The Idea of Justice*. Cambridge, MA: Harvard University Press.

Ristroph, A. (2011) 'Responsibility for the Criminal Law', in *Philosophical Foundations of Criminal Law*, (ed.) R. A. Duff and Stuart P. Green. Oxford: Oxford University Press, 107–124.

Sen, A. (2011) *The Idea of Justice*. Cambridge, MA: Belknap Press.

Sykes, G. (2007) *The Society of Captives*. Princeton, NJ: Princeton University Press.

von Hirsch, A. (1996) *Censure & Sanction*. New York: Oxford University Press.

Williams, B. (1981) 'Practical Necessity' in *Moral Luck*, Cambridge: Cambridge University Press.

2

PUNISHMENT, SUFFERING AND JUSTICE

Matt Matravers

Punishment generally – perhaps conceptually – involves the deliberate infliction of suffering on the punished. In modern liberal democratic states this can take the form of restrictions on liberty (for example, requirements to perform community work or prison) or financial penalties such as fines. To inflict such suffering on a person outside the domain of punishment would normally be to violate his or her rights in important ways. For this reason – *because* punishment involves such 'hard treatment' – punishment calls for a specially robust justification and the main focus of penal philosophers has been to offer such justificatory arguments.

This chapter is addressed to a different, although related matter. Imagine a system of 'punishment' otherwise identical to the current system, but which involves no hard treatment. To borrow from Andrew Ashworth's characterization of 'the rationale for the criminal law', it would 'declare ... serious public wrongs'; it would 'provide for the public censure of those who commit [such wrongs]'; and it would do so 'by means of conviction under a procedure that satisfies due process'. However, it would *not* follow this by providing 'for a punishment up to a proportionate maximum' (all quotations Ashworth, 2011: 129). In short, consider as a thought experiment the possibility that convicted offenders are censured for their criminal acts, but that is as far as it goes (this will be qualified as the chapter progresses).[1] The question is: what, *from the point of view of justice*, would be lost (if anything) were we to adopt such a system?

The question is related to the question of the justification of punishment in a fairly obvious way. If one believes, for example, that the justification for punishment lies in 'offenders getting their just deserts', then this will inform what one believes about the injustice of a situation in which deserved suffering is not in fact inflicted on convicted offenders and, *mutatis mutandis*, for other familiar accounts of the justification of punishment. Nevertheless, there are elements of even these familiar arguments that are brought out by asking the above question rather than the traditional one. That this is so can only be shown by engaging with the arguments.

It is often said that punishing the offender through deliberately imposed suffering is 'owed' to the victim, or to some specified third parties, or even to the offender themselves. These claims provide the structure of much of what follows, but first it is worth confronting two preliminary issues and three more immediate worries that might arise from the proposal to abolish hard treatment; worries grounded in the need to incapacitate, to assure and deter, and to avoid a regression into some kind of pre-social state. In discussing these worries, the chapter is not yet concerned with the perspective of *justice* so much as with the overall plausibility of a system without suffering. After all, if such a system is manifestly unworkable, then it is not worth considering whether it is or is not also unjust.

Finally, it is assumed throughout that the system being assessed is to apply to a society much like those found in the contemporary developed world. Although the discussion is in large part abstract and philosophical, this assumption is critical in what follows. Hegel's comment about penal codes applies equally to broader issues of criminal justice: they are 'primarily the child[ren] of [the] age and the state of civil society at the time' (Hegel, 1942: §218A). A different society, populated by differently motivated persons, might well need a different system.

Preliminary one: is it punishment?

One preliminary issue is whether what is being considered here is a system of 'punishment' or some other thing altogether. This issue arises out of the definition of punishment. For many people one element of the definition of punishment is that it involves the infliction of suffering (see, for example, the famous definition given in Hart, 2008: 5). A social practice that does not involve this element, even if it is otherwise identical to the social practice of punishment, cannot then be punishment but must be something else.

This worry could be met by renaming the social practice being considered here.[2] That seems contrived, but if a critic were to insist on calling what is being discussed something other than 'punishment', then what is at stake here is the question of what from the point of view of justice would be lost if we replaced the system of punishment with the alternative system (whatever it is called).

The point is that no normative consequences follow from such definitional moves; they merely displace rather than resolve the central question(s). That is, the issue of whether a system that involves the deliberate infliction of suffering on an offender for an offence is justified or not cannot be resolved by referring to the definition of punishment (for a discussion of the 'definitional stop' see Hart, 2008: 5–6).

Preliminary two: can we 'say it with words'?

A related, but substantive, issue arises in the claim that the *censuring* or *denunciatory* function of punishment can be retained without the element of hard treatment. That is, the argument presupposes that what Ashworth calls the 'public censure' of those who commit serious public wrongs can be retained and the thought might be that hard treatment is needed in order to express this censure.

There are two possible ways of understanding this claim.[3] On the one hand, hard treatment might be intrinsically connected to the expression of appropriate censure such that no other means of expression are possible.[4] On the other, hard treatment may just happen to be the way we express such censure.

If the intrinsic claim were correct, then the position being investigated here would be nonsensical. We could not retain censure while doing without hard treatment. But is there any reason to believe that it is correct? Of course, censure itself may be something that is experienced by the censured as 'unpleasant' or 'painful', but that is independent of whether the censure itself must be expressed in the form of hard treatment. For example, when I censure you for breaking a promise I express my disapproval verbally. I may be aware that you will find my censure painful – and I may think less of you if you do not do so (for example, if you shrug off my complaint as if it does not matter) – but my intention might be merely to put the facts to you such that you understand how those facts have affected me. I do not need to intend to cause you unpleasantness or pain (indeed, any such intention might be thought inappropriate).

What of the contingent claim? Censure is sometimes appropriately expressed through hard treatment just as romance is through roses. That is, social practices, like words, have meanings and those meanings are not susceptible to Humpty Dumpty's claim that 'When I use a word … it means just what I choose it to mean – neither more nor less' (Carroll, 1897: 123).

Of course, this is true. Censure for the commission of serious public wrongs is often expressed in hard treatment, but surely if there are good reasons to adjust our practices, then this can be done. Consider, as an example, a social practice in which praise, or the marking of a 'rite of passage', has traditionally involved the giving of ivory. Once there is good reason to restrict the use of ivory, there is good reason to change this practice. Of course, this will take time and in the interim some people will misunderstand or misread what is happening, but there is nothing inexplicable or extraordinary about such a change.

The analogy with ivory might be thought misleading. After all, a young man turning eighteen (for example) might be disappointed to find that he has not been given the traditional ivory gift he was expecting, and traditionalists might think it a shame, but the dangers that accompany misreadings of the situation are less pressing than those that might occur in punishment. In both cases a message is sent (or not), but in the case of penal hard treatment the message is more important than in the case of a gift or token.

This worry may take two forms. It might be thought that hard treatment reinforces the message that the wrong done is a serious one. Consider the following from Fitzjames Stephen:

> Some men, probably, abstain from murder because they fear that, if they committed murder, they would be hung. Hundreds of thousands abstain from

it because they regard it with horror. One great reason why they regard it with horror is, that murderers are hung with the hearty approbation of all reasonable men.

(Stephen, 1863: 99)

The question of to what degree the law in general, and penal sanctions in particular, reinforce moral norms is a difficult one, but insofar as that message is conveyed by the law 'declaring wrongs' and by different degrees of 'censuring wrongdoers', the proposal here (to do without hard treatment) secures whatever effect is achieved.[5] The 'horror' of murder is surely secure even without the gallows.

The second, more nuanced, worry is that penal sanctions themselves and not just the declaratory and denunciatory forces of the law have been needed to change the social meanings of certain offences. Domestic abuse and drink driving are often cited as offences that the public only took to be serious once they were punished as serious crimes. Put another way, as described the ivory case has no negative externalities, but a change in sentencing that leaves a sub-set of society thinking that the absence of hard treatment for a domestic abuser or a drink driver indicates a return to the view that these are not serious offences certainly does.[6]

This is a serious worry and any change in the social practice of punishment to one without hard treatment will have to be slow and managed, but this is of course true for many reasons. Penal hard treatment does convey a conventional message. That message is important and must be retained. The claim here is that, if hard treatment and censure can be 'decoupled' – in managed incremental steps – then there is nothing nonsensical in considering a world with censure but without hard treatment.

The above concerns relate to the possibility of having a practice of 'punishment' that fulfils its declaratory and denunciatory functions without involving the deliberate infliction of hard treatment on the offender. I have shown that this is possible. The concerns that follow are of a different order. They derive from the thought that, whatever the issues of justice that might surround hard treatment, its infliction is unavoidable if society is not to become irredeemably unstable. The reasons include the need to incapacitate the dangerous, to deter potential offenders and assure those who obey the law that 'crime does not pay', and to avoid vendettas. Let me take each in turn.

Incapacitation

Clearly, some proportion of offenders are and remain dangerous in the sense that were they simply to be released after conviction they would predictably go on to do serious harm to others. Assuming that such people can be identified or that the rate of false positives is reasonable, there is little option but to incapacitate such people.[7] For some, such incapacitation could be achieved by actual or electronic monitoring, curfews and so on, but for some it may have to involve incarceration. Such restrictions will be deliberately imposed, and will presumably cause the offender to suffer, but nevertheless need not be imposed *as punishment*. Rather, we can model incapacitation on something more akin to quarantine. In other words, the punishment would be complete with the public censuring of the offender after conviction. The incapacitation that follows, if needed, would not be punishment, but merely incapacitation on grounds of future dangerousness.

Does this make a difference? It might seem not. If the offender is found guilty, censured and then incarcerated, it might seem like a distinction that does not make a difference to describe the incarceration as preventive or 'quarantine' rather than punishment. This is perhaps acutely so from the offender's point of view. Yet, of course, there are important distinctions here. Preventive detention is not punishment. An individual is quarantined only for as long as they are dangerous and, while quarantined, they do not lose other rights (such as the right to wear their own clothes). In short, preventive incapacitation should meet Stephen Morse's conditions of being 'maximally humane and minimally intrusive' (1999: 297), including the use of non-incarcerative methods where possible.

Preventive detention of course brings with it dangers and is open to abuse (von Hirsch, 1976). However, our concern here is with a potential world without hard treatment (deliberately inflicted as punishment) and with the worry that any such world would be unable to respond to dangerous individuals within it. That is not so.

Deter and assure

A second worry in response to the proposal to do without suffering may well be that without the threat of hard treatment there would be no deterrence and, relatedly, no assurance for the law-abiding that others are obeying the constraints imposed by the criminal law.

We know comparatively little about the deterrence effects of marginal changes in sanctions and about the general effect that having sanctions attached to the criminal law has on behaviour (von Hirsch, 1999a), but while it is reasonable to assume that we are not all devils whose desires to offend are constrained only by the threat of sanctions, it is implausible to think that we are all such saints that in the absence of any such sanctions we would invariably abide by the law.

To take one example of why saintliness might not be a reasonable standard to which to hold people, consider the return of annual self-assessment tax forms.[8] In England and Wales, these forms are due on a certain date in the year (31 January). Were there no penalty for returning such forms late, or with false information, then general obedience would decline for two reasons. First, some people would give in to the temptation not to fill in the forms or to falsify the information. Second, others would come to believe that their obedience was 'a mug's game'; that they were obeying when others were not. Such a perception − that others are free-riding on one's obedience − gives rise to an assurance problem (for a discussion of the importance of assurance to the justification of punishment, see Matravers, 2000).

To think this through requires us to think about both different categories of crime and of potential criminals. It may be that we need to be very fine-grained about this, but for the moment consider two exemplars of each. In terms of crimes, think of individual tax evasion of the sort just discussed and of murder. In terms of people, think of those who are tempted either directly or by loss of assurance to commit these offences and those who are not so tempted (for whom the threat of sanctions is inert).

Perhaps the number of people who would be tempted to evade paying tax in the absence of any penalties or assurance that others are paying their (fair) share is substantial. That group would include those who are currently tempted to avoid paying but who do so because of the threat of sanctions (call these 'potential direct offenders'), and those for whom the threat is currently inert but who would move from that position to the position of being tempted because of the belief that they were the victims of free-riding (call these 'potential assurance offenders'). If we assume that the number of potential offenders of both kinds is substantial, then the stability of the system requires that there are penalties for late or non-submission and for concealing the truth about one's income. However, must we conceive of such penalties as *punishments*?

Assuming a background that is roughly just, avoiding tax is a moral and criminal wrong, and those who offend are then rightly condemned and censured (they are 'punished' as understood here). Does it follow that an additional penalty that is attached to non-compliance need be thought of as the imposition of suffering as punishment rather than as what it is: a 'prudential supplement' (von Hirsch, 1993) that ensures most of us behave like angels and are not tempted towards devilish behaviour (in this context anyway)?

I think not only do we not have to think of these penalties as punishments but that in many cases we do not do so. Consider the rhetoric around the penalty for non-, or late, return of tax forms (and compare it with that which accompanies other forms of criminality). For example, the following is from an HMRC[9] document on proposed changes to the penalty regime:

> we know that the vast majority of *customers* meet their obligations in full … and that *penalties* are only applied to a small minority … . [W]e want to consider whether we can better differentiate between deliberate and persistent *non-compliers* and those who might make an occasional *error*.

And again,

> Penalties are applied to encourage taxpayers to comply with their obligations, to act as a sanction for those who don't and to reassure the compliant majority that they will not be disadvantaged by those who don't play by the rules… *penalties have a role to play in influencing customer behaviour*, encouraging voluntary compliance and discouraging non-compliance … . Penalties impose additional costs or restrictions on customers, emphasising that non-compliance does not pay.
> (*Emphasis added. All quotations HMRC, 2015*)

That is the language of compliance and non-compliance – of penalties as influencing behaviour – not the language of punishment inflicted for past wrongdoing.[10]

However, whereas the argument might have purchase in the example of tax it might be thought that it will not in our second example: that of actual and potential murderers. This is because the situation seems to be very different in that there are presumably far fewer people who obey the injunction because of the threat of sanctions and there is no assurance problem. That is, the number of 'potential direct offenders' is very small and the number of 'potential assurance offenders' – those who would move from the 'not tempted' to the 'tempted' because of the belief that they are being treated unfairly by free-riding murderers – is zero.

That said, it is possible to rephrase this in line with a well-known theory of punishment so as to generate an assurance problem. Think of obedience to the law generally as a burden, but one worth shouldering because, assuming others also obey, it gives the great benefit of security under the rule of law. In that case, any unlawful behaviour is an instance of free-riding, and were that behaviour not to have sanctions attached to it, others could think of themselves as 'victims' of that free-riding and be tempted themselves to free-ride.[11]

Although such a modification of the position is conceptually possible – and may be an important component in our understanding of crime and punishment – it is surely implausible to think the numbers here are sufficient to render the system unworkable. Those directly tempted – that is those whose obedience to the law of murder is ensured only by the threat of hard treatment – are few in number. As for the modified free-riding problem, for all that we have and often use the familiar phrase 'to get away with murder', it seems implausible to think that there are large numbers of people who would follow up the thought 'he's getting away with murder' with the thought 'so I might as well get away with theft' having otherwise not been so tempted.

Of course, the discussion above involves a number of empirical claims that may or may not turn out to be accurate. Were they not to do so, the conclusions generated would need to be revised. Nevertheless, it is possible to conceptualize the territory independent of the way the numbers work out. That is, the arguments from which any conclusions would follow can be stated independently as follows.

There are classes of legal rules such that absent some penalty beyond public censure for their violation: (1) a sufficient number of people would disobey to threaten social stability; (2) a number of people would disobey and this will lead to others disobeying given the lack of assurance so that the level of disobedience threatens social stability; (3) the effect on obedience will not be sufficient to threaten social stability.

Legal rules that fall into the first two categories would need to be supplemented with penalties. If these are extensive and the penalties needed are large, then the system would resemble a system of punishment as traditionally conceived. Understanding what constitutes an unacceptable level of disobedience (glossed here as 'threatening social stability') is a complicated normative matter, but once this is settled the issues are empirical.

One apparently paradoxical result of such a proposal is that, if we assume that prohibitions on such core offences as murder fall into category 3, then there may be no additional 'penalty' for murder but one for tax evasion (and within the class of offences that have additional penalties, there may be higher penalties for more tempting but less serious offences than for those that are more serious, but less tempting). This result may be not only puzzling but potentially problematic if the 'censuring message' is undermined by the scale of the penalty. That is, the blame and condemnation for murder ought to be much greater than for tax evasion. However, if the murderer is 'merely' condemned and the tax evader is both condemned and fined, then it might be thought that the message being conveyed is that the latter is more serious than the former.

These responses depend on thinking of the penalty as part of the punishment rather than as a technique for securing obedience where people are tempted otherwise. If the *punishment* (which here means the public censure) for tax evasion were more severe than that for murder, then that would be a problem. But what is being discussed is not that. Rather, we might think of the regulative penalty the way we think of paying a deposit at the time of booking a service that is forfeited by parties who do not turn up. Such deposits can be substantial (far in excess of some criminal fines).

Avoiding vendettas

For the sake of completion it is worth mentioning a final possible worry about a criminal justice system without suffering imposed as punishment. Perhaps – possibly for evolutionary reasons – the desire for revenge is a psychological predisposition shared by human beings.[12] If it is, there may be a case for thinking it is best regulated by the state and that, should the state fail in that function, vendetta practices will arise that threaten peace, stability and, insofar as such practices will be error prone, justice.

Such a position has historical antecedents both in the sense that vendetta societies have been replaced by societies of law and in the sense that it has been defended by political philosophers and penal theorists.[13] As Fitzjames Stephen's (1863: 99) famous quip has it, 'the criminal law stands to the passion of revenge in much the same relation as marriage to the sexual appetite'.

However, is it at all plausible that an otherwise working criminal justice system that dispenses with suffering would regress into the chaotic anarchy of vendetta to the degree needed to render the society unmanageable? There are at least two reasons to think not given current circumstances. First, to continue Stephen's analogy, the relative breakdown of marriage as an institution has undoubtedly led to more and more interesting expressions of 'the sexual appetite', but other forms of social regulation have sprung up – or co-opted sexual behaviour – to do some of the regulative work. Second, and more importantly, the passion for revenge is grounded in a particular understanding of what revenge comprises (the equivalent suffering of the person who has harmed you). As noted above, *that* social meaning is what is at stake and if it can be changed then the passion for revenge may be sated by censure (and possibly apology).

In sum, given certain – armchair, but hopefully not entirely false – empirical assumptions, a system without suffering imposed as punishment looks viable given (1) alternative means of incapacitation for the dangerous and (2) penalties imposed as prudential supplements to the moral appeal of the law where these are needed to ensure a threshold level of compliance when there is both significant direct temptation to break the law and the danger that not penalising offenders will create a substantial assurance problem.

That said, the discussion so far might seem odd or idiosyncratic. The issue, surely, to continue with one of the examples, is that someone is a murderer and someone else a victim. The former deserves to suffer – justice demands that he or she does so – and whether they are few or many makes not a jot of difference to that. This returns us to the main theme of the chapter: does justice demand suffering?

Yes, it just does!

One answer is that it is an impersonal moral demand that criminal wrongdoers suffer punishment. This is not merely a definitional claim – that punishment necessarily involves suffering – but rather a substantive moral claim: that it is morally good (morally required) that serious wrongdoers be made to suffer. Such a position was adopted by Kant and Hegel and in the contemporary literature defended by Michael Moore (Kant, 1996; Hegel, 1942; Moore, 1993).

There are many discussions of this kind of retributivism (even about whether it is correctly attributed to Kant and Hegel) but this is not the place to review them. In each case, the argument rests on robust metaphysical commitments – that is, they depend for their plausibility on accounts of the overall nature of moral value. For example, Michael Moore's account – in which the *sole* good of punishment is that 'someone who deserves it gets it' (Moore, 1987: 87) – depends on a rich moral realism according to which there are valid moral claims that we can know through attending to our moral reactions to worldly phenomena (such as crimes) (Moore, 1982; 1992; for discussion see Matravers, 2000: 81–7). Putting to one side whether such metaphysical commitments are at all plausible, they sit uneasily (to say the least) with the kinds of commitment to liberal impartiality that many people find attractive in *political* as against *moral* philosophy. That is, the claim that in pluralist liberal democratic states, states in which we have to live together in circumstances where we differ profoundly on questions of the good or best way to live, the justification for state action ought not to depend on just such controversial metaphysical claims (given reasonable disagreement amongst citizens over those conceptions).

Given the widespread view that the above position is untenable, a second possibility for someone who wishes to defend the position that justice requires offenders to suffer is that 'the "desert thesis" [that justice = retribution in consequence of one's deserts] rather than a "thesis" has, in practice, assumed the status of an "axiom"', rather than being the conclusion, of retributive thinking (Materni, 2013: 277, in response to Matravers, 2011b).

If what is meant by this is that retributive theorizing consists of simply working out what follows from assuming the truth of the desert thesis, then of course that does nothing to justify retributivism as a theory of punishment and leaves us none the wiser as to what ought actually to be done to criminal offenders.[14] If it is a substantive claim – that criminal offenders deserve suffering imposed as punishment as a matter of justice – then its axiomatic status would rest on something like its being 'self-evident' or 'universally acknowledged', and neither of those is at all plausible.[15]

In short, if neither of these arguments stands up and the suffering of the offender is not an impersonal good, then perhaps it is better understood as owed to someone: to the victim; the wider society; or to the offender himself.

Is the suffering of the offender owed to the victim?

What sense can be made of the claim that the victim is owed the suffering of the offender? Such a claim is widespread – particularly in the negative form that a 'light' sentence fails to give justice to the victim – but is it plausible? One possibility returns to the fairness claim given above. If there is, as it were, suffering to be distributed, then it is better that as much as is possible falls on the offender rather than the victim. A second is that the victim is damaged in some way beyond the material loss done to him or her and the suffering of the offender repairs (insofar as it is possible) this damage.

Fairness and the distribution of suffering

Above it was noted that a 'desire for revenge' might be a psychological predisposition of human beings. It was expressed that way in relation to a particular argument about vendettas. A more precise form is that there appears to be a (near) universal 'fairness norm' that (among other things) demands a proportionate response to wrongdoing.

If so, it might be that one reason for the emergence of systems of punishment is the need to re-establish a fair relation between the victim and the offender. And one possibility would be to argue that *merely* censuring the offender (even taking into account collateral damage of the kind discussed in endnote 1) will leave the victim with a residual sense of unfairness that itself is a form of suffering.[16]

In this case, we might model it as a zero-sum game (just for ease of exposition) and argue that, if there is some quantum of suffering to be distributed (either in the form of a residual feeling of unfairness on the part of the victim or in the form of that amount of penal hard treatment for the offender that would negate the victim's feeling of unfairness), then it is prima facie plausible that it is morally better to direct the suffering to the offender (it is the offender who did the wrong and the victim has already suffered that wrong).

This is a powerful position that – as we will see below – takes a number of philosophical forms, but just as stated it cannot do the required work for the reason given above in the discussion of vendettas. The claim that the 'fairness norm' demands a proportionate response to wrongdoing can be granted without granting the claim that the proportionate response must (at least sometimes) take the form of penal hard treatment. It is that second claim that motivates the argument. The victim is said to suffer from residual feelings of unfairness *because* the offender has not been made to suffer penal hard treatment. But that need not be so (or at least nothing in this argument shows it to be so). If social meanings can change – and they can – then the victim may come to be satisfied with, for example, the censure of the offender, an apology or compensation. The important question is 'what will properly satisfy the requirements of fairness?', and we cannot assume the answer to that is penal hard treatment without begging the question.

Negating the injury and re-establishing the victim's worth

A different way of pursuing the same underlying thought about the balance between the offender and the victim has been forcefully argued by Jean Hampton.[17] For Hampton, the punishment of the offender negates the moral injury done to the victim and 'vindicates the value of the victim' (Hampton, 1992: 1686).

As with the general fairness argument above, there is much in that claim that is right, but what is the connection to the suffering of the offender? Take first 'negating the moral injury done to the victim' (where such a moral injury is present). One possibility is to think of the 'negation' in fairly prosaic terms. We might think, for example, of victim compensation schemes that try, insofar as it is possible, to restore to the victim the value of what was lost. Justice is indeed served by such compensation and there is injustice where it is not, or cannot, be offered. Cases of the latter include cases where compensation is not possible because the harm in some important way cannot be compensated for financially. Another, implicit in ideas of apology, is that the victim is owed an apology; a public recognition of the wrong done to him or her. However, this does not capture the sense of 'negation' to which Hampton is appealing. Rather, the sense of negation is one tied to the sense of 'vindication'. The offender's moral injury done to the victim must be negated so as to vindicate (through the vindication of) the victim.

The difficulty is that this is not at all obvious. The vindication of the value of the victim can be achieved in many ways. Imposing suffering on the offender *might* be one – although it is hard to see why – but there are others that do not involve imposing suffering on the offender and for that reason are to be preferred.

Of course, *given current social meanings*, it may be that in some cases – cases of serious public wrongful harms – the victim has a legitimate entitlement to see the offender suffer because only that will vindicate their status in their own eyes and in the eyes of the community. In such a case, given that justice requires that people's legitimate entitlements are met, for the offender not to suffer would be an injustice. However, as noted above, this does not show that we have no reason to change those social meanings and generate different legitimate entitlements. Legitimate entitlements emerge *from* a theory of justice and (again) it begs the question to say that the correct theory of justice is one in which the offender must suffer.

In short, the victim *is* entitled to the vindication of his status, an apology and compensation. However, it is an instance of Hart's 'mysterious piece of moral alchemy' to think that the victim is entitled to the offender's suffering (Hart, 2008: 234–5, writes of retributivism that 'it appears to be a mysterious piece of moral alchemy in which the combination of the two evils of moral wickedness and suffering are transmuted into good').

Is the suffering of the offender owed to the offender?

In the *Gorgias* (1979), Plato (through) Socrates famously argues that the wrongdoer is necessarily unhappier than the virtuous person and that still worse off is the wrongdoer whose wrongs go unpunished. Punishment, he argues, is owed to the wrongdoer. How can we understand this claim?

In Plato's account, punishment is owed to the offender because he has made a mistake about the best way to live. For Plato, to live in accordance with the demands of justice is (the only way) to live well. In educating the offender, then, we return him to a just and therefore better life.

This position, like some of the retributive positions described earlier, obviously depends on a robust account of the good life. But, even if one grants that – and we might perhaps grant a weaker version in which offending is linked to a life that is not being lived well – it is not obvious why restoring the offender to a life of non-offending is connected to *suffering*. Perhaps it is true, as is held by some religions, that suffering enables contemplation and aids self-understanding and improvement, but, as noted above, such controversial claims about the good life have no place in the justification of public policy in pluralistic liberal democratic societies.[18] In any case, it is surely more plausible that if anything is owed to the offender on this account it is education, rehabilitation, help with addictions, and so on, not the infliction of suffering.

Reference to education, addiction therapy and suchlike might spark a second interpretation of the claim that the suffering of the offender is owed to the offender. This is that it is 'punishment' as against, for example, 'treatment' that is owed to the offender as a mark of respecting him or her as a choosing agent who is entitled to be thought of as bearing responsibility for his or her acts (arguably, this is critical in Kant's retributivism – and the contrast between a 'desert' and a 'treatment' model of the criminal law continues to be important in the literature; see, for example, Morse, 2013). However, this is consistent with the proposal under examination here. The agent is censured as just such a mark of respect. It is the blame and censure that convey the message that the offender is responsible for his or her past acts.

In the end, perhaps the best sense of the claim that suffering is owed to the offender is a Dostoyevskian one in which the soul of the offender can only rest when they have acknowledged what they have done, but such an account is not suitable for a public justification of *imposed* suffering.

Is the suffering of the offender owed to the wider society?

Criminal wrongs are, of course, famously (if not perspicuously) '*public* wrongs'. They are prosecuted by the Sovereign, the Commonwealth, the People, and so on, and thus, if the suffering of the offender is owed to anyone or any body, perhaps it is owed to the public (on the assumption that it would not be owed to the Sovereign herself, for example, other than as a proxy for the public). To evaluate this claim we need to be able to make sense of it, and the idea of a 'public wrong' is notoriously hard to pin down (see, for example, Marshall and Duff, 1998).

To public values

One possibility is that those things that are properly criminalized as public wrongs are (only) those things that violate important public values. Murder, for example, violates the core liberal value of the sanctity of human life (a value that has exceptions but is nevertheless central to our shared life in a liberal polity).

Such an argument seems analogous to the one offered by Hampton examined above and is subject to exactly the same set of objections. We should, and do, condemn the offender and reaffirm the values that he or she has violated, and nothing in the proposal being examined here changes that, but there is no compelling reason to think that is best achieved – or, in some cases, achieved at all – by imposing suffering on the offender.

To potential victims

A different account of public wrong thinks of us all as potential victims (and, of course, potential offenders) who are entitled to live in ways that are relatively secure and stable and in which risks of criminal harm are limited. Perhaps, then, the thought is that were we to follow through on this proposal we would, for example, increase the risk of being murdered for all (by those few who are at present directly tempted and who obey only because of the risk of hard treatment) and, critically, would fail in our duty to protect those who become actual victims.

This captures a common intuition that the offender and victim do not inhabit the same space of moral concern (although of course both remain of some moral concern). Imagine that we could identify a particular individual who would not have been victimized had we continued to use penal hard treatment, but who is victimized following its abolition. To put some flesh on this, imagine a society with extremely low levels of crime – in addition, one in which abolishing (the threat of) penal hard treatment would increase crime rates by only a very small amount (for discussion of a similar example, see the debate between Duff (1999) and von Hirsch (1999b) in Matravers, 1999). The society carries out the suggestion being examined here and abolishes penal hard treatment. The criminal code continues to declare what ought not to be done and courts continue to condemn and censure offenders. The abolition of hard treatment is not done because the citizens think that things previously prohibited are no longer serious public wrongful harms – it is not that they believe the freedom to do such things is a value – but as a result there are a small number of victims who would not otherwise have been victims, and the individual mentioned above is one. The question is, does such a person have a complaint of having been treated *unjustly*?

The answer is no (or at least it is not straightforwardly yes). He is of course unfortunate and he is treated unjustly in some sense by his victimizer, but the state has not acted unjustly. This is because there is no particular substantive level of security that is owed in justice by the state to its citizens. To see this, consider the claim that the state has a duty of justice to reduce the risk of being the victim of a criminal offence to zero. That cannot be right for two reasons. First, even to attempt to do so would require the violation of other aspects of justice. Second, the state's resources are scarce. With those resources the state must provide a range of services such as welfare, health care, defence, foreign aid, education and so on. How much of each it ought in justice to provide depends on one's theory of justice or of legitimacy. One might, for example, think the question is to be answered by considering a hypothetical decision point where suitably constituted individuals ask what principles could not be reasonably rejected for the general regulation of society (Barry, 1995; Scanlon, 1998). Or one might think the question is to be answered by a suitably arranged democratic decision. The point is that, however one thinks the question is to be answered, the demands of justice at this level are what Samuel Scheffler calls 'holistic'. That is, 'the justice of any assignment of economic benefits to a particular individual always depends – directly or indirectly – on the justice of the larger distribution of benefits in society' (Scheffler, 2001: 190). In short, in the imagined society, the decision has been made in order that the massive amounts of money saved may be spent on other policies that promote justice and well-being. That is not unjust (although similarly it may not have been unjust had the citizens decided otherwise).

There are two important caveats to be made, but neither undermines the overall position. First, although there is no substantive answer to the question of 'how much security?', there is a formal answer. Whatever the decision – whether arrived at through a contractualist thought experiment, by democratic decision, or whatever – each citizen is entitled to be treated as an equal in its distribution (and, in some way or other, in the making of the decision concerning its distribution). Second, any plausible theory of justice (whether or not entwined with a theory of democracy) will require a minimum level of security for moral and prudential reasons. Morally, given adequate resources overall, each citizen has a claim to a level of security compatible with living a decent life (however understood). Prudentially, security makes other goods possible – it 'pays in the long run' – and, as we have seen, responds to potential assurance problems.

There is no immediate sense, then, in which the suffering of offenders is owed to potential victims. Of course, and as admitted above, if as a matter of fact there are many potential direct or assurance offenders, then it will be true that an adequate account of justice will have due regard to how to deter the potential direct offenders and reassure the potential assurance ones. That account will have to justify the use of threats in so doing and may well appeal to the fact that it is better overall that potential offenders are threatened and actual offenders penalized than that non-offenders suffer as a consequence of social instability, but it need not make any reference to the claim that the suffering of the offender is in itself good, or even less important than the suffering of victims.

Rather, the claim might be that each of us has reason to endorse a system of rules and, given certain empirical conditions, supplement some of those rules with an appropriate sanction for those who contravene them (even given that we might suffer those sanctions). We also have reason to endorse those things that will reduce the risk of our falling foul of those sanctions such as moral education and the protection of the rule of law and the rules of criminal law (such as rules of evidence and a high burden of proof). (I have tried to develop such an account over some time. See Matravers, 2000; 2011c; 2011d; 2013.)

Having come this far, one might wonder why it is that punishment and suffering have been so closely coupled together in both penal theory and dominant social meanings. Why, if suffering is only contingently connected to punishment, has it had such a long and continuing grip on us?

Answering that question would require a book-length treatment by someone with skills other than mine. However, it might be worth gesturing at a number of possibilities. One, of course, is that for much of human history human beings have believed in supernatural powers and what might have been mechanisms of social control needed in less secure times became imbued with moral and 'religious' meanings that outlived their location in wider schemes of belief; moral and religious meanings that often involved the regulation of women and sex (Berkowitz, 2012).

Another is that the demands of social control, the assurance of stability, are more easily achieved now through means other than punishment, and that societies – at least the kinds of societies I have been discussing here – are now less violent than in the past, but the social meaning attached to suffering is necessarily slow to catch up.

Nietzsche once declared:

> The 'creditor' always becomes more humane to the extent that he has grown richer. ... It is not unthinkable that a society might attain such a consciousness of power that it could allow itself the noblest luxury possible to it – letting

those who harm it go unpunished. 'What are my parasites to me?' it might say. 'May they live and prosper: I am strong enough for that!'

(Nietzsche, 1956: 72)

Conclusion: is there anything to learn from this thought experiment?

I do not think we have reached the stage described by Nietzsche. We are not in the imaginary society discussed above. The idea of 'social stability' invoked above was left deliberately vague, but for many reasons it is unlikely we could abolish penal hard treatment here and now without unjustifiably increasing the risks of future criminal harms. Some of those reasons are, I believe, grounded in distributive injustice, but the victims of those criminal harms would of course mainly consist of many people who also suffer from that distributive injustice.

Moreover, as was pointed out several times above, as long as the expression of appropriate censure does as a matter of social meaning require hard treatment, the seriousness of the wrong, the censuring of the offender and the recognition of the wronged status of the victim will all require that such treatment is dispensed.

Finally, the argument has lumped together penal hard treatments, and a more nuanced account of such treatments – for example, one that included community sentences – would complicate the picture still further. It is *not* that the argument was meant to apply only to prison – it is the imposition of suffering as punishment that is in question – but undoubtedly the focus on prison has made the argument simpler. Given all that, one might ask what the point was in working through the thought experiment.

At the abstract level, the point of the thought experiment was twofold: first, to see what happens if one reframes the question of penal hard treatment as one of what would be lost if we stopped doing it. This question – the question of whether the offender's suffering is *owed* to anyone – offers a different perspective on traditional questions. Second, the argument against ending hard treatment depends on understanding that, were we now to abolish all hard treatment, we would act unjustly because we would have failed to balance properly the various interests each of us has in living in a certain kind of society (one that taxes and spends appropriately so as to ensure a number of goods, including the good of security). We would in that sense not be living in a just society. However, so long as the mistake was one within our appropriate reasoning rather than because we had reasoned inappropriately (for example, a mistake made when calculating the effects of the policy when voting rather than because we denied the vote to people of a certain colour), we would all be 'victims' of this injustice. Of course, the tangible cost of this injustice would fall most visibly on those who suffer from criminal wrongs that they would otherwise have avoided (just as now we all live in an unjust society the most visible costs of which – relevant to the topic here – are borne by those who suffer penal hard treatment that is not warranted by a proper balance of interests).

At a more particular, perhaps parochial, level, the point was to respond to the ways in which we in the UK, following the US, are seemingly wedded to punishment and hard treatment. We live at a time when our politicians engage in an 'arms race' to convince the voters of their 'toughness' when it comes to crime (Lacey, 2008). Reform, I think, starts with imagination. Other countries do things differently and even within our own community the meanings of social practices can change and have changed (think, for example, about the meaning of the vow to 'obey' in marriage or of what is involved in being a (particularly male) parent). The emphasis we currently give to suffering seems to me to be unhealthy and unreasoned. But it is not only those things. It is also ineffective.

Many of the objections to the thought experiment considered above have behind them the thought that if we abolished penal hard treatment crime would flourish and society would fail. If so, this would obviously be a bad thing. But if we are serious about reducing crime and its devastating effects on victims, communities, offenders and offenders' families, we ought to be less concerned with continuing to inflict suffering on offenders and more with redirecting some of the huge sums of money currently spent on imposing suffering to education, welfare, improving social mobility and so on. To the extent that we do not do this because of the strange grip that imposing suffering has on us, the thought experiment is meant to help to loosen that grip.

Acknowledgement

My thanks to the audience of the University of Newcastle's Ethics, Legal and Political Philosophy Seminar Series for comments on a very rough draft of this paper and to Derek Bell for the invitation. Also to Ian Loader for probing comments and corrections, which have led to numerous changes in the argument. Work on this paper was made possible by a Mid-Career Fellowship from the Independent Social Research Foundation for which I am very grateful.

Notes

1 Of course, it may well be that the experience of censure and the possible consequences for, say, loss of reputation are painful. However, the paper is concerned with the suffering of the offender that is deliberately imposed by the state as punishment. Thus, I am not concerned with other forms of suffering even if it is a predictable by-product of punishment or with any other suffering endured by the offender (for example, should they have a particularly aggressive and painful cancer).
2 This is Rawls's strategy in 'Two Concepts of Rules', where he uses the term 'telishment' to describe a practice that is not 'of an offender for an offence' (Rawls, 1955 (1999)).
3 What follows draws on my 'Duff on Hard Treatment' (Matravers, 2011a). That paper examined and rebutted the claim that penal censure and hard treatment are intrinsically connected.
4 In one way, if expressing censure and hard treatment are intrinsically connected, this would be a version of the definitional stop discussed earlier. A practice without hard treatment would *ipso facto* be a practice without censure and a practice without censure

would not be punishment. The difference here is that the argument sets out to ask what a system of punishment would look like *with* censure but *without* hard treatment.

5 The relationship of the law, penal sanctions and moral norms is examined in many places but is of particular concern to penal sociologists such as Durkheim (1983) and those in the Scandinavian tradition such as Johannes Andenaes (1974) (for a discussion of these see Matravers, 2011e), and to legal moralists such as Devlin (Devlin, 1965).

6 I am very grateful to Kathryn Hollingsworth for pressing me hard on this argument in an email exchange following the presentation at Newcastle.

7 In a discussion of preventive detention, Stephen Morse claims that the justification of any such measures depends upon '(1) if the potential harm were sufficiently grave; (2) if the prediction technology were sufficiently accurate; (3) if the preventive response were maximally humane and minimally intrusive under the circumstances; and (4) if the preventive action was preceded by adequate due process' (Morse, 1999: 297). For the most part, condition (2) is not met. A recent discussion of 'punishment' modelled on preventive incapacitation (in this case in response to scepticism about free will and 'basic desert') can be found in 'Free Will Scepticism and Criminal Punishment'.

8 The Conservative government elected in 2015 has promised to abolish these, but this makes no difference to the argument here as they are being discussed only as an example.

9 Her Majesty's Revenue and Customs, the UK Government office responsible for tax and customs and excise.

10 Interestingly, one 'penalty' that has been criminal in England and Wales is that imposed for failing to have a television licence (and possessing a television or watching television online). During the election campaign of 2015, this was declared an anomaly and 'heavy handed' by the prime minister, David Cameron (Swinford, 2015).

11 This idea underpins the so-called 'Fair Play' theory of punishment. The account was pioneered by Morris (1968) and Murphy (1973) and was more recently defended by Dagger (1993; 2011). For criticism, see Duff, 1986: chapter 8; Matravers, 2000: 52–72.

12 I am very grateful to John Lazarus at the University of Newcastle for suggesting this term (and for explaining to me why my original choice of 'hard-wired' was inappropriate). He also suggested the fairness-based argument discussed below.

13 The idea of course dates back to Greek mythology (for a fascinating discussion see Allen, 1999) and is important in Locke's *Second Treatise*.

14 The claim that serious moral wrongdoing (other things equal) deserves moral criticism might be taken as axiomatic in that it captures something in the 'logic' of moral language (of course, it does not follow that such criticism ought always to be uttered).

15 The claim that the desert thesis is an axiom seems to me to amount to the claim that we ought not to give up searching for a justification of punishment (since we can just stipulate whatever axiom suits us best).

16 I am grateful to John Lazarus for pressing me on this argument.

17 For an extended critical discussion of Hampton's argument, from which this section borrows, see my *Justice and Punishment* (2000: 75–81).

18 One religiously inspired account of the connection between suffering and reform – an account that prefigures in some ways Antony Duff's communicative theory – was offered by Sir Walter Moberly in 1968. Moberly writes of penal suffering as bringing home to the offender 'the real nature of his deed', of its foreshadowing 'the pain of mind [the offender] will have to undergo' if he is to recover, and of its inducing him 'to rue his deed and to be ashamed of himself'. In short, Moberly thinks, 'penal pain must ultimately be transmuted into penitential pain' (Moberly, 1968: 221). Although interesting, the account suffers from the same flaws when it comes to the connection between suffering and penitence as Duff's later theory (Matravers, 2011a).

References

Allen, D. S. (1999) *The World of Prometheus: The Politics of Punishing in Democratic Athens*. Princeton, NJ: Princeton University Press.

Andenaes, J. (1974) *Punishment and Deterrence*. Ann Arbor, MI: University of Michigan Press.

Ashworth, A. (2011) 'Attempts', in *The Oxford Handbook of Philosophy of Criminal Law*, J. Deigh and D. Dolinko. Oxford: Oxford University Press, 125–146.

Barry, B. (1995) *Justice as Impartiality*, vol. 2 of *A Treatise on Social Justice*. Oxford: Clarendon Press.

Berkowitz, E. (2012) *Sex and Punishment: Four Thousand Years of Judging Desire*. Berkeley, CA: Counterpoint.

Carroll, L. (1897) *Through the Looking Glass and What Alice Found There*. London: Macmillan & Co.

Dagger, R. (1993) 'Playing Fair with Punishment', *Ethics*, 103, 473–488.

Dagger, R. (2011) 'Social Contracts, Fair Play, and the Justification of Punishment', *Ohio State Journal of Criminal Law*, 8, 341–368.

Devlin, P. (1965) *The Enforcement of Morals*. London and New York: Oxford University Press.

Duff, R. A. (1986) *Trials & Punishments*. Cambridge: Cambridge University Press.

Duff, R. A. (1999) 'Punishment, Communication and Community', in *Punishment and Political Theory*, in (ed.) M. Matravers. Oxford: Hart Publishing, 48–68.

Durkheim, É. (1983) 'The Evolution of Punishment', in *Durkheim and the Law*, S. Lukes and A. Scull. Oxford: Oxford University Press.

Hampton, J. (1992) 'Correcting Harms versus Righting Wrongs: The Goal of Retribution', *UCLA Law Review*, 39, 1659–1702.

Hart, H. L. A. (2008) *Punishment and Responsibility: Essays in the Philosophy of Law*. Oxford: Oxford University Press.

Hegel, G. W. F. (1942) *Hegel's Philosophy of Right*. Oxford: Clarendon Press.

HM Revenue & Customs (2015) *HMRC Penalties: A Discussion Document*. London: HMRC.

Kant, I. (1996) 'The Metaphysics of Morals', in *The Cambridge Edition of the Works of Immanuel Kant: Practical Philosophy*, M. J. Gregor. Cambridge: Cambridge University Press, 353–603.

Lacey, N. (2008) *The Prisoners' Dilemma: Political Economy and Punishment in Contemporary Democracies*. Cambridge: Cambridge University Press.

Marshall, S. and R. A. Duff (1998) 'Criminalization and Sharing Wrongs', *Canadian Journal of Law & Jurisprudence*, 11(1): 7–22.

Materni, M. (2013) 'Criminal Punishment and the Pursuit of Justice', *British Journal of American Legal Studies*, 2(1): 263–304.

Matravers, M. (1999) *Punishment and Political Theory*. Oxford: Hart Publishing.

Matravers, M. (2000) *Justice and Punishment: The Rationale of Coercion*. Oxford: Oxford University Press.

Matravers, M. (2011a) 'Duff on Hard Treatment', in *Crime, Punishment and Responsibility*. R. Cruft, M. Kramer and M. Reiff. Oxford: Oxford University Press.

Matravers, M. (2011b) 'Is Twenty-First Century Punishment Post-Desert?', in *Retributivism Has a Past: Has it a Future?* in (ed.) M. Tonry. New York: Oxford University Press.

Matravers, M. (2011c) 'Mad, Bad, or Faulty? Desert in Distributive and Retributive Justice', in *Responsibility and Distributive Justice*, in (eds) C. Knight and Z. Stemplowska. Oxford: Oxford University Press, 136–151.

Matravers, M. (2011d) 'Political Theory and the Criminal Law', in *Philosophical Foundations of the Criminal Law*. R. A. Duff and S. Green. New York: Oxford University Press, 67–82.

Matravers, M. (2011e) 'Reassurance, Reinforcement, and Legitimacy', in *Handbook of Crime and Criminal Justice*, in (ed.) M. Tonry. New York: Oxford University Press.

Matravers, M. (2013) 'On Preventive Justice', in *Prevention and the Limits of the Criminal Law: Principles and Policies*, in (eds) A. Ashworth, L. Zedner and P. Tomlin. Oxford: Oxford University Press.

Moberly, W. H. (1968) *The Ethics of Punishment*. London: Faber & Faber.

Moore, M. (1982) 'Moral Reality', *Wisconsin Law Review*, 1061–1156.

Moore, M. (1987) 'The Moral Worth of Retribution', in *Responsibility, Character and the Emotions*, F. Schoemann. New York: Cambridge University Press, 179–219.

Moore, M. (1992) 'Moral Reality Revisited', *Michigan Law Review*, 90, 2424–2533.

Moore, M. (1993) 'Justifying Retributivism', *Israel Law Review* 27, 15–49.

Morris, H. (1968) 'Persons and Punishment', *Monist* , 52, 475–501.

Murphy, J. (1973) 'Marxism and Retribution', *Philosophy and Public Affairs* 2, 217–243.

Morse, S. J. (1999) 'Neither Desert Nor Disease', *Legal Theory*, 5, 265–309.

Morse, S. J. (2013) 'Compatibilist Criminal Law', in *The Future of Punishment*, in (ed.) T. Nadelhoffer. Oxford: Oxford University Press, 107–131.

Nietzsche, F. (1956) *On the Genealogy of Morals*. New York: Doubleday.

Pereboom, D. (2013) 'Free Will Skepticism and Criminal Punishment', in *The Future of Punishment*, in (ed.) T. Nadelhoffer. Oxford: Oxford University Press, 49–78.

Plato (1979) *Gorgias*. Oxford: Clarendon Press.

Rawls, J. (1955 (1999)) 'Two Concepts of Rules', in *Collected Papers*. J. Rawls and S. R. Freeman. Cambridge, MA: Harvard University Press, 20–46.

Scanlon, T. M. (1998) *What We Owe to Each Other*. Cambridge, MA: Harvard University Press.

Scheffler, S. (2001) *Boundaries and Allegiances: Problems of Justice and Responsibility in Liberal Thought*. Oxford: Oxford University Press.

Stephen, J. F. (1863) *A General View of the Criminal Law of England*. London and Cambridge: Macmillan & Co.

Swinford, S. (2015) 'David Cameron Pledges to Decriminalise Licence Fee'. Available at: www.telegraph.co.uk/news/bbc/11600972/David-Cameron-pledges-to-decriminalis e-licence-fee.html [accessed May 2015].

von Hirsch, A. (1976) *Doing Justice: The Choice of Punishments: Report of the Committee for the Study of Incarceration*. New York: Hill and Wang.

von Hirsch, A. (1993) *Censure and Sanctions*. Oxford: Oxford University Press.

von Hirsch, A. (1999a) *Criminal Deterrence and Sentence Severity: An Analysis of Recent Research*. Oxford: Hart Publishing.

von Hirsch, A. (1999b) 'Punishment, Penance, and the State: A reply to Duff', in *Punishment and Political Theory*, M. Matravers. Oxford: Hart Publishing, 69–82.

3

PUNISHMENT, LEGITIMACY AND THE ROLE OF THE STATE

Reimagining more moderate penal policies

Sonja Snacken

Introduction: Punishment and state power

Punishment is without doubt one of the most coercive forms of the exercise of state power. It expresses the powers of the state in a very direct and even brutal way. It cuts deep into the lives, fundamental rights and freedoms of suspects or convicted offenders, such as the right to life (cf. death penalty), to freedom (cf. imprisonment), to private and family life (cf. most sanctions and measures, including those imposed in the community). This has long been recognized (see, for example, Beccaria, 1764/1972; Garland and Young, 1983; Garland, 1990; Whitman, 2003) and is exemplified by some recent definitions of punishment:

'the conscious inflicting of pain'

(Christie, 1981: 4)

'the organized infliction of pain by the State upon an individual in response to that individual's criminal wrong-doing'

(Loader, 2010: 353)

'the authorized imposition of deprivations – of freedom or privacy or other goods to which the person otherwise has a right, or the imposition of special burdens – because the person has been found guilty of some criminal violation, typically (though not invariably) involving harm to the innocent'

(Bedau and Kelly, 2010 n.p.)

Punishment is hence a *human* institution, in which a political authority has the *power* to impose certain *pains, deprivations of rights or burdens* on persons believed to have acted wrongly (Snacken, 2012: 248). This has important implications for its legitimacy. In western liberal democracies (or democratic constitutional states), state power is subjected to the rule of law and to several checks and balances. However, several of these western democracies have over the last decades also been characterized by penal inflation, new forms of punitiveness, expressive justice and mass/hyperincarceration of certain groups of offenders, often driven by populist punitiveness. Reimagining more moderate penal policies and practices hence requires tackling the question of the legitimacy of such policies and the relation between state power and public opinion. I first look into these questions from a theoretical point of view through a dialogic approach to legitimacy. I then illustrate the values and options at stake through the example of parole for serious offenders.

Legitimacy of penal power

In his influential analysis of the legitimation of power, political scientist David Beetham (1991) describes 'legitimacy' as a multidimensional concept, used differently by different professionals. Constitutional lawyers refer to the legal and constitutional validity of the acquisition and exercise of power. Moral and political philosophers will look at the moral justifiability of the exercise of power. This will often express a universalising claim to define legitimacy. Social scientists, on the contrary, will focus on the empirical consequences of legitimacy in a particular social context. Beetham is very critical though of the major impact that Max Weber's definition of legitimacy as 'belief in legitimacy by relevant social actors' (Weber, 1968: 213) has had on the social sciences, as it seems to reduce legitimacy to a mere description, without any objective reference or moral content. According to Beetham, Weber's definition misrepresents the relationship between beliefs and legitimacy:

> a given power relationship is not legitimate because people believe in its legitimacy, but because it can be justified in terms of their beliefs; [the emphasis should be on] the degree of congruence, or lack of it, between a given system of power and the beliefs, values and expectations that provide its justification.
>
> *(Beetham, 1991: 11)*

He hence distinguishes different levels of legitimacy: the legal/constitutional validity of the acquisition and exercise of power; the justifiability of the rules governing a power relationship in terms of the beliefs and values current in a given society; and the evidence of consent derived from actions by subordinates expressive of it. Let us now look into these forms of legitimacy.

Legal/constitutional validity of penal power

In *democratic constitutional states*, i.e. democracies governed by the rule of law, the exercise of state power must be limited, controlled and justified. This principle goes back to the major founding documents of the democratic constitutional state in England (1688 Bill of Rights), the USA (1776 Declaration of Independence and 1788–1791 US Constitution) and France (1789 Déclaration des droits de l'homme et du citoyen). They put an end to the arbitrary and absolute power of the former sovereigns and laid the basis for a new constitutional system in which individual liberty would prevail. The project of the democratic constitutional state has engendered a specific concept of state in which power is by definition limited. The aims of the democratic constitutional state are generally translated, expressed and concretized through the enactment of three basic constitutional principles, namely the recognition of fundamental rights and liberties, the rule of law (constitutionalism) and democracy (De Hert and Gutwirth, 2004; Gutwirth, 1998; Gutwirth and De Hert, 2002; Snacken, 2012; 2013).

Democratic constitutional states recognize a set of fundamental *human rights* and liberties that are deemed to be at the very core of the political construct. In principle, the state is not allowed to encroach upon or to interfere with these rights ('negative' state obligations). They work as a shield or a bulwark; they express the recognition of the power of the individual, drawing the limits and frontiers of the power of the state and of state intervention. They therefore protect individuals against excessive steering of their lives and entitle them to autonomously determine their lives and choices and to participate in the political system (cf. De Hert and Gutwirth, 2004). Besides these 'negative' obligations, it has increasingly been argued, including by the European Court of Human Rights (ECtHR), that states also have 'positive' obligations to actively protect the human rights of individuals by taking 'necessary' or 'reasonable and suitable' measures (Snacken, 2013). An example can be found in the case-law of the ECtHR on states' obligation to protect prisoners' family life by granting family visits (van Zyl Smit and Snacken, 2009).

Democratic constitutional states enshrine the *rule of law*. This expresses the idea of 'government by law, not by men': our societies are governed by rational and impersonal laws, not by arbitrary and/or emotional commands of humans. The constitutional recognition and implementation of the rule of law again aims to limit the power of government, but this time through a system of imposed weighing, checking and balancing powers. The main idea of the rule of law is the subjection of government and other state powers to a set of restricting constitutional rules and mechanisms. The rule of law hence provides for the principle of legality of government: public authorities are bound by their own rules and can only exercise their powers in accordance with the law. It implies that government is accountable and that its actions must be controllable, and thus transparent (Gutwirth, 1998; Snacken, 2013).

Democracy recognizes the people's sovereignty or self-determination and the principles of democratic representation. The only valid justification of power must be sought in the citizens' consent or will. This crucial link is expressed through the different variations upon the theme of the social contract (Beccaria, Locke, Rousseau). However, social contract theories can legitimize very different forms of government: from a minimal liberal state (in the line of Locke and Beccaria) to a more republican nation (in the line of Rousseau and Kant). These variations have been invoked in order to understand differences between respectively Anglo-Saxon and Continental European legal systems (Garapon and Papadopoulos, 2003).

Democracy entails that government must be in line with the public or general interest and must take into account the will of the majority. However, there is no democratic constitutional state without a multitude of (individual) viewpoints, opinions, projects, behaviours, life-styles and so on. Decision-making, therefore, requires a debate in which these diverging interests are openly discussed and where the policies resulting from these debates are framed in the general interest. Hence, systems of representation and accountability are of crucial importance, which again calls for transparency of public decision-making and policies (Gutwirth, 1998; Snacken, 2012).

Although all contemporary western states recognize the above three sources of legal/constitutional legitimacy, their application is a complex matter, as they may often seem contradictory. Indeed, tensions may occur between these three basic elements, for example when increased feelings of insecurity and fear of crime lead a majority of the citizens to prioritize crime control over respect for human rights and the rule of law. In the US, for example, the 'war on crime' has led to a 'virulent culture of demonization of convicts' (Wacquant, 2008) and to punitive laws and measures (for example three-strikes laws, Megan's law) that 'suggests a complete disregard for the rights or humanity of those being sanctioned' (Garland, 2001: 133). Such tensions hence result from the fact that a democratic constitutional state aims at guaranteeing both a high level of individual freedom and a social order in which such freedom is made possible and guaranteed (Gutwirth, 1998; De Hert and Gutwirth, 2004; Snacken, 2013).

A dialogic approach to legitimacy in criminal justice

Bottoms and Tankebe (2012) have further developed Beetham's thinking about the legitimacy of power through a dialogic approach to legitimacy in criminal justice, distinguishing 'audience legitimacy' from 'power-holder legitimacy' (see also Snacken, 2015).

Legitimacy is seen as the recognition of the right to govern within a structured bilateral (or multilateral) relationship; if successfully established it 'simultaneously justifies the actions of both the power-holder and the obedient subject' (Bottoms and Tankebe, 2012: 125). Beetham's three dimensions of legitimacy – legal/constitutional validity, shared beliefs and values, and consent – are seen as constitutive of audience legitimacy. Power-holder legitimacy refers to the legal/constitutional validity of the exercise of power and to the cultivation of 'their self-legitimacy with reference to the beliefs shared by them and their audience' (ibid., 2012: 151). It can be summarized as the 'cultivation of self-confidence in the moral rightness of power-holders' authority, within a framework of both official laws and regulations, and societal normative expectations' (ibid., 2012: 154).

Fostering the legitimacy of a particular policy may require 'skilful negotiation' though, as laws do not necessarily mirror values, and different groups may hold very different core values in our globalized and multicultural societies (ibid., 2012: 144). Within the dialogic process that legitimation requires, part of the skill of power-holders will then be to negotiate the acceptance of a particular policy through identification of shared values (ibid., 2012: 143). Bottoms and Tankebe distinguish between general 'core' values and 'specific' criminal justice values. 'Core' values relate 'to essential values and basic institutions, which are the object of a consensus that lies beyond discussion and [have] a type of validity that is foundational' (ibid., 2012: 141). Procedural justice and effectiveness are described as fairly universal 'specific' values of criminal justice systems (ibid., 2012: 144–147).

Punishment, legitimacy and conflicting values: the example of parole

Punishment and contradictory values

Penality is related to a variety of contradictory values and emotions. While the criteria for legal/constitutional legitimacy emphasize the need for a rational and restrictive use of penal power, many authors have described the fundamentally irrational, passionate and emotional feelings aroused by crime and punishment (Durkheim, 1902; Garland, 1990; Loader, 2010). Effectiveness as a specific value of criminal justice (Bottoms and Tankebe, 2012) may well conflict with the emotional, expressive and non-utilitarian aspects of punishment (Garland, 1990; 2001; Falcon y Tella and Falcon y Tella, 2006). Punishment is also an expression of censure, moral indignation, solidarity with victims, concerns for personal and community safety, fear of the 'Other', etc. (Garland, 1990; Pratt, 2002; Boutellier, 2004). It can even offer the gratification and sheer pleasure of (indirectly) exercising power over and degrading fellow humans, thus reinforcing our own feelings of superiority (Whitman, 2003). The choice of penal power-holders hence lies in which (balance of) values they invoke to legitimize particular policy choices.

Parole for serious offenders

Parole for serious offenders is a good example of such contradictory values. Parole for serious offenders is often 'unpopular', as it allows prisoners sentenced to relatively long prison sentences to be conditionally released before the end of their sentence. In the Belgian 'Justice Barometer' survey, for example, 60 per cent of respondents oppose conditional release for offenders, while only 36 per cent support it (Hoge Raad voor Justitie, 2010: 69). Parole illustrates the inherent contradictions between several official aims of imprisonment. Retribution and incapacitation call for the implementation of the full sentence, while special prevention and reducing the risk of recidivism are often better served by a gradual transition from deprivation of liberty to re-entry into society (Kensey and Tournier, 2000; Goethals and Bouverne-De Bie, 2000; Ostermann, 2013; Wan et al., 2014; Shute, 2004).

Two examples illustrate these tensions: the Belgian parole reforms following a case that received extensive media coverage, and the 'life without parole' policy and practice in the United Kingdom in the context of European standards.

The Belgian parole reform: one case, two policies

The Belgian Dutroux case, involving the rape and murder of several young girls in 1996, led to overwhelming popular demand for the abolition of parole for serious crimes. A 'White March' demanding justice and solidarity with the victims brought 300,000 people to the streets of Brussels on 20 October 1996. As M. Dutroux was under parole when allegedly committing these crimes, a petition demanding the abolition of parole for serious offenders collected three million signatures (out of a population of ten million). Both initiatives were taken by victim organizations. A fierce and emotional debate followed in Parliament, and several drafts were presented to abolish parole for serious offenders. The then Minister of Justice secured the survival of parole by emphasizing its *effectiveness* in protecting the public and potential victims through individual guidance and control, supported by scientific evidence provided by academics and practitioners. The parole legislation was reformed in 1998 and 2006, transferring decision-making from the Minister of Justice to independent 'parole commissions' (Acts 5 and 18 March 1998), which were eventually transformed into 'sentence implementation courts' (Act 17 May 2006). The legitimacy of parole for victims and the public was reinforced through emphasizing *procedural justice*: the legal position of the victims (but also of the prisoners) in the parole procedure was strengthened, victims had to be informed of the possibility of parole of 'their' offender and could be heard by the parole commission on the question of conditions to be imposed in their interest. Parole had to be considered for all prisoners, the initiative to start the procedure being taken automatically by the prison director. The multidisciplinary composition of the parole commissions, headed by an acting judge and including an expert in social reintegration and an expert in prison matters, was advocated as guaranteeing more scientific and effective decision-making. Demands by the victim organizations to include an expert member on victim issues, and to allow victims to have an impact not only on the conditions to be imposed but also on the decision of whether to grant release at all, were not accepted by Parliament, as it was thought this could distort the necessary and difficult equilibrium between the interests of the victims (protection), the offender (reintegration) and society at large (community safety). Despite demands from opposition parties and victim organizations to increase the proportion of time to be served by prisoners before being eligible for parole, the existing proportions of one-third of the sentence (two-thirds for legal recidivists[1]) and ten years for lifers (14 years for legal recidivists) were maintained. But protection of the public was also reinforced by making parole conditions and supervision stricter and by increasing opportunities to impose preventive detention on sex offenders (Snacken, 2007).

Sixteen years later (2012), the conditional release of M. Dutroux's former wife and accomplice M. Martin by an independent sentence implementation court again sparked popular outcry and outrage, with victims trying to interfere with the release decision. The political reaction was very different on this occasion. Despite opposition by academics and practitioners (including chief public prosecutors), the parole conditions were made much stricter in 2013 for prisoners serving very long (30 years) or life sentences, raising the minimum to be served to 15 years for first offenders and 19 or 23 years for different types of recidivists (Act 17 March 2013). The definition of 'legal recidivism' was broadened in order to cover cases such as M. Martin,[2] and the role of the prison director in initiating the parole procedure was abolished. The composition of the multidisciplinary courts was enlarged by two additional criminal court judges when dealing with the most serious cases (30 years or life sentence coupled with preventive detention, as is the case for M. Dutroux), and release now requires unanimity of the five members.

The reform following the Martin case has nothing to do with effectiveness or community safety. There was never any suggestion that Dutroux's former wife was at risk of reoffending or a threat to the victims or to community safety. The reform cannot undo her release and will only affect future parole decisions about other prisoners. It was defended by the minister in order to ensure a 'more punitive and more socially acceptable approach to certain categories of sentenced offenders' (Explanatory Memorandum to the 2013 Act; see also Scheirs, 2014: 280). It appeared to comprise a purely *populist punitive* reaction, and a motion of censure against the independence and multidisciplinarity of the sentence implementation courts (Snacken, 2014).

This example shows how in the same case – M. Dutroux in 1996, his former wife M. Martin in 2013 – Belgian political leadership has chosen to appeal to very different values and emotions, resulting in different penal policies: a 'skilful negotiation' based on procedural justice and effectiveness in the first part, expressive justice based on emotional outrage and populist punitiveness in the second.

Life without parole in the United Kingdom and in European standards

The United Kingdom has the highest percentage of life-sentenced prisoners of all European countries: 10.7 per cent in England and Wales, 14.1 per cent in Northern Ireland and 15.4 per cent in Scotland in 2013, with a European mean of 3.1 per cent (Aebi and Delgrande, 2013: 116, Table 7). Life imprisonment is not in itself incompatible with European standards. The European Court of Human Rights has found it not to breach the Convention (ECHR) if it is imposed for the most serious crimes (see *Sawoniuk v United Kingdom*, 29 May 2001, concerning war crimes committed against Jews in Poland during the Nazi occupation).

But life without parole does raise an issue under the Convention. In recent years, the Court has slowly moved towards the position that life without any possibility of parole constitutes *inhuman and degrading treatment* violating Article 3 ECHR. In 2001, it cautiously did 'not rule out that the imposition of an irreducible life sentence may raise an issue under Article 3 of the Convention' (*Einhorn v France* 16 October 2001, §27). In 2008, it did not find a violation as long as there is some, even remote and uncertain prospect of release, as '[i]t is enough for the purposes of Article 3 that a life sentence is *de jure* and *de facto* reducible' (*Kafkaris v Cyprus* [GC] 12 February 2008, §98) (see also van Zyl Smit and Snacken, 2009: 328–332). In *Vinter a.o. v UK* (9 July 2013, §130), the Court eventually concluded that, in 'the absence of any dedicated review mechanism for the whole life orders' in the Criminal Justice Act 2003, whole life sentences in England and Wales could not be regarded 'as reducible for the purposes of Article 3 of the Convention'. The Court (and the applicants themselves) accepted though that 'even if the requirements of punishment and deterrence were to be fulfilled, it would still be possible that they could continue to be detained on grounds of dangerousness' (ibid., §131).

The tensions between different values are obvious here. If life sentences really are limited to the most serious crimes, then release of some individuals may face considerable opposition because of the extreme heinousness of their crimes or because of the danger that they are alleged to pose to society (van Zyl Smit and Snacken, 2009: 328).

In the case of *Vinter*, the UK government argued that 'The penal policy of England and Wales was long-standing and well-established. It reflected the view, both of the domestic courts and Parliament, that there were some crimes so grave that they were deserving of lifelong incarceration for the purposes of *pure punishment*' (§92; my emphasis). The Court retorted that

> [the] legitimate penological grounds for detention (…) include punishment, deterrence, public protection and rehabilitation. Many of these grounds will be present at the time when a life sentence is imposed. However, the balance between these justifications for detention is not necessarily static and may shift in the course of the sentence. What may be the primary justification for detention at the start of the sentence may not be so after a lengthy period into the service of the sentence. It is only by carrying out a review of the justification for continued detention at an appropriate point in the sentence that these factors or shifts can be properly evaluated.
>
> *(§111)*

The Court approvingly referred to the German Federal Constitutional Court's decision in the *Life Imprisonment* case (21 June 1977) that

> it would be incompatible with the provision on *human dignity* (…) for the State forcefully to deprive a person of his freedom without at least providing him with the chance to someday regain that freedom. (…) prison authorities had the duty to strive towards a life sentenced prisoner's rehabilitation and that rehabilitation was constitutionally required in any community that established human dignity as its centerpiece. (…) Similar considerations must apply under

the Convention system, the very essence of which, as the Court has often stated, is respect for human dignity.

(§113; my emphasis)

The Court found further ample support in European and international law for the principle that all prisoners, including those serving life sentences, be offered the possibility of rehabilitation and the prospect of release if that rehabilitation is achieved (§114). It recalled (§115–116) that this follows from the Council of Europe's 'legal instruments' (such as the European Prison Rules, Recommendation 2003(23) on the management by prison administrations of life sentence and other long-term prisoners, Recommendation 2003(22) on conditional release and the standards of the European Committee for the Prevention of Torture (CPT)), that

> while punishment remains one of the aims of imprisonment, the emphasis in European penal policy is now on the *rehabilitative* aim of imprisonment, particularly towards the end of a long prison sentence.
>
> *(§115; my emphasis)*

It concluded that

> in the context of a life sentence, Article 3 must be interpreted as requiring reducibility of the sentence, in the sense of a review which allows the domestic authorities to consider whether any changes in the life prisoner are so significant, and such progress towards rehabilitation has been made in the course of the sentence, as to mean that continued detention can no longer be justified on legitimate penological grounds.
>
> *(§119)*

The values involved here are hence on the one hand 'pure punishment' (retribution) and protection of the public against 'dangerous' offenders (incapacitation), and on the other hand human dignity (a right to hope) and rehabilitation or reintegration. But parole and other community sanctions are also supposed to reinforce community safety by reducing the risk of reoffending through supervision, control, guidance and assistance, aiming at the social inclusion of an offender (Council of Europe Probation Rules, Basic Principle 1).

What does this mean in view of Beetham's legal/constitutional validity and social justifiability of the exercise of power and Bottoms and Tankebe's distinction between audience and power-holder legitimacy?

Legitimacy of parole for serious offenders

The European Court of Human Rights is now quite clear on this issue. Life without parole may be legally enforced in England and Wales through the Criminal Justice Act 2003, but it has no *constitutional validity* as it violates the absolute prohibition on inhuman and degrading treatment or punishment enshrined in Article 3 ECHR. While this installs a 'right to hope' for all prisoners, including those serving life sentences, it does not guarantee a 'right to release', as state authorities also have the duty to protect the public and potential victims from harm. In cases where temporarily released offenders had relapsed into murder, the Court recognized the 'legitimate aim of a policy of progressive social reintegration of persons sentenced to imprisonment (...) even where they have been convicted of violent crimes' (*Mastromatteo v Italy* (GC) 24 October 2002 §72). The Court would, however, look closely into the way in which release had been applied in the individual case, in view of the duty of care that the government owes to potential victims under Article 2 ECHR (right to life). While it found no such violation by the Italian authorities in the case of *Mastromatteo*, it reached the opposite conclusion in *Maiorano v Italy* (15 December 2009), where authorities had failed to react appropriately when serious problems arose in the supervision of the released prisoner (Snacken, 2011).

While *protection of the public* is a legitimate counter rationale for releasing offenders, '*public opinion*' in general is not. In the case of *Stafford v UK* (GC, 28 May 2002), the secretary of state refused to release an offender, sentenced to life imprisonment following a conviction for murder, who had subsequently returned to the community but had then been sentenced to imprisonment for fraud. The refusal of release after serving the second sentence was based on the breach of the conditions of his initial life sentence. The Court held that a conviction for fraud, a non–violent offence, did not justify the further detention of the applicant on the murder charge (see also van Zyl Smit and Snacken, 2009: 332–333). While reference had been made by secretaries of state to the 'public acceptability of release', the Court made it quite clear that this was not a *legitimate* criterion:

> It is not apparent how public confidence in the system of criminal justice could *legitimately* require the continued incarceration of a prisoner who had served the term required for punishment for the offence and was no longer a risk to the public.
>
> *(§80; my emphasis)*

This was repeated a few years later in a different context, when the UK government referred to 'public opinion' in its refusal to grant the right to vote to any sentenced prisoner:

> Nor is there any place under the Convention, where tolerance and broad-mindedness are the acknowledged hallmarks of democratic society, for automatic disenfranchisement based purely on *what might offend public opinion*.
>
> (Hirst *v* United Kingdom *(no 2) [GC] 6 October 2005, §70; my emphasis)*

'Democracy' is obviously defined here through the basic requirements of a democratic constitutional state, where human rights and the rule of law are not dependent on 'public opinion' (see also Snacken, 2010). 'Power-holder legitimacy' cannot be based on the emotional outrage of 'public opinion' if this violates the fundamental rights and human dignity of offenders, no matter how heinous their crimes. But that is of course exactly what populist punitiveness entails, as illustrated by the UK examples of *Stafford* and *Hirst* and the Belgian Martin case.

This means that 'power-holder legitimacy', based on constitutional validity, will require policymakers to enter into 'skilful negotiation' with 'the public' on the topic of parole for serious offenders. Let us first look into the significance of 'public opinion'.

Skilful negotiation: 'Public opinion' and the values inherent in parole for serious offenders

'Public opinion'

When policymakers refer to 'the public' or 'public opinion', they may use such terms as a purely rhetorical tool, independent or without knowledge of what people's opinions really are, in order to serve their own political purposes (Verfaillie, 2012). 'Populist punitiveness' thus refers to politicians tapping into and using for their own purposes what they believe to be the public's generally punitive stance (Bottoms, 1995). Or it may refer to 'real' people's opinions, as derived from everyday conversations or from (more or less sophisticated) opinion polls. There is a growing tendency for politicians to refer to public opinion polls, such as the Crime Survey for England and Wales, the Scottish Crime and Justice Survey, the Security Monitor and the Justice Barometer in Belgium.

Several authors have argued, however, that people seem very ambivalent about how we should punish (Stalans, 2002; Roberts et al., 2003; Roberts and Hough, 2002; Hutton, 2005; Verfaillie, 2012). There are methodological issues linked to how questions are framed: single-item surveys lead to more punitive responses than complex deliberations based on detailed information about a case (Freiberg and Gelb, 2008; Elffers and de Keijser, 2008; de Keijser and Elffers, 2009; Verfaillie, 2012; Snacken, 2013). But more importantly, opinions are situated, dynamic and complex. They are formed through reference to different sources of authority (for example personal experience, the media). They vary in interaction with concrete events and occurrences in space and time (Meert et al., 2004; Blommaert, 2005; Verfaillie, 2012). They are influenced by emotions and processes of identification – the authority of a source increases with the strength of the emotion and the level of personal identification (Verfaillie, 2012).

In that sense, opinions which seem at first sight contradictory can sometimes be logically explained. Let us take the example of the finding in the Belgian Justice Barometer that 30 to 90 per cent of the respondents (depending on the offence) demand harsher punishment, but 81 per cent of respondents are also in favour of more community sanctions (especially community service). The degree to which respondents can identify with either the victim or the offender correlates with their demands for more or less punishment. Young adults are hence less punitive towards drug offences, while women demand increased punishment for sex offences. Respondents voting for rightwing political parties are more punitive than respondents voting for leftwing parties – with the exception of financial crimes. But only 30 per cent of respondents demand harsher punishment of traffic offences, while 16 per cent feel these are already punished too harshly (Hoge Raad voor Justitie, 2010: 64–72).

With parole for serious offenders, one can assume that identification and emotions work in the direction of empathy for the victims of serious crime, not the offenders. But can the other values involved in parole – human dignity/human rights, reintegration/social inclusion and community safety – be invoked by power holders within the 'skilful negotiation' required to attain audience legitimacy?

Public opinion and human rights/dignity

'Public opinion' within the European Union is measured on a regular basis by the European Union Standard Eurobarometer. We can see from these measurements that human rights score highly within the values held by EU respondents (Table 3.1).[3]

Out of the given list, human rights stand on top of the 'personal values' held by European respondents (47 per cent). This is confirmed by the next question concerning which values best represent the EU, where the top answers also relate to democracy and human rights, both at 38 per cent (Table 3.2).

Of course, these answers relate to human rights in general, not human rights for offenders or prisoners. Respondents may think about human rights for themselves, or in international affairs, or for victims of crime. But within the dialogic approach to legitimacy advocated by Bottoms and Tankebe (2012), we can conclude that

TABLE 3.1 Standard Eurobarometer 74 (autumn 2010): three most important personal values (per cent)

Human rights	47
Peace	44
Respect for human life	41
Democracy	29
Individual freedom	23
Rule of law	22
Equality	19
Solidarity	15
Tolerance	15
Self-fulfilment	10
Respect for other cultures	8
Religion	6

Source: Adapted from European Commission, Standard Eurobarometer 74, 2011: 32.

TABLE 3.2 Standard Eurobarometer 74 (autumn 2010): three values which best represent EU (per cent)

Democracy	38
Human rights	38
Peace	35
Rule of law	25
Solidarity	20
Respect for other cultures	18
Tolerance	11
Self-fulfilment	4
Religion	3

Source: Adapted from European Commission, Standard Eurobarometer 74, 2011: 33.

human rights are not only an important aspect of the legal/constitutional legitimacy of the exercise of penal power (Beetham, 1991) but also an important 'shared' value with the European audience. Their application to offenders and prisoners may then be the object of 'skilful negotiation' by power holders in order to convince their audience that all humans, including offenders, are entitled to protection of their fundamental rights. The abolition of the death penalty in Europe has thus been described as an example 'where governments lead by example' in the construction of a European identity (Girling, 2006: 72).

Public opinion and reintegration/social inclusion

A similar finding applies to EU respondents' attitude to social exclusion (European Commission, Special survey 321 on poverty and social exclusion, October 2009). Tables 3.3 and 3.4 show the European average and the figures for the UK (per cent of respondents). The questions relate to who is seen most at risk of poverty, what is seen as the most important cause of poverty, and what measures might best tackle poverty.

The groups who are most at risk for poverty according to Europeans are the unemployed, then the elderly, and then those with a low level of education. In the UK, elderly people score highest. For the causes of poverty, interestingly, social injustice scores highest. Laziness scores higher in the UK than the European average. But asked about the solutions for poverty, the UK is very much in line with the EU average, emphasizing the importance of government and social policy in tackling poverty and social exclusion.

The responses all over Europe, including in the UK, suggest a 'social' rather than a 'neo-liberal' approach to solutions for social-economic problems, referring to traditional social democratic values of 'more government', 'more health care' and 'free education'. The UK scores even more strongly in these responses than the

TABLE 3.3 Special survey 321 on poverty and social exclusion (October 2009): poverty (per cent)

	EU	UK
Who is at risk of poverty?		
Unemployed	56	38
Elderly	41	47
Low-level education	31	37
Causes of poverty?		
Injustice	47	33
Laziness	16	26
Solutions for poverty?		
Action by government	89	85
Reduce income inequality	88	82
Redistribution of wealth by government	82	74
Higher taxes by well off	75	65
No point, poverty will always exist	35	43

European average, especially with regard to health care, minimal wages and free education. Only with regard to the division of responsibility between 'government' and 'self' does the UK score differently.

Again of course, these surveys on poverty and social exclusion are not about offenders. But as with human rights, they illustrate that addressing social exclusion is an important value and concern in Europe.

But we also know that public attitudes towards reintegration of former prisoners are generally negative, although variations have been found relating to the type of offence (e.g. violent and sex offences versus property and white-collar crime) and personal characteristics of the respondents (age, gender, socio-economic background, education level, political orientation, religion: see Reynolds et al., 2009). Arguing

TABLE 3.4 Special survey 321 on poverty and social exclusion (October 2009): social and economic problems (per cent)

Solving social and economic problems?	EU	UK
More health care, education, social spending, even if it means raising taxes	63	77
Minimal wages, even if less jobs	62	72
Free education, even if less quality	60	69
More responsibility government/self	55/34	40/51
National government to provide jobs for unemployed	54	57

for parole on the basis of community safety or protection of the public may therefore be more successful – as in the first Belgian example.

Public opinion and community safety

Community safety is mentioned as part of the definition of 'probation' and an explicit aim of all community sanctions and measures in the 2010 Council of Europe Probation Rules (CM/Rec (2010) 1):

> Probation: relates to the implementation in the community of sanctions and measures, defined by law and imposed on an offender. It includes a range of activities and interventions, which involve supervision, guidance and assistance aiming at the social inclusion of an offender, as well as at contributing to *community safety* (my emphasis).

The Council of Europe Recommendation Rec(2003)22 on conditional release (parole) equally emphasizes in its Preamble the positive effect of parole on reoffending:

> Recognising that conditional release is one of the most effective and constructive means of *preventing reoffending* and promoting resettlement, providing the prisoner with planned, assisted and supervised reintegration into the community (my emphasis).

This is reiterated in its first General Principle:

> Conditional release should aim at assisting prisoners to make a transition from life in prison to a law-abiding life in the community through post-release conditions and supervision that promote this end and contribute to *public safety* and the *reduction of crime* in the community (my emphasis).

Defending parole on the basis of community safety can therefore be seen as an illustration of Bottoms and Tankebe's (2012) reference to 'effectiveness' as a specific criminal justice value. It will still require 'skilful negotiation' in order to attain audience legitimacy, as the public may well feel that it is better protected by the incapacitation of offenders through imprisonment than by their supervision and guidance through parole. This will require discussion of the short-term versus long-term protection of the public, i.e. incapacitation by the prison versus reduction of recidivism after prison.

The growing insights into desistance processes from crime can offer helpful arguments in this respect. We know that imprisonment is counterproductive regarding nearly all the elements that help offenders desist from crime: human and social capital, positive relationships, generativity, decreased pressure of deviant peer groups (Farrall and Calverley, 2006; McNeill, 2006). But are such rational arguments sufficient to tackle public emotions surrounding parole for serious offenders?

Public opinion and emotions

In their report to the National Offender Management Service (NOMS), *Changing Lives? Desistance Research and Offender Management*, McNeill and Weaver (2010) explicitly tackle the question how desistance can reinforce the credibility of offender management. Community sanctions such as parole have the difficult task of combining 'internal' legitimacy (offenders and victims) in order to foster compliance by the offender, with 'external' legitimacy, aimed at audiences outside offender management (especially the courts and the public). It may well be established that parole reduces reoffending and promotes community safety, but such rational arguments will have to confront public emotions raised by serious crimes:

> Justice is, at its heart, an emotional, symbolic process, not simply a matter of effectiveness and efficiency (…) Desires for revenge and retribution, anger, bitterness and moral indignation are powerful emotive forces, but they do not raise confidence in probation work – just the opposite. To do that, one would want to tap in to other, equally cherished, emotive values, such as the widely shared belief in redemption, the need for second chances, and beliefs that all people can change.
>
> *(McNeill and Weaver, 2010: 44; citing Maruna and King, 2008: 347)*

Probation and parole may then be defended as 'more constructive punishment', mediating between the different and conflicting aims of punishment: retribution, reparation and rehabilitation; but also mediating between the different stakeholders in the justice process: courts, communities, victims and offenders (McNeill and Weaver, 2010: 46).

This is exactly what Belgian policymakers did in the first Dutroux case. Did it diminish their political legitimacy? The then minister of justice resigned in 1998, not because of the legislation that saved the parole system but because M. Dutroux managed to escape from the court where he was being interrogated … . The minister was back in office ten years later (2008–2011). His successor, who more fundamentally restricted the parole system in 2013 after the second Martin case, had disappointing results in the next election in 2014 and only narrowly managed to secure another post as regional minister.

Political legitimacy through populist punitiveness?

This latter example illustrates that populist punitiveness does not necessarily guarantee electoral success or political legitimacy. Lappi-Seppälä (2011; 2012) has demonstrated that countries with higher prison rates do not necessarily enjoy higher political legitimacy and trust – quite the contrary. The Scandinavian countries have the lowest prison rates and highest welfare expenditures in Europe, and enjoy the highest levels of public trust and political legitimacy. Conversely, countries with the highest prison rates and lowest welfare expenditures – i.e. the UK and most eastern European countries – have the lowest levels of public trust and legitimacy and the highest level of fear. The high levels of trust and legitimacy are hence positively correlated with welfare investments and social equality but not with more punitive penal policies.

What can we learn from these contrasts? Some authors have argued that the Scandinavian model is intrinsically linked to the typical characteristics and histories of the Scandinavian societies (Pratt, 2008). Others have argued to the contrary (Kuhnle, 2012) that the Scandinavian welfare states can and actually sometimes do serve as a positive model for other countries because they are successful in terms of values and objectives highly regarded by many: limited poverty, a relatively high degree of income equality, and social stability.

This seems to be corroborated by the findings on the most important concerns of European respondents in the Standard Eurobarometer. The survey distinguishes between the main concerns of respondents for their respective countries and their main personal concerns. Concerns may be influenced by recent incidents, so Table 3.5 shows a period of 1.5 years (spring 2013 – autumn 2014).

Figures fluctuate over the 1.5-year period but concerns for economic issues clearly dominate the responses all over Europe, with unemployment ranking first. Half of the respondents (51 per cent in 2013, 48–45 per cent in 2014) mention unemployment as the main concern for their country. Crime ranks fifth, with only 12 per cent of respondents citing it as one of two main concerns, decreasing to 9 per cent in autumn 2014 (in autumn 2009, crime ranked third, equal to rising prices and inflation). The UK figures are more or less comparable to European averages, with the exception of immigration, which scores much higher in the UK (three times higher in 2013), but is also increasing all over Europe (from 10 per cent in 2013 to 18 per cent in 2014). Terrorism ranks last in the European average, but sharply increased in the UK in autumn 2014 (from 3 per cent in spring to 16

TABLE 3.5 Main concerns for your country: Standard Eurobarometer 79, 81, 82 (per cent)

Main concerns	EB 79 (Spring 2013)		EB 81 (Spring 2014)		EB 82 (Autumn 2014)	
	EU	UK	EU	UK	EU	UK
Unemployment	51	36	48	29	45	22
Economic situation	33	23	29	19	24	13
Inflation	20	10	15	15	14	17
Government debt	15	19	13	7	14	12
Crime	12	18	12	12	9	9
Health & soc sec	11	13	14	17	16	22
Immigration	10	32	15	41	18	38
Pensions	9	7	11	8	11	6
Terrorism	3	8	2	3	6	16

Source: Adapted from European Commission, Standard Eurobarometer 79, 2013: 45; Standard Eurobarometer 81, 2014a: 39; Standard Eurobarometer 82, 2014b: 50.

per cent in autumn). This picture is confirmed for the main personal concerns (Table 3.6).

Crime further decreases to eighth position, with only 5–6 per cent of respondents mentioning it as one of their personal main concerns. This seems to indicate that, although crime and punishment are occasionally highly emotional topics in media, public and political debates, the more constant personal concerns of the respondents are with the economic situation and its repercussions in their daily lives. This could then explain the higher levels of trust and political legitimacy enjoyed by the more welfare-oriented Scandinavian political system compared to the Anglo-Saxon system.

Conclusion

Punishment is one of the most coercive forms of the exercise of state power. Reimagining penal policies should hence tend to more moderate penal policies. This exercise requires legitimation within a democratic constitutional state. Following Beetham (1991), I distinguished different levels of legitimacy: the legal/constitutional validity of the exercise of penal power and its justifiability in terms of the values current in society. I applied these levels of legitimacy to the topic of parole for serious offenders, a rather 'unpopular' penal practice, which often generates emotional outrage. The Belgian parole reforms and the European standards concerning 'life without parole' illustrate the different values and emotions raised by this practice.

Following Bottoms and Tankebe (2012), I applied a dialogic approach to the legitimacy of parole for serious offenders. This means considering the interaction between power-holder legitimacy and audience legitimacy and the importance of

TABLE 3.6 Main personal concerns: Standard Eurobarometer 79, 81 (per cent)

Main concerns	EB 79 (Spring 2013)		EB 81 (Spring 2014)	
	EU	UK	EU	UK
Inflation	41	34	32	34
Unemployment	22	16	21	12
Economic situation country	18	14	15	9
Taxation	16	9	17	15
Financial situation household	16	21	16	10
Health & social security	15	16	15	16
Pensions	14	17	15	17
Crime	6	8	5	6
Immigration	3	10	4	6
Terrorism	1	3	1	1

Source: Adapted from European Commission, Standard Eurobarometer 79, 2013: 16; Standard Eurobarometer 81, 2014a: 20.

'skilful negotiation' by power holders on the basis of shared core values or values specific to criminal justice. The example of the subsequent Belgian parole reforms illustrates the impact that political leaders, in casu the different ministers of justice, can have in dealing with highly publicized and emotional events, depending on which emotions and shared values they invoke in the public and political debates: public protection and procedural justice in the first case, pure retribution in the second case. 'Pure punishment' was also invoked by the UK government in legitimizing life without parole before the European Court of Human Rights, but found to constitute inhuman and degrading punishment. Even if it were supported by 'public opinion', such a practice can thus confer no constitutional legitimacy to power holders. But parole for serious or life-sentenced offenders must still be justifiable in terms of the values current in our societies. The European standards justify parole, including for serious offenders, on the basis of the fundamental values of human rights, reintegration into society and community safety. I have argued that these values are sufficiently shared to allow for 'skilled negotiation' by power-holders. This allows entering into debate with the emotions raised by serious crimes – not avoiding them altogether (Loader, 2010). It means understanding and responding to the legitimate concerns of the public, but also taking political responsibility to offer solutions that really answer those concerns.

Notes

1   Legal recidivism refers to two specific categories of recidivism: conviction for felony after an earlier felony; and conviction for misdemeanour after an earlier felony (Art. 54–56 Penal Code).
2   A third category of 'legal recidivism' has been added: conviction for misdemeanour within five years after an earlier conviction for a misdemeanour resulting in at least 12 months of imprisonment.
3   The questions about personal and EU 'values' were rephrased differently into 'issues' in subsequent Eurobarometers, where human rights were no longer mentioned.

References

Aebi, M. and Delgrande, N. (2014) *Council of Europe Annual Penal Statistics. SPACE I Prison Statistics, Survey 2013*, 15 December, Strasbourg, PC-CP (2014) 11. Available at: http://wp.unil.ch/space/files/2015/02/SPACE-I-2013-English.pdf.

Beccaria, C. (1764/1972) *Dei delitti e delle pene*, translated by J. M. Michiels, *Over misdaden en straffen*, Antwerpen: Standaard wetenschappelijke uitgeverij.

Bedau, H. A. and Kelly, E. (2010) 'Punishment', in *The Stanford Encyclopedia of Philosophy*, Zalta, Edward N. (ed.). Available at: http://plato.stanford.edu/archives/spr2010/entries/punishment/.

Beetham, D. (1991) *The Legitimation of Power*. London: MacMillan Publishers.

Blommaert, J. (2005) *Discourse: A Critical Introduction*. Cambridge: Cambridge University Press.

Bottoms, A. (1995) 'The Philosophy and Politics of Punishment and Sentencing', in C. Clarkson and R. Morgan (eds), *The Politics of Sentencing Reform*, Oxford: Oxford University Press, 17–49.

Bottoms, A. and Tankebe, J. (2012) 'Beyond Procedural Justice: A Dialogic Approach to Legitimacy in Criminal Justice', *Journal of Criminal Law & Criminology*, 102: 119–170.

Boutellier, H. (2004) *The Safety Utopia: Contemporary Discontent and Desire as to Crime and Punishment*. Dordrecht: Kluwer Academic Publishers.

Christie, Nils (1981) *Limits to Pain*, Oslo: Universitetet I Oslo.

De Hert, P. and Gutwirth, S. (2004) 'Rawls' Political Conception of Rights and Liberties: An Unliberal but Pragmatic Approach to the Problems of Harmonisation and Globalization', in Van Hoecke, M. (ed.), *Epistemology and Methodology of Comparative Law*. Oxford, Portland: Hart Publishers, 317–357.

Durkheim, E. (1902) 'Deux lois de l'évolution pénale', *L'Année Sociologique*, 4: 65–95.

Elffers, H. and Keijser, J. W. de (2008) 'Different Perspectives, Different Gaps: Does the General Public Demand a More Responsive Judge?', in Kury, H. (ed.), *Fear of Crime – Punitivity: New Developments in Theory and Research* (Crime and Crime Policy, vol. 3). Bochum: Universitätsverlag Brockmeyer, 447–470.

European Commission (2009) *Special Survey 321 on Poverty and Social Exclusion*, October. Brussels: TNS Opinion & Social.

European Commission (2011) *Standard Eurobarometer 74: Public Opinion in the European Union*, Autumn 2010. Brussels: TNS Opinion & Social.

European Commission (2013) *Standard Eurobarometer 79: Public Opinion in the European Union*, Spring. Brussels: TNS Opinion & Social.

European Commission (2014a) *Standard Eurobarometer 81: Public Opinion in the European Union*, Spring. Brussels: TNS Opinion & Social.

European Commission (2014b) *Standard Eurobarometer 82: Public Opinion in the European Union*, Autumn, Brussels: TNS Opinion & Social.

Falcon y Tella, M. J. and Falcon y Tella, F. (2006) *Punishment and Culture: A Right to Punish?* Leiden: Martinus Nijhoff Publishers.

Farrall, S. and Calverley, A. (2006) *Understanding Desistance From Crime: Theoretical Directions in Resettlement and Rehabilitation*. Crime and Justice Series. Oxford: Oxford University Press.

Freiberg, A. and Gelb, K. (eds) (2008) *Penal Populism, Sentencing Councils and Sentencing Policy*. Cullompton: Willan Publishing.

Garapon, A. and Papadopoulos, I. (2003) *Juger en Amérique et en France: Culture juridique et common law*. Paris: Odile Jacob.

Garland, D. (1990) *Punishment and Modern Society: A Study in Social Theory*. Chicago, IL: Chicago University Press.

Garland, D. (2001) *The Culture of Control: Crime and Social Order in Contemporary Society*. Oxford: Oxford University Press.

Garland, D. and Young, P. (1983) *The Power to Punish: Contemporary Penalty and Social Analysis*. London: Heinemann Educational Books.

Girling, E. J. (2006) European Identity, Penal Sensibilities, and Communities of Sentiment, in S. Armstrong and L. McAra (eds), *Perspectives on Punishment: The Contours of Control*. Oxford: Oxford University Press, 69–82.

Goethals, J. and Bouverne-De Bie, M. (eds) (2000) *Voorwaardelijke invrijheidstelling: wetgeving, predictie en begeleiding*. Gent: Academia Press.

Gutwirth, S. (1998) 'De polyfonie van de democratische rechtsstaat', in Elchardus, M. (ed.), *Wantrouwen en onbehagen*. Brussels: VUBPress, 137–193.

Gutwirth, S. and De Hert, P. (2002) 'Grondslagentheoretische variaties op de grens tussen het strafrecht en het burgerlijk recht. Perspectieven op schuld-, risico- en strafrechtelijke aansprakelijkheid, slachtofferclaims, buitengerechtelijke afdoening en restorative justice'. in Boonen, K., Cleiren, C. P. M., Foqué, R. and de Roos, Th. A. (eds), *De weging van 't Hart: Idealen, waarden en taken van het strafrecht*. Deventer: Kluwer, 121–170.

HogeRaadvoorJustitie (2010) *Belgische Justitiebarometer 2010.* Available at: www.belgium.be/nl/publicaties/publ_justitiebarometer-2010.jsp.

Hutton, N. (2005) 'Beyond populist punitiveness', *Punishment & Society*, 7/3, 243–258.

Keijser, J. de, and Elffers, H. (2009) 'Punitive public attitudes: a threat to the legitimacy of the criminal justice system?', in M. E. Oswald, S. Bieneck and J. Hupfeld (eds), *Social Psychology of Punishment of Crime*. Chichester: John Wiley & Sons, 55–74.

Kensey, A. and Tournier, P.-V. (2000) *Placement à l'extérieur, semi-liberté, libération conditionnelle: Des aménagements d'exception*. Paris: CESDIP.

Kuhnle, S. (2012) 'The Scandinavian Path to Welfare', in Snacken, S. and Dumortier, E. (eds), *Resisting Punitiveness in Europe? Welfare, Human Rights and Democracy*. London and New York: Routledge, 73–85.

Lappi-Seppälä, T. (2011) 'Explaining Imprisonment in Europe', *European Journal of Criminology*, 8/4: 303–328.

Lappi-Seppälä, T. (2012) 'Explaining National Differences in the Use of Imprisonment', in Snacken, S. and Dumortier, S. (eds), *Resisting Punitiveness in Europe? Welfare, Human Rights and Democracy*, London and New York: Routledge, 35–72.

Loader, I. (2010) 'For Penal Moderation: Notes Towards a Public Philosophy of Punishment', *Theoretical Criminology*, 14/3: 349–367.

Maruna, S. and King, A. (2008) 'Selling the Public on Probation: Beyond the Bib', *Probation Journal*, 55: 337–351. Available at: www.academia.edu/5231747/Selling_the_Public_on_Probation_Beyond_the_Bib.

McNeill, F. (2006) 'A Desistance Paradigm for Offender Management', *Criminology and Criminal Justice*, 6(1): 39–62.

McNeill, F. and Weaver, B. (2010) 'Changing Lives? Desistance Research and Offender Management', *Scottish Centre for Crime and Justice Research*, March. Available at: http://www.sccjr.ac.uk/wp-content/uploads/2012/11/Report_2010_03_-_Changing_Lives.pdf.

Meert, H., Blommaert, J., Stuyck, K., Peleman, K. and Dewilde, A. (2004) *Van Balen tot Onthalen: De geografische en discursieve dimensies van attitudes tegenover asielzoekers*. Gent: Academia Press.

Ostermann, M. (2013) 'Active Supervision and its Impact upon Parolee Recidivism Rates', *Crime and Delinquency*, 59/4: 487–509.

Pratt, J. (2002). *Punishment and Civilization: Penal Tolerance and Intolerance in Modern Society*. London: Sage.

Pratt, J. (2008) 'Scandinavian Exceptionalism in an Era of Penal Excess. Part I: The Nature and Roots of Scandinavian Exceptionalism', *British Journal Criminology* 48/2: 119–137.

Reynolds, N., Craig, L.A. and Boer, D. P. (2009) 'Public Attitudes towards Offending, Offenders and Reintegration', in Wood, J. and Gannon, T. (eds), *Public Opinion and Criminal Justice*. Cullompton: Willan Publishing, 166–186.

Roberts, J. V. and Hough, M. (eds) (2002) *Changing Attitudes to Punishment: Public Opinion, Crime and Justice*. Cullompton: Willan Publishing.

Roberts, J. V., Stalans, L. J., Indermauer, D. and Hough, M. (2003) *Penal Populism and Public Opinion*. Oxford: Oxford University Press.

Scheirs, V. (2014) *De strafuitvoeringsrechtbank aan het werk*. Antwerp and Apeldoorn: Maklu.

Shute, D. (2004) 'Does Parole Work? The Empirical Evidence from England and Wales', *Ohio State Journal of Criminal Law*, 2: 315–331.

Snacken, S. (2007) 'Penal Policy and Practice in Belgium', in Tonry, M. (ed.), *Crime, Punishment and Politics in Comparative Perspective*, Crime and Justice: A Review of Research no. 36. Chicago: University of Chicago Press, 127–216.

Snacken, S. (2010) 'Resisting Punitiveness in Europe?', *Theoretical Criminology*, 14/3: 273–292.

Snacken, S. (2011) *Prisons en Europe: Pour une pénologie critique et humaniste*. Collection Crimen. Brussels: Larcier.

Snacken, S. (2012) 'Conclusion: Why and How to Resist Punitiveness in Europe', in Snacken, S. and Dumortier, E. (eds), *Resisting Punitiveness in Europe? Welfare, Human Rights and Democracy*, London and New York: Routledge, 247–260.

Snacken, S. (2013) 'Legitimacy of Penal Policies: Punishment between Normative and Empirical Legitimacy', in Crawford, A. and Hucklesby, A. (eds), *Legitimacy and Compliance in Criminal Justice*. London and New York: Routledge, 50–70.

Snacken, S. (2014) 'De Commissie Holsters dan toch buitenspel?', in T. Daems, K. Beyens and E. Maes (eds), *Exit gevangenis? Werking van de strafuitvoeringsrechtbanken en de wet op de externe rechtspositie van gevangenen*. Antwerp: Maklu, 155–176.

Snacken, S. (2015) 'Punishment, Legitimate Policies and Values: Penal Moderation, Dignity and Human Rights', *Punishment and Society*, 17/3: 397–423.

Stalans, L. (2002) 'Measuring Attitudes to Sentencing', in Roberts, J. V. and Hough, M. (eds), *Changing attitudes to punishment. Public Opinion, Crime and Justice*. Cullompton: Willan Publishing, 15–32.

van Zyl Smit, D. and Snacken, S. (2009) *Principles of European Prison Law and Policy: Penology and Human Rights*. Oxford: Oxford University Press.

Verfaillie, K. (2012) 'Punitive Needs, Society and Public Opinion: An Explorative Study of Ambivalent Attitudes to Punishment and Criminal Justice', in Snacken, S. and Dumortier, E. (eds), *Resisting Punitiveness in Europe? Welfare, Human Rights and Democracy*. London and New York: Routledge, 235–246.

Wacquant, L. (2008) 'Racial Stigma in the Making of the Punitive State', in Loury, G. C. with Karlan, P., Shelby, T. and Wacquant, L. (eds), *Race, Incarceration and American Values* (The 2007 Tanner Lecture Symposium). Cambridge, MA: MIT Press, 59–70.

Wan, W.-Y., Poynton, S., van Doorn, G. and Weatherburn, D. (2014) 'Parole Supervision and Reoffending', *Trends and Issues in Crime and Criminal Justice no. 485*, September. Canberra: Australian Institute of Criminology. Available at http://www.aic.gov.au/p ublications/current per cent20series/tandi/481-500/tandi485.html.

Weber, M. (1922/1968) *Economy and Society*. New York: Bedminster Press.

Whitman, J. Q. (2003) *Harsh Justice: Criminal Punishment and the Widening Divide between America and Europe*. Oxford: Oxford University Press.

4

WHAT GOOD IS PUNISHMENT?[1]

Fergus McNeill

Introduction

Sociologists of punishment have long recognized that both crime and punishment serve important and useful social functions. Perhaps most famously, Emile Durkheim (1984) argued that social solidarity depends on the unity of moral beliefs in social groups. Punishment of crime is always a passionate collective reaction to violations of these core, shared beliefs; its rituals are important as a means of allowing us to communicate, reaffirm and reinforce them. As Garland (2013a: 25) puts it in a recent re-examination of Durkheim's work on punishment, offending shocks 'healthy' (i.e. well-socialized) consciences into punishment as a reaction:

> The essence of punishment, [Durkheim] claims, is irrational, unthinking emotion driven by outrage at the violation of sacred values or else by sympathy for fellow individuals and their sufferings.
>
> *(Ibid.: 25)*

The notions of crime and punishment as, respectively, a stimulus for and crucible of moral communication suggest the possibility of positive framings of the challenges posed by crime. Yet contemporary penal policy tends to be preoccupied merely with reducing harms by preventing crime, protecting the public or reducing reoffending. The unlikely analogy of plumbing might help to make clear the differences between these positive and negative perspectives. Most of the time, when we think about plumbing – and when we call plumbers – it is because we are concerned about flaws (or leaks) in our plumbing systems. We know that, left unattended, even very minor leaks have the capacity to destroy the fabric of our homes and diminish their value. Major leaks can do serious damage very quickly and can make life in our homes intolerable. A good plumber, we tend to think, is one who fixes leaks swiftly and efficiently – minimising our losses and restoring our comforts.

But there is another way to think about plumbing; the way that architects, for example, might think about it. For them, plumbing is a central design feature in any property, the purpose of which is to bring two of the necessities for human life – heat and water – to wherever they are needed (and, of course, to remove some of the waste that human life inevitably produces). Perhaps for architects, the 'true' purpose of plumbing is to make human life comfortable in a given space and thus to allow humans dwelling in the space to thrive.

My suggestion is that, much of the time, when we think and talk about criminal justice, we think and talk as if its institutions are like leak-repair or leak-prevention services. For example, we talk about the importance of crime reduction, tackling the fear of crime, reducing reoffending, managing serious and dangerous offenders, reducing risk. In contrast, the central argument I want to advance in this short chapter is that perhaps *we should judge criminal sanctions not so much by the evils (or harms) they reduce as by the goods they promote*. In other words, I want us to think like architects of justice.

That said, the problem with architects is that they have a tendency to build edifices; at their worst, ambition or vanity gets the better of them and they build large, wasteful and unsustainable buildings that the next generation has to tear down. So it has been with punishment. In the middle of the twentieth century, the ambition to do something positive with punishment, and the vanity of assuming too readily that we knew what to do, constructed an intrusive and expansionist penal welfarism (Garland, 1985). Despite its benign intentions, welfarism often neglected the human dignity and rights of the subjects it aimed to rehabilitate or reform. Counter-movements pressed the case for a much less ambitious and, they hoped, a much less harmful philosophy of just deserts (von Hirsch and Ashworth, 2005) and of limiting retributivism (Morris and Tonry, 1991; Frase, 2004). Yet what we have witnessed at least in some western jurisdictions in the last 30 years is not a shrinking penal state that accepts a modest assessment of its limits and an expanded conception of its duties but rather the opposite. At least in Anglophone jurisdictions we more commonly find an expanding penal state with a hollowed-out sense of its obligations, and a desire to contract out or otherwise devolve to others any obligations it can (Wacquant, 2009). If nothing else, the story of mass incarceration makes clear enough that penal expansionism has no need of a positive narrative; on the contrary, it feeds on fear and insecurity rather than on hope and aspiration.

So, while my instinct is to heed the injunctions of critical criminologists (like Christie, 1993) and to favour penal reductionist and (wherever possible) abolitionist strategies, and while I recognize that a positive agenda can become an expansionist one, I aim here to consider whether and how the articulation of a positive agenda for criminal justice might in fact exercise a moderating and modifying effect on the penal state. In seeking to develop these arguments, I will focus primarily on the sanctioning end of the justice system, and more specifically on the relationships between punishment and rehabilitation (for a more detailed discussion, see McNeill, 2014).

What sort of good is (criminal) justice?

One of the twentieth century's pre-eminent political philosophers, John Rawls, famously wrote in his magnum opus *Theory of Justice* that 'Justice is the first virtue of social institutions, as truth is of systems of thought' (Rawls, 1971). Those familiar with his work will understand that he was discussing justice in the broadest sense. His mechanism for exploring the nature and meaning of justice required us to imagine ourselves as rationally self-interested amnesiacs deliberating about social institutions from behind a 'veil of ignorance' (that is, to imagine ourselves capable of reasoned argument but freed from privileging our own interests and positions). From this position, he argued, we could intelligently but disinterestedly work out how to order society and to address the enduring tensions between liberty, equality and welfare. His conclusions need not concern us here; the central point is that he saw justice as the core virtue (or quality) of social institutions and not merely as a mechanism for delivering *other* social goods. In this he drew perhaps on Aristotle who, in the *Nicomachean Ethics*, distinguished between constitutive and productive ends. The latter are ends that are good only insofar as they produce some other good; the former are good in and of themselves.

However, even if justice is properly understood as a constitutive good of the good society, it is also a productive good for humanity. Perhaps the simplest way to sum this up is in the common slogan 'Without justice there is no peace'. In other words, reciprocal social relations of cooperation are essential to human and social life (just as they were to human evolution); without an established network of reasonably reliable reciprocities, we can enjoy peaceful co-existence at neither the level of the community nor the level of the state. In a similar vein, at a recent Howard League conference, the British historian Bettany Hughes explained that the oldest surviving human text (from Ancient Babylon) contains the text 'Ana shulmi u balaatu', meaning 'To peace and to life'; the phrase is interpreted as a greeting or salutation that was used when social or kinship groups came together. It is perhaps a statement of mutual respect that had to be uttered to make discussion (and trade) possible between unfamiliar groups for their mutual benefit.

This brief and superficial excursion into philosophy and ancient history is offered simply to recall what is at stake both in 'offending' and in punishment (see also Atwood, 2008). Offending (whether by individuals, groups, corporations or states) offends because and to the extent that it violates these fundamental principles of mutual recognition and respect, as well as the reciprocal social relations that recognition and respect should permit and entail. Offending thus constitutes an unjust distribution (of recognition, respect and/or reciprocity), as the offender fails to return the recognition, respect and/or bonds of reciprocity from which she/he has benefited. The classical explanation of retributivist punishment (which also dates back at least to Aristotle) is that it seeks to secure or to restore a 'just order' of things. In this sense, punishment is a productive good; it aims to remedy an imbalance (in the scales of justice or in the honouring of obligations of reciprocity) and to restore the proper equilibrium in human and social relationships.

However, as we have already seen, following Durkheim, punishment is also a *communicative* good; by affirming and expressing our values, it says something to us and about us as a community; it reminds all of us how we understand our common obligations of respect, recognition and reciprocity. Even so, Durkheim also argued that we can punish in ways that are '*pathological*' or ill-adapted to our social and political circumstances and to the state of development of our society (see McNeill and Dawson, 2014). For Durkheim (1973), the development of moral individualism in modernity, amongst other influences, should have produced a shift from repressive to restitutive forms of law and punishment.

More generally, it is clear that there are many possible ways to restore balance and to communicate and affirm values. Most fundamentally, we can punish in ways that wilfully damage offenders and their interests, or we can punish (or rehabilitate) in ways that elicit a more positive form of redress. The choices we make about the forms of penal power and the penal mechanisms we deploy in this respect are historically, sociologically and politically contingent. And they have profound consequences.

Two forms of penal power

In a recent paper that offers a compelling argument for the development of comparative analyses of the contours of 'penal states', Garland (2013b) identifies 'modes of penal power' as one of the key dimensions of any comparison:

> Penal power takes different forms and may be oriented toward different ends. The power to kill, the power to incarcerate, the power to supervise, the power to levy fines, the power to transform individual conduct, and the power to transform families or communities are distinct forms, and they each may be deployed as means to different ends. For purposes of comparison, one wants to know which modes of exercising power are deployed by a particular penal state and in what proportion.
>
> (Ibid.: 500–501)

Garland also notes, following Foucault (1975/1977), that these modes of penal power are also inevitably modes of 'power-knowledge'; the discourses, rationalities and technologies of punishment in any society and in any system will have profound consequences.

Leaving the comparative project aside on this occasion (but see McNeill and Beyens, 2013), Garland's brief account of 'negative' and 'positive' forms of penal power speaks directly to the project of 'positive criminology'. For him, negative penal power is incapacitating; positive penal power is capacity-building.

This distinction is not difficult to comprehend; indeed, it is implicit not just in sociological analyses of penal discourses and practices but also in the philosophy of punishment itself. Retributive punishment remedies the imbalance that crime creates by taking something away from the offender; it slices something off – or cuts the offender off from or out of society altogether. It may take life, liberty, time, property or reputation and status – or some combination of these. In essence, retributive punishment imposes some form of loss or suffering on the offender as a negative compensation for the unfair advantage that offending has illicitly produced. Though this is negative power, the term 'incapacitation' is perhaps too clinical or managerial a term for what is going on in this kind of punishment, since retribution is also demonstrative and communicative. Psychologically and etymologically, retribution is not far away from revenge (in Latin, *revindicare*), though the latter term also implies that the purpose of the pain imposed on the offender is to release (or more literally to 'vindicate') the victim's pain or loss.

Positive approaches to punishment, whether rehabilitative, reparative or restorative, tend to aim at grafting the offender back into the social body rather than severing him or her from it. There are important differences in the methodologies and priorities of these three approaches. Rehabilitation – to the extent that it focuses on the offender and not the victim – requires no metaphor of balance, whereas reparation and restoration can and do share retribution's desire for justice-as-balance. But, like rehabilitation, reparation and restoration aim to sanction in ways which build capacity rather than imposing loss; they aim to enable and elicit goods from (and sometimes for) the offender; to enhance life, (positive) liberty, time, property, reputation and/or status. These enhancements are conditional, to be sure – but they are in theory made available in and they are valued by these penal philosophies and practices. If (and only if) the offender 'makes good', then the balance is restored without the need for exacting loss upon him or her.

There are risks involved with both forms of power. The problem with the exercise of negative penal power is obvious; it harms those upon whom it operates. Moreover, it does a great deal of unintended collateral damage to others associated with the offender (principally their partners and children, on which see Condry, 2007; Comfort, 2007). Additionally, since most of those on whom this incapacitating, diminishing power operates have to return to (or continue in) life in the community, it risks damaging their ability to do so lawfully and constructively. Garland (2013b: 478) makes this point himself in commenting on the multiple 'disqualifications and disabilities that follow felony conviction' in the USA. He adds:

> In all societies, the stigma of criminal convictions and sentences of imprisonment creates difficulties for ex-offenders when they try to secure employment, find housing, form relationships, or resettle in the outside world. But in the United States, these de facto social consequences of conviction are exacerbated by a set of de jure legal consequences that extend and intensify the sanction in multiple ways. Disfranchisement, either temporary or permanent; disqualification from public office and jury service; ineligibility for federal housing

benefits, education benefits, and welfare assistance; liability to court costs and prison fees; exclusion from various licensed occupations; banishment from specified urban areas; and where the offender is a noncitizen, deportation – all of these are concomitants of a criminal conviction for millions of individuals ... the result [is] that potential employers, landlords, and others are legally permitted to discriminate against an individual on the basis of his or her prior convictions, or on the basis of prior arrests, even when these were for minor offenses or offenses that occurred many years previously.

(Ibid.: 478–479)

If, as some have argued (e.g. Jolliffe and Hedderman, 2015), the consequence of these civil disqualifications and disabilities is that the exercise of negative penal power is itself criminogenic, then ironically it harms not just the offender but the punishing community itself.

The dangers of positive penal power are somewhat different – although also familiar. As I noted in the introduction, too optimistic and enthusiastic an assertion of positive penal power (especially of the rehabilitative sort) can easily become decoupled from the constraints of the metaphor of balance. If punishment is doing the offender good (and thus doing us all some good in some way), then why set limits of proportionality upon it? Of course, this is the lesson of history; rehabilitation's infamous (if often over-stated) demise in the 1970s and 1980s was at least partly the result of a failure to season optimism about the 'appliance of science' with, first, respect for human rights and, second, a thorough, cautious and critical appraisal of research evidence.

Garland (2013b) also makes an important practical point about the exercise of these two forms of penal power. For all its disadvantages, the exercise of negative penal power – precisely because of the limit of its ambition (to incapacitate) – lies wholly within the ambit of the penal system; penal actors can incapacitate without cooperation from other social systems and services, or from civil society more broadly. Exercising the positive form of penal power, by contrast, depends to a very great extent on collaboration not just between justice agencies (policing, prosecution, courts, probation, prisons), but with services, systems and actors outside of the penal system (e.g. education, health, housing, welfare, etc.). The penal system has it within its own grasp to exclude, but not to integrate.

Four forms of integration

In some recent papers (McNeill, 2012a, 2014; Kirkwood and McNeill, 2015), I have been seeking to refine an understanding of what rehabilitation and reintegration might mean and what they might require. My ideas first evolved in the context of a somewhat technical debate about evidence-based practice in 'offender rehabilitation' (McNeill, 2012a). In that paper, I began with a review of current arguments about what a credible 'offender' rehabilitation theory requires, exploring some aspects of current debates about different theories, before going on to locate this specific kind of contemporary theory-building in the context of historical arguments about and critiques of rehabilitation as a concept and in practice. More pertinent in the context of the current discussion, in the third part of the paper I examined the nature of the relationship between 'desistance' theories (explaining how and why people stop offending and progress towards social integration) and rehabilitation theories, so as to develop my concluding argument: that narrowly conceived debates about the merits of different forms of 'psychological rehabilitation' have been hampered by a failure to engage fully with debates about at least three other forms of rehabilitation (legal, moral and social) that emerge as being equally important in the process of desistance from crime. The concluding discussion of the paper is introduced with a quote that deploys the metaphor of mobility:

> To the extent that felons belong to a distinct class or status group, the problems of desistance from crime can be interpreted as problems of mobility – moving felons from a stigmatized status as outsiders to full democratic participation as stakeholders.
>
> *(Uggen et al., 2006: 283)*

Drawing on evidence from desistance studies – which often examine and rely upon the lived experience of rehabilitation and reintegration – I argued that rehabilitation is a social project as well as a personal one. Whether cast in deontological terms as being concerned with the requalification of citizens, or in utilitarian and correctional terms as being concerned with their re-education or resocialization, rehabilitation raises profound political questions about the nature of (good) citizenship, about the nature of society, about the relationship between citizenship, society and the state, and about the proper limits of legitimate state power.

The practical challenges of 'delivering' or 'transforming' rehabilitation ultimately rest upon these shaky and under-articulated philosophical foundations, and at least some of rehabilitation's problems come from the failure of some of its proponents and practitioners to engage adequately with these moral and political questions. Such engagement requires 'psychological or correctional rehabilitation' (which is principally concerned with promoting positive individual-level change in the 'offender', developing his or her motivation, skills and capacities) to articulate its relationships with the three other forms.

The first of these concerns the practical expression of Cesare Beccaria's (1764/ 1963) concern with the requalification of citizens; this is the problem of 'legal or judicial rehabilitation' – when, how and to what extent a criminal record and the stigma that it represents can ever be set aside, sealed or surpassed. Maruna (2011) has recently argued cogently that efforts to sponsor rehabilitation and reform must address the collateral consequences of conviction – most notably its stigmatizing and exclusionary effects – or be doomed to fail. No amount of supporting people to change themselves and their behaviour can be sufficient to the tasks and challenges of rehabilitation and desistance, if legal and practical barriers to reintegration are left in place. The most obvious of these barriers relates to the effects of criminal records in terms of labour market exclusion (Armstrong, McGuinness and McNeill, 2013).

However, I also argue that such barriers are not just legal – they are moral and social too. A solely psychological conception of rehabilitation is inadequate to the moral and social offence that crime represents. In simple terms, doing something for or to the 'offender', even something that aims to somehow change them so as to reduce future victimization, fails to engage with other key aspects of dispensing justice. Perhaps most importantly in moral terms, as I noted above, rehabilitation offers no moral redress *per se*; it operates only on the individual 'offender', not on the conflict itself and not on the victim or the community (Zedner, 1994). Critically, reparation – and reparative work in particular – seems capable of fulfilling this function in ways rehabilitation cannot, perhaps principally because reparation seems better able to convey (not least visibly) that redress is being actively provided. Rehabilitation, by contrast, is typically a private and secretive business, incapable of responding to the late-modern re-emergence of appetites and demands for more expressive forms of justice (Freiberg, 2001; Pratt, 2007).

Reparation perhaps speaks to the insistence that moral demands have to be satisfied, and moral communication secured, before 'moral rehabilitation' can be recognized (see also Duff, 2001). In simple terms, a person who has offended has to pay back before she/he can trade up to a restored social position as a citizen of good character; as Bazemore (1998) has argued, redemption needs to be earned. This is not necessarily bad news for rehabilitation; as the Scottish Prisons Commission (2008, para. 33) noted, 'one of the best ways for offenders to pay back is by turning their lives around'. But it does mean that rehabilitation theories and practices need to engage much more explicitly with questions of justice and reparation.

In a later paper further developing the model (McNeill, 2014), this time with reference to the philosophy and sociology of punishment, I add more explicit recognition of the reciprocal duties implied in moral rehabilitation; duties that are owed by the 'offender', the community and the state to one another. In addition to the offender's obligation to make good, the community and the state must accept a duty to support reintegration that rests on two principles. First, to the extent that the community and the state bear some complicity in permitting or exacerbating criminogenic social inequalities, they too must make good. Second, even under a retributivist approach to punishment, the polity has a duty to make sure that the punishment ends and that there is no punishment beyond the law ('nulla poena sine lege'). Yet, as I have already argued here, following Garland (2013b), criminological and sociological evidence about the enduring unintended effects of punishment both for individuals and for their families suggests that this duty is commonly neglected *de facto* and *de jure*.

Ultimately, even where psychological issues are tackled, legal requalification is confirmed and reciprocal moral debts are settled, the question of 'social rehabilitation' remains. In European jurisprudence, the concept of 'social rehabilitation' entails both the restoration of the citizen's formal social status and the availability of the personal and social means to do so (van Zyl Smit and Snacken, 2009). But in using the term, I mean something that is 'broader, deeper and more subjective; specifically, the informal social recognition and acceptance of the reformed ex-offender' (McNeill, 2012a: 15). That, rather than the advancement of the 'science' of personal reform, is perhaps the ultimate problem for rehabilitation in practice. It lies at the root of the hostile correctional climate that bedevils and undermines rehabilitation (Garland, 2001; 2013b), and it lies behind the mistranslation, corruption and misuse of rehabilitation theories.

Conclusions: judging sanctions

In a very recent paper on 'pathways to integration', Steve Kirkwood and I compare models of and data about 'ex-offender' and asylum-seeker reintegration (Kirkwood and McNeill, 2015). In looking at the latter population, we draw heavily on the work of Ager and Strang (2004), who were commissioned by the UK Home Office to develop a framework and indicators for integration to be used in evaluating the work of projects that assist asylum seekers and refugees in the UK. Ager and Strang did so on the basis of extensive empirical work with asylum seekers themselves. They outline ten 'domains' of integration, clustered in four categories:

- Means and markers: employment; housing; education; health.
- Social connections: social bonds; social bridges; social links.
- Facilitators: language and cultural knowledge; safety and stability.
- Foundation: rights and citizenship.

The first category is described as 'means and markers' because these are both indications of the extent to which an individual is 'integrated', as well as being resources or opportunities that should assist people to integrate in other ways. The second category draws on research and theory into social capital, which is constituted by the social resources available to a person through their formal and informal social networks, including family members, friends and work colleagues, etc. (Coleman, 1988). Ager and Strang (2004: 4) define the three domains as follows:

1. social bonds (connections within a community defined by, for example, ethnic, national or religious identity);
2. social bridges (with members of other communities); and
3. social links (with institutions, including local and central government services).

The third category (language and cultural knowledge and a sense of safety and stability) relates to aspects that are necessary for facilitating integration, whereas the fourth category asserts the role of formal rights and obligations, including legal grounds to remain in the host society, and political engagement.

Ager and Strang (2004: 5) define someone as being integrated when they achieve public outcomes within employment, housing, education, health and so on, which are equivalent to those achieved within the wider host communities; when they are socially connected with members of a (national, ethnic, cultural, religious or other) community with which they identify, with members of other communities and with relevant services and functions of the state; and when they have sufficient linguistic competence and cultural knowledge, and a sufficient sense of security and stability, to confidently engage in that society in a manner consistent with shared notions of nationhood and citizenship.

This overall framework conceives of integration as a *process* as well as defining successful integration as *achievement* across a range of domains (Ager and Strang, 2008). The authors also point out that if this definition was applied to members of the host society it would inevitably highlight that not all members are equally – if at all – 'integrated'. However, they suggest that the benefits of integration are such that this is a goal that should be worked towards for *all* members (Ager and Strang, 2004). This framework therefore functions as a sort of 'ideal' that might be used to guide service development and evaluation in terms of policies and practices directed at asylum seekers and refugees, although it holds the potential to be applied to other members of society as well.

There have been criticisms of Ager and Strang's model. Behind its elegance and simplicity lies a set of highly complex problems that face late-modern societies: how do we understand nationhood, citizenship and belonging? Exactly what sorts of reciprocity, trust and social connection are invoked in the concept of social capital? Is that capital available where it is needed or not? Perhaps most importantly, whose responsibility is reintegration? As I have already noted above, in criminal justice the responsibility tends to be placed squarely on the offender or the community (Miller, 2014) but the state has duties too (McNeill, 2012b).

Without dismissing the seriousness and complexity of these problems, I want to conclude by arguing that, if nothing else, the concept of integration at least invites us to ask some challenging questions about our approaches to punishment – and to set those charged with imposing and administering sanctions a positive and challenging metric within which to assess their achievements or failures. I doubt that many criminologists or practitioners would suggest that our present systems and practices of punishment would score positively against these measures of integration.

Perhaps if, instead of asking whether a sanction prevents an offender from reoffending, we were to ask whether it supports his or her longer-term reintegration, we might come to judge punishment and rehabilitation differently. We might also come to recognize our own moral involvement with punishment as citizens. In the process, we might also be compelled to address some difficult questions about whether and why we think we have any right to punish (in an unjust society), and what the ways in which penal power is exercised on our behalf say about us, to us and for us. I can't help but suspect that it is from confronting these questions – rather than questions about what might work best to reduce crime – that we will learn most about how to be architects of safer and peaceful societies, as opposed to plumbers of leaky ones.

Note

1 This paper was initially delivered as a speech at the Howard League's 'What is Justice?' conference at Keble College, Oxford, 1 October 2013. It was then adapted and published as a book chapter in a collection on 'Positive Criminology' edited by Natti Ronel and Dana Segev and published by Routledge in 2015. I am grateful to the editors for permission to re-use some of the material here. In this collection, the text is returned more or less to the form in which it was first delivered.

References

Ager, A. and Strang, A. (2004) *Indicators of integration: Final report*. Available at: http://weba rchive.nationalarchives.gov.uk/20110218135832/http://rds.homeoffice.gov.uk/rds/pdfs0 4/dpr28.pdf [accessed May 2015].

Ager, A. and Strang, A. (2008) 'Understanding integration: a conceptual framework', *Journal of Refugee Studies*, 21, 166–191.

Armstrong, S., McGuinness, P. and McNeill, F. (2013) *The use and impact of the Rehabilitation of Offenders Act (1974): Final Report*. Glasgow: Scottish Centre for Crime and Justice Research. Available at: http://www.sccjr.ac.uk/wp-content/uploads/2013/07/SCCJR-ROA-Final-Report-26-June-2013.pdf.

Atwood, M. (2008) *Payback: Debt and the Shadow Side of Wealth*. London: Bloomsbury Publishing.

Bazemore, G. (1998) 'Restorative justice and earned redemption: communities, victims, and offender reintegration', *American Behavioral Science* 41(6): 768–813.

Beccaria, C. (1764/1963) *On Crimes and Punishment* (trans. Pallouci, H.). Indianapolis, IN: Bobbs-Merrill.

Christie, N. (1993) *Crime Control as Industry: Towards Gulags, Western Style*. Abingdon: Routledge.

Coleman, J. S. (1988) 'Social capital in the creation of human capital', *American Journal of Sociology* 94: S95–S120.

Comfort, M. (2007) *Doing Time Together: Love and Family in the Shadow of the Prison*. Chicago: University of Chicago Press.

Condry, R. (2007) *Families Shamed: The Consequences of Crime for the Families of Serious Offenders*. Cullompton: Willan.

Duff, A. (2001) *Punishment, Communication and Community*. New York: Oxford University Press.

Durkheim, E. (1973) 'Two laws of penal evolution', *Economy and Society*, 2(3): 285–308.

Durkheim, E. (1984) *The Division of Labour in Society*. London: Palgrave Macmillan.

Foucault, M. (1975/1977) *Discipline & Punish*. (English trans. 1977). London: Allen Lane.

Frase, R. (2004) 'Limiting Retributivism' in Tonry, M. (ed.) *The Future of Imprisonment*. Oxford: Oxford University Press.

Freiberg, A. (2001) 'Affective versus effective justice: instrumentalism and emotionalism in criminal justice', *Punishment and Society*, 3(2): 265–278.

Garland, D. (1985) *Punishment and Welfare*. Aldershot: Ashgate.

Garland, D. (2001) *The Culture of Control*. Oxford: Oxford University Press.

Garland, D. (2013a) 'Punishment and Social Solidarity', in Simon, J. and Sparks, R. (eds) *The Sage Handbook of Punishment and Society*. London and New York: Sage.

Garland, D. (2013b) 'Penality and the penal state: the 2012 Sutherland Address', *Criminology*, 51(3): 475–517.

Jolliffe, D. and Hedderman, C. (2015) 'Investigating the impact of custody on reoffending using propensity score matching', *Crime & Delinquency*, 61(8): 1051–1077.

Kirkwood, S. and McNeill, F. (2015) 'Integration and reintegration: comparing pathways to citizenship through asylum and criminal justice', *Criminology & Criminal Justice*, first published 16 March as doi: 10.1177/1748895815575618.

McNeill, F. (2012a) 'Four forms of 'offender' rehabilitation: towards an interdisciplinary perspective', *Legal and Criminological Psychology*, 17(1): 18–36.

McNeill (2012b) 'Whose responsibilities are rehabilitation and reentry', *Discovering Desistance* blog, posted 21 November: http://blogs.iriss.org.uk/discoveringdesistance/2012/11/21/whose-responsibilities-are-rehabilitation-and-reentry/ [accessed May 2015].

McNeill, F. (2014) 'Punishment as Rehabilitation', in Bruinsma, G. and Weisburd, D. (eds) *Encyclopedia of Criminology and Criminal Justice*. New York: Springer Science and Business Media.

McNeill, F. and Beyens, K. (eds) (2013) *Offender Supervision in Europe*. Basingstoke: Palgrave.

McNeill, F. and Dawson, M. (2014) 'Social solidarity, penal evolution and probation', *British Journal of Criminology* 54(5): 892–907.

Maruna, S. (2011) 'Reentry as a rite of passage', *Punishment & Society*, 13(1): 3–28.

Miller, R. (2014) 'Devolving the carceral state: race, prisoner reentry, and the micro politics of urban poverty management', *Punishment and Society*, 16(3): 305–335.

Morris, N. and Tonry, M. (1991) *Between Prison and Probation: Intermediate Punishments in a Rational Sentencing System*. Oxford: Oxford University Press.

Pratt, J. (2007) *Penal Populism*. London: Routledge.

Rawls, J. (1971) *A Theory of Justice*. Cambridge, MA: Harvard University Press.

Scottish Prisons Commission (2008) *Scotland's Choice*. Edinburgh: Scottish Prisons Commission.

Uggen, C., Manza, J. and Thompson, M. (2006) 'Citizenship, democracy, and the civic reintegration of criminal offenders', *Annals AAPSS* 605: 281–310.

van Zyl Smit, D. and Snacken, S. (2009) *Principles of European Prison Law and Policy*. Oxford: Oxford University Press.

von Hirsch, A. and Ashworth, A. (2005) *Proportionate Sentencing: Exploring the Principles*. Oxford: Oxford University Press.

Wacquant, L. (2009) *Punishing the Poor: The Neoliberal Government of Social Insecurity*. Durham, NC and London: Duke University Press.

Zedner, L. (1994) 'Reparation and retribution: are they reconcilable?', *Modern Law Review*, 57: 228–250.

5

CIVIC REPAIR AND PENAL REFORM

The role of the state in rebuilding trust

Vanessa Barker

Introduction: 'I can't breathe'

On August 9, 2014, a white police officer shot and killed an unarmed young black man, Michael Brown, following a convenience store robbery in Ferguson, Missouri. In the wake of the shooting, black youth filled the streets of Ferguson to protest the blatant disregard of black life. One year later, they are still marching and marching alongside thousands of other Americans, black and white, who have joined this mass movement against police brutality. A new civil rights movement has emerged to protest not only the Ferguson shooting but a rapid succession of police shootings of unarmed black men and boys in which no one was held accountable for the violence, the loss of life, or the breach of the social contract. Protesters around the country have taken another police fatality Eric Garner's last words, 'I can't breathe', as their rallying call and staged spontaneous 'die-ins' in highly visible public places to show solidarity with fellow Americans killed by the police and voice moral outrage at unchecked police brutality. Eric Garner died from a police chokehold, an asphyxiation that was videotaped and broadcast around the country. 'Black lives matter,' protestors chanted, plainly reasserting the value of black lives and demanding human dignity for all. In response, President Obama has called for equality before the law, comparing contemporary protests to the anti-lynching struggle over one hundred years ago, and naming discrimination an 'American problem', not a black problem (2014a, 2014b). He continued: 'We are not going to let up until we see a strengthening of the trust and a strengthening of the accountability' (2014b).

This is a pivotal moment in the United States, a moment in which public demands for serious and substantial changes in the criminal justice system are literally spilling out onto the streets, across social media, into courthouses, police departments, legislative chambers, and across Lafayette Park into the White House, demands that include an end to police brutality and 'freedom from mass incarceration' (Ferguson Action, 2014). This is a rare chance for civic repair. Obama has pointed to the need to dissolve distrust between the police and communities of colour. This point has been scoffed at by some critics as just talk. But, as I argue below, trust is a necessary building block in the making of a fair and more equitable criminal justice system. Criminal justice is not simply a matter of crime control: it is a matter of civil rights (Alexander, 2010). Rebuilding trust is essential for the recognition of such rights and the transformation of criminal justice.

This paper is about trust, its centrality to a less repressive, milder and minimalist criminal justice system, and the specific role of the state in rebuilding trust. It proceeds with a definition of trust, its relation to punishment, and four elements of civic repair that include: accountability; responsiveness; participation; and shared future. These four elements include some practical suggestions, many of which are attainable in the immediate present (e.g. citizen advisory boards; 311 for Justice; mobile youth forums), and other suggestions that involve a fundamental change in perspective away from the past towards the future. It may take time, but it is entirely feasible to end this era of mass incarceration and de-carcerate young people. Political theorist Danielle Allen, in her analysis of American democracy and distrust (2004), suggests the need to cultivate a belief in a 'shared future', not a 'common' or 'identical' future but a shared one that recognizes the 'wholeness' of society and one where majority rule works to maintain the allegiance of the minority. When a society no longer sees its future together, she explains, this breakdown has historically been linked to civil war (Allen, 2004: xviii). Like Allen, I think the need to restore trust and imagine a shared future is a serious and pressing issue, especially in diverging societies like the US that have been relying on repressive means to resolve social conflicts for the past 30 years. This chapter is informed by and takes inspiration from political theorists such as Allen, but also academics who are engaged in the public debate about mass incarceration (e.g. National Academy of Sciences' 2014 report on *The Growth of Incarceration in the United States* and its critics), the empirical literature on policing and trust, the sociology of punishment, the sociology of trust, and perhaps most importantly, the new civil rights movement for justice. It aims, in a modest way, to contribute to the growing public debate about how justice might be achieved.

What is trust and why is it important for penal reform?

Trust is a basic building block of society. It is about having confidence in others. It is a feeling of being safe with others: 'Trust in one's fellow citizens consists in the belief, simply, that one is safe with them' (Allen, 2004: xvii). As many social theorists have noted, it is a way to decrease the uncertainty and risk inherent in modern life (Misztal, 2011; Luhmann, 1988). Perhaps most importantly, trust, as Robert Putnam (1993: 2000) made clear, is intimately tied to norms of reciprocity, the practice of mutual exchange between interdependent parties. It holds societies together by making cooperation possible. By having confidence in others, believing that others will not take advantage of one's vulnerability (Misztal, 2011), and engaging in reciprocity, trust eases our more mundane daily exchanges and enables more complex forms of collaboration across all areas of social, economic, political and private life. Trust makes it possible to realize collective goods. Trust in others, as political scientists have explained, 'makes it less risky and more rewarding for [citizens] to participate in community and civic affairs, and helps to build the social institutions of civil society upon which peaceful, stable and efficient democracy depends' (Zmerli and Newton, 2008: 707). In other words, it is the 'social glue' that holds communities and nations together (see review in Trägårdh, 2013: 182).

There is a lively and healthy debate about the nature and character of trust – its cognitive, emotional, rational (Hardin, 2001; Coleman, 1990) and moral dimensions (Uslaner, 2002) (review in Sztompka, 1999) – and its origins (individual, social, historical, religious). For our purposes here, however, it may be more fruitful to focus on its social and political forms and its effects because, as I will argue below, both social trust and public trust are critical to the production of penal order. Social trust refers to trust in other people whereas public trust refers to confidence in state institutions and authorities. As discussed below, societies with high degrees of social trust tend towards more minimalist approaches to punishment (Lappi-Seppälä, 2008). Societies with high degrees of confidence in state authorities tend towards less crime, high norm compliance and policing that is less brutal and fairer (Goldsmith, 2001; Jackson et al., 2012). If we want to move towards a society with fewer victims and safer communities, as the Howard League for Penal Reform advocates, we need to better understand the role of trust and how to rebuild it. Because trust is not an intrinsic characteristic of individuals but a property of social relations (Sztompka, 1999), it is not fixed or essentialist, and this means we can in fact rebuild it.

In his landmark study on American democracy, *Bowling Alone*, Robert Putnam (2000) defined social capital as how well people connect and cooperate with one another through civic engagement to bring about collective goods. Norms of reciprocity and high degrees of social trust, key components of social capital, facilitate a sense of civic duty and the exchange of information and resources. In places with high degrees of social capital, for example, people tend to be active in community life: they are more likely to participate in neighbourhood events; show up at community meetings; volunteer for local organizations; belong to local clubs or associations; and vote in local and national elections (Putnam, 2000). Civic engagement, Putnam explains, allows people to create and build different kinds of social ties (some dense and tight-knit and others loose and open), social ties that are necessary for cooperation and which over time and through repeated interaction can reinforce mutual trust. Subsequent and related research has found that the ability to make ties across groups – what Putnam calls 'bridging' social capital, rather than thick ties within a group ('bonding' social capital) – is more effective in generating inclusive public policies. In *Bowling Alone*, Putnam meticulously documented and analysed a wide range of historical and statistical data to show how social capital was on the decline with perilous results for American democracy.

Informed by Putnam's work, I have tried to develop a connection between social capital and penal order to understand US imprisonment variation. I have been particularly influenced by Putnam's earlier comparative study on Italy, *Making Democracy Work* (1993), in which he found regions with higher rates of social capital associated with higher economic prosperity, more generous social welfare and less coercive social control. In *The Politics of Imprisonment*, I found that higher rates of social capital – including higher rates of social trust and civic engagement – were associated with milder penal sanctioning and lower imprisonment rates. Higher rates of social trust meant that polity members were less likely to inflict state coercion against others (Barker, 2009: 177). These findings were based on an extensive historical and comparative analysis of three case studies (Washington State, California and New York), that went back to the late nineteenth century to trace the political histories of these states and then focused on the period 1965–2005, which saw significant changes and variation in state responses to rising crime.

To understand the dynamic between social capital and punishment in a place such as Washington State, I showed how norms of reciprocity and trust tended to support a shared sense of civic duty, making polity members less willing to inflict harsh penal sanctions on others (for details and evidence about the political and legislative histories of crime and punishment in Washington and how social capital played a decisive role in this analysis, see Barker, 2009: chapter four). Social capital provided a kind of protective mechanism against state repression in response to crime. What is important to note here is that polity members were not unwilling to sanction criminal offenders; they did not tolerate violations of criminal law but rather demanded that the harm done to victims was repaired and repaid through punishment. Yet this moral payback was not meted out with brute force but instead with the least repressive sanction possible. Criminal offenders were included in a shared moral universe with the rest of the polity – their violations, rights, liberties and social ties all figured in the conceptualization and realization of justice. High degrees of social trust indicate the capacity and willingness to recognize others, to treat others with respect – even those who are different, even those who break the law. We know from Zygmunt Bauman's (1989) work on social distancing that casting out perceived others relieves the rest of us from shared moral obligation and responsibility, not only leading to social exclusion but also leaving those on the outside at the mercy of state power (Barker 2015; Eriksson, 2015). The inclusion of criminal offenders, their rights and liberties, into notions of justice and punishment can also be seen as an illustration of what Danielle Allen (2004) calls the importance of imagining a shared future. In stark contrast to the dynamics of mass incarceration in California, for example, which depends on the expulsion of offenders from a shared future and is associated with a denial of reciprocity and low social trust, Washington State tended towards a minimalist approach to justice, using the least repressive sanctions possible, echoing the late Norval Morris's (1974) call for penal parsimony.

In a broad cross-national study of trust and penal order, Finnish criminologist Tapio Lappi-Seppälä (2008) found a similar pattern: high trust and low imprisonment. By analysing crime and punishment trends across a wide range of regions, including the Nordic, Baltic, Anglo and Eastern and Western European countries, Lappi-Seppälä investigated how varying levels of trust, welfare and political culture were statistically related to the intensity and severity of punishment, measured here as imprisonment rates. In explaining his findings, he states: 'the most powerful predictors' of penal moderation (low intensity, low severity, low imprisonment rates) are 'high confidence in fellow citizens and in government' (ibid.: 313). Strong welfare states and consensus politics were also significant findings (see also Pratt, 2008). The Nordic countries with high levels of social trust and confidence in political institutions contrast most sharply with their Eastern European counterparts. A relatively recent European Social Survey on 'Trust in Justice' found the same pattern (Jackson et al., 2011: 8). Referring to the literature on trust, Lappi-Seppälä (2008) explains how high levels of social trust ease cooperation and make those societies more effective at informal social control, decreasing the need to enact repressive forms of social control. In his analysis of Durkheim, a foundational figure in understanding the complex relationship between punishment and social institutions, David Garland (2012) makes a related point: societies with organic solidarity based on inter-group cooperation and respect for individualism rather than strong group identity tend to promote generous welfare states and less punitive policies. Margaret Levi (1998) made a similar argument: more inclusive democracies tend to govern through agreement and restrict coercion. In contrast, as Lappi-Seppälä argues, declining solidarity indicates support for harsher sanctions.

In a series of related studies that examine the effects of harsh punishment on trust (rather than the effects of trust on punishment), some interesting and disturbing results have emerged. Harsh punishment can decrease trust. As Lubell and Scholz found, harsh penal regimes 'destroy trust where (reciprocal) relations of trust already exist' (Lubell and Scholz, 2001: 175). Recently, writing in the *Annals of the American Academy*, sociologists Christopher Muller and Daniel Schrage (2014) investigated the effects of mass imprisonment, specifically its scale and pervasiveness in the lives of African Americans, on trust. Analysing the General Social Survey, they found that mass imprisonment drives down public trust in criminal justice. In high-imprisonment states, for example, respondents were more likely to believe that the courts were too harsh. Focusing on the particular experience of African Americans, they found that people of colour who had contact with prison through family, close friends or themselves had lower trust in criminal justice, believing the courts and police to be racially biased (Muller and Schrage, 2004: 150; see also Lee, Porter and Comfort, 2014). These findings, although the authors do not highlight or suggest it, have implications for eroding the notion of penal populism, the argument that the public always and already wants to get tough on crime. Clearly, substantial parts of the US have moved away from this position, just as substantial parts never subscribed to it in the first place (Miller, 2008).

Moreover, Muller and Schrage (2014) reflect on their finding and try to think through the consequences of low trust in criminal justice. They suggest that lower rates of trust could lead to increased political mobilization against mass incarceration, a process that is already underway across the United States. While the authors highlight the trigger of a white backlash to mass incarceration due to high rates of white imprisonment, I think recent anti-police protests linking criminal justice reform to a broader civil rights agenda may strengthen and expand the appeal of this movement. For our purpose here, political mobilization may be a positive outcome and source for reform. However, it is important to note the authors make an explicit link between low trust and increased crime, a distinct possibility as low trust erodes norm compliance and may support overzealous policing in minority neighbourhoods, the very issue we are trying to resolve.

Before moving on to think about ways we might rebuild trust, I want to highlight the importance of public trust in state institutions. A leading expert on trust in Sweden, Bo Rothstein (2011), argues that social trust is created through fair and universal public institutions, with corrupt and unfair institutions the principal sources of distrust. As indicated above, public confidence in the police and the courts, for instance, can have significant effects on penal order and efforts to bring about penal reform. In a now classic text, David Garland (1996) explained how a legitimacy crisis – the loss of confidence in democratic governments that followed in the wake of rising crime, social protests, expanding but seemingly ineffective welfare states in the late 1960s and early 1970s – pushed states towards regressive criminal justice policies; that is, an overreliance on repression to resolve problems of order and reassert their right to rule (see also Garland, 2001). Similarly, Lappi-Seppälä (2008) argues that declining trust in public institutions has led states to use repressive means to close the legitimacy gap (see also Simon, 2007). This state strategy has been, certainly from our view in 2015 on the collateral damages of mass imprisonment (Western, 2007; Clear, 2008), a colossal failure. The effect of this strategy has been the erosion of trust rather than its renewal. As Vesla Weaver and Amy Lerman (2010) write, aggressive and repressive criminal justice policies and practices, especially when perceived or experienced as 'hostile, invasive' tend to 'breed [...] political alienation, distrust, and withdrawal', with devastating consequences for American democracy (Weaver and Lerman, 2010: 203).

What is more, the research on policing and trust suggest the very opposite approach to crime control. In his seminal work on policing, Tom Tyler showed how trust in the police was highly contingent on how well the police treated people and whether or not people perceived their treatment as fair and equitable (Sunshine and Tyler, 2003; Tyler, 2006). In what has become known as 'procedural justice', a series of empirical studies in different contexts have confirmed this finding: fair, equitable, responsive and respectful policing can generate trust in policing and increase compliance (Goldsmith, 2005; Van Craen and Skogan, 2014; Jackson et al., 2012; Lerman and Weaver, 2014; Myhill and Bradford, 2012). Researchers analysing policing data from the European Social Survey likewise found that compliance and cooperation with the police were more likely when people were treated fairly and respectfully and less likely when the police resorted to coercive or aggressive tactics, which were associated with defiance (Jackson et al., 2012: 10–11). This type of policing, also referred to in the literature as 'policing by consent' (Goldsmith, 2005), may not only increase cooperation with the police but have the distinct possibility of decreasing crime. And on a more grandiose scale, as political scientists Weaver and Lerman argue, it has the potential to rebuild 'community peace and well-being', as basic order is essential for a democratic way of life (Weaver and Lerman, 2010: 204).

Four elements to civic repair and penal reform

How can we rebuild trust and how can we rebuild it in ways that reduce reliance on repressive means but make communities safer? Below I offer four basic elements to rebuilding trust that are based on my reading of key social science research on policing and punishment, political theory on citizenship, and social activism for justice. This list of suggestions is not meant to be all-inclusive or a definitive plan of action. But it does point to what I see as necessary steps for any serious criminal justice reform. Others, of course, may disagree and I welcome the dialogue.

The four elements include:

1. Accountability
2. Responsiveness
3. Participation
4. Shared Future.

On accountability

Here I take the lead from research on policing and trust. As noted above, there is a substantial body of policing literature that places the relationship between policing and trust at the core of healthy, well-functioning democracies. Many researchers such as Ian Loader (2014), Vesla Weaver and Amy Lerman (2010), and Andrew Goldsmith (2005) have provided guidelines for policing reform. What becomes immediately clear is the central role accountability plays in rebuilding trust in public institutions. As Goldsmith explains, even low-trust governments can generate trust by earning it the 'old fashioned way' through 'honest and effective performance' (Mishler and Rose, cited in Goldsmith, 2005: 457–458). He specifically highlights the importance of fairness, transparency and respect where the police take responsibility for their actions, demonstrate their commitment to the rule of law, limit the use of force and institute third-party oversight such as independent citizen advisory boards. In New York, a federal judge recently ruled in *Floyd v City of New York* against the New York Police Department's 'stop-and-frisk' policing as a violation of the constitutional rights of minorities. In *Floyd v City of New York*, the judge called for the establishment of a federal monitor to oversee policing reforms in the city, an example of a third party that can hold state authorities accountable for their actions. Citizen advisory boards can play much the same role and involve locals and those most affected by crime, punishment and policing in a governing role.

In terms of punishment, the National Academy of Sciences (2014) recently released a 500-page assessment of the causes and consequences of mass incarceration in the United States, and in chapter 12, 'The Prison in Society: Values and Principles', proposed a number of reforms that would reduce not only the unprecedented scale of mass confinement but its social concentration among severely disadvantaged communities. Drawing upon Norval Morris's theory of punishment, the report calls for parsimony: the restricted use of repression and responses to criminal violations that would value and prioritize liberty (Travis and Western, 2014: 326). Here we might think of parsimony as a way to enact 'honest and effective performance' that is perceived to be fair, transparent and respectful. In this way, the principle of parsimony may also promote trust as it reduces repressive and unnecessary penal sanctions. A more minimalist approach, an approach that would seriously limit the use of imprisonment, may be more responsive to citizens' concerns about justice. Additionally, as Travis and Western claim: parsimony may also 'limit the negative and socially concentrated effects of incarceration, thereby expanding the distribution of rights, resources, and opportunities more broadly throughout the US' (ibid.: 327). In comparative terms, societies with more parsimonious sanctions such as the Nordic countries tend towards higher trust (Pratt, 2008). But as these societies change in response to globalization and mass migration, we have seen a slight decrease in trust (Wallman Lundåsen and Wollebaek, 2013) and increased use of repression. Although repressive measures have always been a component of punishment in welfare states (Scharff Smith, 2012; Barker, 2013a), these new developments, along with the criminalization of migration, only verify the need for parsimony.

On responsiveness: a 311 for Justice

A state can rebuild trust by being responsive to the needs and demands of its people, particularly those most marginalized by aggressive policing and mass incarceration. Demonstrating a sincere concern for the safety of all citizens and treating people fairly, for example, is a straightforward way for the police to repair broken trust. In order to record, monitor, analyse and respond to public concerns, states could establish more direct lines of communication and interaction that are non-threatening and civically oriented. I have in mind here a variation on New York City's '311' initiative. What began as a way to record local complaints about potholes and broken pipes and communicate government information in non-emergency situations has become a gateway for civic engagement, helping to close the gap between remote and unresponsive city officials and local residents. Cities could develop their own version of 311 for Justice, a hotline and online app that records, monitors and analyses concerns about justice, ranging from police surveillance to police brutality. This could record and systematically analyse and make transparent complaints about racial profiling, discrimination and the security gap in minority neighbourhoods, which entails being both over-policed and under-served by public institutions (on the security gap, see Miller, 2013). Cities could develop a separate hotline for non-emergency situations that would enable citizens to register specific complaints against the police and make specific demands for police action. A basic feature of democratic policing is the ability for citizens to call the police and expect action, a basic feature that is not realized in many parts of the world but is also not realized in many neighbourhoods in democratic societies. The ability to call the police and expect a response is an expression of full and equal citizenship; it is a demand on the state to fulfil its obligation to provide security not just for certain segments of the population but for everyone in the population and territory.

The first 311 for Justice might register and respond to calls from the new civil rights movement: 'we want freedom from mass incarceration'; we want the 'de-militarization of local law enforcement across the country'; we want 'an immediate end to police brutality'; we want a 'comprehensive review by the Department of Justice into systematic abuses by police departments and the development of spe-cific use of force standards'; we want the 're-purposing of law enforcement funds to support community-based alternatives to incarceration'; we want a 'Congres-sional hearing investigating the criminalization of communities of color'; we want the 'passage of the End Racial Profiling Act'; we want the 'development and enactment of a National Plan of Action for Racial Justice' (Ferguson Action, 2014). Effective and meaningful responses from local, state and national governments are really the only way forward. Denial and deferment will only break trust and delay justice.

On participation: civic engagement and mobile justice

States can rebuild trust by reinvigorating democracy, a government for and by the people. Civic engagement is not only a necessary factor to reform but may be the key factor in ending mass incarceration. There is now a substantial body of litera-ture on punishment that supports the argument that more public debate, more public involvement, more public deliberation, more public input and more public trust can reduce state repression (Dzur, 2012; Barker, 2009; 2013b; Green, 2006; Miller, 2008; Loader and Sparks, 2012; Rowan, 2012; Taslitz, 2012).

Calls for public participation are not naïve or intended to belittle sincere con-cerns about fear of crime and demands for vengeance. Quite the contrary: calls for public participation are based on the premise that the public must grapple with these moral dilemmas together in order to come to terms with the pain, suffering, loss of life and violence caused by crime and punishment, to recognize the limits of state power, the right to life, liberty and human dignity. There are no easy answers. And this is what makes public participation necessary in democratic societies: to come to terms with these conflicts and inconsistencies and try to reconcile them. Ian Loader and Richard Sparks (2012) similarly invoke the need for public parti-cipation as a matter of 'democratic responsibility' (Boyte cited in Loader and Sparks, 2012: 33). They explain that crime control is about the distribution of public goods such as safety, security, justice and rights, and as such, the public –

particularly those most affected by crime – have an obligation to contribute to this resource allocation. Loader and Sparks' 'democratic responsibility' bears a close resemblance to Albert Dzur's (2012) concept of 'load-bearing' citizenship in which the public takes an active and responsible role in the meting out of justice, learning what it is really like to 'live among others' (Dzur, 2012: 123). These recent developments in our thinking about participation resonate with foundational texts in the sociology of punishment. For instance, we know from Émile Durkheim (1984 [1933]) and classic sociology that crime is a violation of our deeply held beliefs and punishment is the expression of that outrage. Resolutions to crime must come from public sentiment in order to make them meaningful and legitimate. In his classic *Limits to Pain*, Nils Christie (1981), the late internationally known critical criminologist, argued that participatory justice would help to clarify our values as they are expressed through the gradation and distribution of pain. As Dzur argues, the public has a responsibility to monitor and regulate criminal justice institutions because these state institutions have 'potential for great harm to human develop-ment' and are now 'so marked by both racial and socio-economic bias' (Dzur, 2012: 123; see also Western, 2001; Wacquant, 2009). Civic engagement, as a form of democratic responsibility, provides the legitimacy, social meaning and critical checks and balances to the uses and abuses of state power. It can act as an accel-erator but more importantly for our purposes here it can put a break on repression. Civic engagement, moreover, following Putnam, builds trust.

In addition to those arguments outlined above, there is compelling empirical evidence to suggest that the counter trend, the breakdown of democracy, was responsible for much of the mass incarceration phenomenon, making it imperative to reverse that trend. In response to David Scott's (2013) query, *Why Prison?*, I presented this claim as evidenced by the process of de-democratization, the failure of the parity principle and the privatization and commodification of public life (Barker, 2013b: 131–134). Briefly, I argue that the collapse of the public sphere has left the repressive powers of the state unchecked and mobilized against the most marginal by special rather than public interests. With historical declines in social capital, low rates of voter turnout (an average of 53 per cent in national elections since the mid-1970s), and significant decreases in civic engagement across all areas of social life (Putnam, 2000), it is difficult to see how a 'runaway democracy' led to mass incarceration (Barker, 2013b: 131; see also Tonry, 2007; on diminished democracy see Skocpol, 2002). Instead, Americans retreated into the private sphere, consumed by social media, resisting face-to-face interaction, existing 'alone together', as Sherry Turkle (2011) so powerfully captures this transformation of daily social interaction. Thomas Mathiesen (2001) has similarly marked the decline in the public sphere, the loss of sincere deliberation and respectful debate, a shift he argues 'corrodes values like civil rights, the rule of law and humanity' (Mathiesen in Barker, 2013b: 132). As noted in the previous section, the 'collapse of commu-nity', as Putnam puts it, has serious consequences for building trust, particularly trust that reaches across diverse social groups, a necessary element to supporting and maintaining more inclusive, less coercive public policies.

This collapse and its consequences are painfully made obvious in the lives of those most affected by crime and punishment, severely disadvantaged racial and ethnic minorities. Jeff Manza and Chris Uggen's (2006) path-breaking study of offender disenfranchisement captures this dilemma well, showing how civil penalties on ex-offenders negatively affect their ability to participate in public, social and economic life. This work set the stage for an emerging literature on negative effects of mass incarceration on democracy (Loury, 2008; Lerman and Weaver, 2014; Weaver, Hacker and Wildeman, 2014; Lee, Porter and Comfort, 2014). Uggen, Manza and Melissa Thompson argue that the absence of former offenders from the political process essentially means their concerns, interests and demands are excluded from the public arena: 'The major political parties need not attend to the concerns of more than five million citizens – mostly poor and people of color – who are currently locked out of the democratic process' (Uggen et al., 2006: 298). This is a gross violation of the parity principle, what Ian Loader and Richard Sparks identified as the necessity of including those most affected by crime and punishment into the public debate about the distribution of goods. Bruce Western (2007) has called this exclusion second-class citizenship, what should be an unthinkable reference to the antebellum South.

Where do we go from here? How do we reverse these trends? Again, the only way forward is to restore public participation. There are several emerging trends at grassroots level that suggest a growing movement not only for penal moderation but also an end to mass incarceration. In line with Western's concern about second-class citizenship and Michelle Alexander's (2010) breakthrough and national bestseller *The New Jim Crow*, we are witnessing the strong return of an Abolitionist movement. Groups such as Critical Resistance (Oparah, 2013), Families Against Mandatory Minimums (FAMM) and Mothers Reclaiming our Children (Gilmore, 2007), the Drop the Rock campaign in New York, and responsive politicians, frontline prosecutors and judges and local residents have all played a role in recent reform movement (Gottschalk, 2012: 225). Michael Leo Owens (2014) has documented how ex-offenders have similarly engaged in the community, organizing to restore voting rights and challenge the civic degradation of punishment. Since 2009, more than half of American states have reduced their prison populations in direct response to reform (Greene and Mauer, 2010). In 2013, the former US attorney general Eric Holder made profound and moving statements against mass incarceration as he pushed for federal legislation to decrease drug penalties. To critics this legislation is not enough, but his words were powerful and highly charged symbolic statements about the immorality of the current penal regime:

> Too many Americans go to too many prisons for far too long and for no good law enforcement reason. ... Although incarceration has a role to play in our justice system, widespread incarceration at the federal, state and local levels is both ineffective and unsustainable. ... It imposes a significant economic

burden – totaling $80 billion in 2010 alone – and it comes with human and moral costs that are impossible to calculate.

(Holder, 2013)

Continued protests against police brutality indicate the new civil rights movement is gaining momentum and clearly advocates an end to mass incarceration. Groups such as Ferguson Action have proposed a six-point national action plan to realize a more equitable fair justice system that is no longer based on the repression of African American men (Ferguson Action, 2014).

This moment presents a major opening in the American political system for significant penal reform. In order to maximize the potential for transformative politics, I suggest that it is just as important to create new institutions that can channel and incorporate this renewed public spirit into decision-making about criminal justice. Otherwise it may be difficult to sustain public input when pro-testors eventually go home. Political institutions significantly shape the character and trajectory of social reform as they channel certain demands into action while blocking others (Barker, 2009; Savelsberg, 1994; Sutton, 2013). Whereas Dzur highlights the critical role of the jury as a practice and institution in reinvigorating public participation, others have pointed to the role of deliberative forums to facilitate face-to-face interaction, access, communication, dialogue, parity and accountability (Johnstone, 2000; Barabas, 2004; Miller, 2008; Green, 2006; Taslitz, 2012; Rowan, 2012; Barker, 2009). The more moderate penal regime achieved in Washington State, for example, depended in part on hybrid state–citizen commis-sions, community meetings, citizen advisory boards, and a Sentencing Guidelines Commission, which included public participation. Smaller face-to-face settings can support what social theorist Jürgen Habermas (1984) calls 'communicative action', the open exchange of differing views, opinions and interests that are expressed in a respectful way. In its ideal form, it can promote dialogue and understanding of others' opposing views and lead to outcomes that uphold individual rights and liberties even as compromises are made (Gutman and Thompson, 2004).

In order to close the participation gap and extend deliberative democracy, I propose the creation of Mobile Justice, a kind of mobile deliberative forum that would bring young people into the political process for justice. Young people, particularly poorer minority youth, experience the full force of law's repression – aggressive policing, criminalization and penalization – but have very little say in the actual workings of justice. Following the parity principle, those most affected by crime and its control should have an equal say in the distribution, application and realization of security and justice. Mobile Justice could reach young people in ways that make law, courts, politics and governing more accessible, more relevant and less remote. They would be mobile in two distinct ways. First, they would be mobile in the sense of using information technology and different forms of social media to reach young people; they would provide a platform for sharing information and producing ideas. Second, they would be mobile in the sense of changing the location of face-to-face meetings in response to events on the ground. This degree of spontaneity could encourage new people to get involved or help make tight connections between the forum's discussion and proposals and related justice events as they unfold, an example of the sociological imagination at work. The Howard League's U R Boss programme was an exemplar of this type of initiative to connect and incorporate young people into the responsibility and act of governing; young people were at the forefront pressing for the de-carceration of their fellow youth (Howard League, 2014), incarceration which we should soon see as a gross violation of human rights.

On a shared future

In this final section, I turn to citizenship studies to think about new ways to restore trust. Here I follow Danielle Allen (2004) in her mesmerizing analysis of American citizenship in the aftermath of *Brown* v *Board of Education*. In *Talking to Strangers*, she explains how the erosion of trust has weakened the capacity of American democracy to solve its collective problems. Moreover, she argues that interracial distrust has tended to distort 'all public policies aimed at issues coded as "race" problems (welfare, employment, crime, drugs, gangs)' and 'any that require the implementation across race lines (health care, abortion, housing and real estate, city planning, public education' (Allen, 2004: xv). In response to this series of political failures, she interweaves the history of Little Rock, Emmerson's *Invisible Man*, with classic political theory ranging from Aristotle, Hobbes and Hannah Arendt to find a way out. What she discovers and develops is the novel concept of 'political friendship'.

Political friendship as a new form of citizenship and citizenship practices, she explains, can provide an effective tool to dissolve distrust that is so corrosive to American race relations. Allen explains how new kinds of citizenship habits must be developed so that majorities do not continue to dominate and alienate minorities. For example, new habits must cultivate political decisions that are mutually beneficial to all parties and majorities must work harder to maintain minorities' attachment to the polity. As noted in the introduction, when polity members no longer see a future together, it becomes nearly impossible to govern as the society is literally torn apart. Through the practice and habits of friendship, Allen argues, citizens can begin to recognize each other and the shared life they live together. They do not live the same life but live as friends who impact on and interact with one another in a shared environment. Here we can see how norms of reciprocity are critical to maintaining friendship: friends are keenly aware of how their actions impact on each other. Reciprocity, furthermore, is to some degree future-orientated, as it sets out expectations of ongoing and future exchanges. Political friendship, as Allen explains, means learning to 'negotiate loss and reciprocity' (Allen, 2004: 165). Political friends are attentive to how present decisions impact one another and guard against patterns of dominance with precisely this shared future in mind.

This friendship metaphor was invoked during the struggle for civil rights. For example, Martin Luther King, Jr. explained the social dynamics of nonviolent resistance in these terms: 'the point of nonviolent resistance is not to humiliate the opponent, but instead to gain his friendship and understanding' (King, 1958). The goal of nonviolence is 'redemption and reconciliation' (ibid.) as King recognized the importance of imagining a shared future, one in which reciprocity and understanding would be vital. This same dynamic underlies 'truth and reconciliation' commissions as post-conflict societies try to come to terms with past violations but still imagine a future together. This dynamic is related to what Bauman identified as a shared moral universe in which the essence of being human means the recognition of others, it means recognizing the duty to care for others (Bauman, 1989). When this duty to care is obliterated or when perceived others are cast out of a shared moral universe, the consequences are devastating, as his analysis of the Holocaust made painfully clear.

Allen's concept of a shared future and political friendship is certainly relevant for justice. If we were to seriously imagine a shared future together, this fundamental shift in perspective would most likely alter our calculations of what constitutes just punishment and the appropriate penal sanctions. Rather than moral payback for past harms, we might think of future dividends. If we were to imagine criminal offenders as part of a shared moral universe, part of a moral and political community, we might be less likely to inflict such repressive, harsh and degrading punishments on them, to expel or banish them from society. The findings of a commission established by the National Academy of Sciences placed much moral weight on the principle and value of citizenship as a restraining factor on punitive penal sanctions. As rights-bearing members of the polity, citizens are guaranteed a 'minimum standard of human dignity' (Travis, Western and Redburn, 2014: 328). But perhaps what is more noteworthy here is the commissions' emphasis on the 'human connectedness' that citizenship evokes. It is the 'human connectedness among members of a political community that serves to limit the penal power of the state' and provides the necessary social support to the 'temporary and dignified character of punishment' (ibid.: 328). Here a shared future is imagined with criminal offenders, one that seeks to avoid returning broken people to society unable to contribute, function or participate as full members (ibid.: 330).

The principles of citizenship and human dignity can provide powerful motivators and sources of cultural and political support for major penal reform (see also Simon, 2014). Although it is necessary and important, it is not enough to make prisons more dignified. I think we can take a more expansive approach to imagining a shared future together. In this future, we would close prisons. And begin to think more seriously about human security, freedom from want and the realization of human rights. The National Academy of Sciences' final principle of social justice, which seeks to address entrenched inequalities at the root of much crime, begins to move us in that direction. Rebuilding trust is one such way to rebuild our society that may bring us closer to this preferred future.

Acknowledgement

I would like to express my thanks to Anita Dockley, Barry Goldson, Stephen Farrall and Ian Loader for inviting me to the Howard League's 'What is Justice?' conference and for inviting me to contribute to this innovative collection. And thanks to Ian Loader for his helpful editorial suggestions on a previous draft of this paper and to the conference participants for their questions and comments.

References

Alexander, M. (2010) *The New Jim Crow: Mass Incarceration in the Age of Colorblindness*. New York: The New Press.

Allen, D. (2004) *Talking to Strangers: Anxieties of Citizenship since Brown v Board of Education*. Chicago, IL: University of Chicago Press.

Barabas, J. (2004) 'How deliberation affects public opinion', *American Political Science Review*, 98(4): 687–701.

Barker, V. (2009) *The Politics of Imprisonment: How the Democratic Process Shapes the Way American Punishes Offenders*. New York: Oxford University Press.

Barker, V. (2013a) 'Nordic exceptionalism revisited: explaining the paradox of a Janus-faced penal regime', *Theoretical Criminology*, 17(1): 5–25.

Barker, V. (2013b) 'Prison and the public sphere: toward a democratic theory of penal order', in D. Scott (ed.) *Why Prison?* Cambridge: Cambridge University Press.

Barker, V. (2016) 'On Bauman's moral duty: population registries, REVA, and eviction from the Nordic Realm', in A. Eriksson (ed.) *Punishing the Other*. New York: Routledge.

Bauman, Z. (1989) *Modernity and the Holocaust*. Cambridge: Polity.

Christie, N. (1981) *Limits to Pain*. Oxford: Martin Robertson.

Clear, T. (2008) *Imprisoning Communities: How Mass Incarceration Makes Disadvantaged Neighborhoods Worse*. New York: Oxford University Press.

Coleman, J. (1990) *Foundations of Social Theory*. Cambridge, MA: Harvard University Press.

Durkheim, É. (1984 [1933]) *The Division of Labor in Society*. New York: The Free Press.

Dzur, A. (2012) 'Participatory democracy and criminal justice', *Criminal Law and Philosophy*, 6(2): 115–129.

Eriksson, A. (2016) *Punishing the Other*. New York: Routledge.

Ferguson Action (2014) 'Demands', http://fergusonaction.com/demands/ (accessed 17 December 2014).

Floyd v City of New York, www.nytimes.com/interactive/2013/08/12/nyregion/stop-and-frisk-decision.html [accessed December 2014].

Garland, D. (1996) 'Limits of the sovereign state: strategies of crime control in contemporary society', *British Journal of Criminology* 36(4): 445–471.

Garland, D. (2001) *Culture of Control: Crime and Social Order in Contemporary Society*. Chicago, IL: University of Chicago Press.

Garland, D. (2012) 'Punishment and social solidarity', in J. Simon and R. Sparks (eds) *The SAGE Handbook of Punishment and Society*. London: Sage Publications, 23–39.

Gilmore, R. (2007) *The Golden Gulag: Prisons, Surplus, Crisis and Opposition in Globalizing California*. Berkeley, CA: University of California Press.

Goldsmith, A. (2005) 'Police reform and the problem of trust', *Theoretical Criminology*, 9(4): 443–470.

Gottschalk, M. (2012) 'The carceral state and the politics of punishment', in J. Simon and R. Sparks (eds) *The SAGE Handbook of Punishment and Society*. London: Sage Publications, 205–241.

Green, D. (2006) 'Public opinion versus public judgment about crime: correction the "comedy of errors"', *British Journal of Criminology*, 46: 131–154.

Greene, J. and Mauer, M. (2010) 'Downscaling prisons: lessons from four states', The Sentencing Project. Available at: www.sentencingproject.org/ [accessed October 2012].

Gutman, A. and Thompson, D. (2004) *Why Deliberative Democracy*. Princeton, NJ: Princeton University Press.

Habermas, J. (1984) *The Theory of Communicative Action, vol. 1: Reason and the Rationalization of Society*, trans. T. McCarthy. Boston, MA: Beacon (original work published 1981).

Hardin, R. (2001) 'Conceptions and explanations of trust', in K. S. Cook (ed.) *Trust in Society*. New York: Russell Sage.

Holder, E. (2013) 'US Attorney General delivers remarks at annual meetings of the American Bar Association', www.justice.gov/opa/speech/attorney-general-eric-holder-delivers-remarks-annual-meeting-american-bar-associations [accessed December 2014].

Howard League (2014) 'Use your situation to change your destination: evaluation of the Howard League for Penal Reform's U R Boss'. London: Howard League. Available at: https://d19ylpo4aovc7m.cloudfront.net/fileadmin/howard_league/user/pdf/Publicati ons/use_your_situation_final.pdf [accessed July 2015].

Jackson, J., Hough, M., Bradford, B., Hohl, K. and Kuha, J. (2011) 'Trust in justice: topline results from Round 5', European Social Survey. Available at: www.europeansocialsurvey. org/essresources/findings.html [accessed December 2014].

Jackson, J., Hough, M., Bradford, B., Hohl, K. and Kuha, J. (2012) 'Policing by consent: understanding the dynamics of police power and legitimacy', European Social Survey. Available at: www.europeansocialsurvey.org/essresources/findings.html [accessed December 2014].

Johnstone, G. (2000) 'Penal policy making: elitist, populist, or participatory?', *Punishment & Society*, 2(2): 161–180

King, Martin Luther, Jr. (1958) *Stride toward Freedom: The Montgomery Story*. New York: Beacon Press.

Lappi-Seppälä, T. (2008) 'Trust, welfare and political culture: explaining differences in national penal policies', *Crime and Justice*, 37(1): 313–387.

Lee, H., Porter, L. C. and Comfort, M. (2014) 'Consequences of family member incarceration: impacts on civic participation and perceptions of the legitimacy and fairness of government', *The ANNALS of the American Academy of Political and Social Science*, 651: 44–73.

Lerman, A. and Weaver, V. (2014) 'Staying out of sight? Concentrated policing and local political action', *The ANNALS of the American Academy of Political and Social Science*, 651: 202–219.

Levi, M. (1998) 'A state of trust', in V. Braithwaite and M. Levi (eds) *Trust and Governance*. New York: Russell Sage, 77–101.

Loader, I. (2014) 'In search of civic policing: recasting the Peelian principles', *Criminal Law and Philosophy*, May 30. Available at: http://link.springer.com/article/10.1007% 2Fs11572-014-9318-1 [accessed 23 November 2015].

Loader, I. and Sparks, R. (2012) 'Beyond lamentation: towards a democratic egalitarian politics of crime and justice,' in T. Newburn and J. Peay (eds) *Policing: Politics, Culture and Control*. Oxford: Hart Publishing, 11–41.

Loury, G. (2008) *Race, Incarceration and American Values: The Tanner Lectures*. Cambridge, MA: MIT Press.

Lubell, M. and J. T. Scholz (2001) 'Cooperation, reciprocity, and the collective action heuristic', *American Journal of Political Science*, 45(1): 175.

Luhmann, N. (1988) 'Familiarity, confidence, trust: problems and alternatives', in D. Gambetta (ed.) *Trust: Making and Breaking Cooperative Relations*. Oxford: Basil Blackwell, pp. 94–107.

Manza, J. and Uggen, C. (2006) *Locked Out: Felon Disenfranchisement and American Democracy*. New York: Oxford University Press.

Mathiesen, T. (2001) 'Television, public space and prison population: a commentary on Mauer and Simon', *Punishment & Society*, 3(1): 35–42.

Miller, L. (2008) *The Perils of Federalism: Race, Poverty and the Politics of Crime Control*. New York: Oxford University Press.

Miller, L. (2013) 'Power to the people: Violent victimization, inequality and democratic politics', *Theoretical Criminology*, 17(3): 283–313.

Misztal, B. (2011) 'Trust: acceptance of, precaution against and causes of vulnerability', *Comparative Sociology* 10(3): 358–379.

Morris, N. (1974) *The Future of Imprisonment*. Chicago, IL: University of Chicago Press.

Muller, C. and Schrage, D. (2014) 'Mass imprisonment and trust in the law', *Annals of the American Academy of Political and Social Science* 651(1): 139–158.

Myhill, A. and Bradford, B. (2012) 'Can police enhance public confidence by improving quality of service? Results from two surveys in England and Wales', *Policing and Society* 22(4): 397–425.

Obama, B. (2014a) 'President Obama speaks on Eric Garner decision', White House Press Office, Washington, DC. Available at: www.whitehouse.gov/photos-and-video/video/2014/12/03/president-obama-speaks-eric-garner-decision [accessed December 2014].

Obama, B. (2014b) 'Excerpts President Obama's BET interview on race relations', White House Press Office, Washington, DC. Available at: www.whitehouse.gov/blog/2014/12/10/excerpts-president-obamas-bet-interview-race-relations-and-progress-we-still-have-ma [accessed December 2014].

Oparah, J. (2013) 'Why no prisons?' in D. Scott (ed.) *Why Prison?* Cambridge: Cambridge University Press.

Owens, M. L. (2014) 'Ex-felons' organization-based political work for carceral reform', *Annals of the American Academy of Political and Social Science*, 651: 256.

Pratt, J. (2008) 'Scandinavian exceptionalism in an era of penal excess', *British Journal of Criminology*, 48(2): 119–137.

Putnam, R. (1993) *Making Democracy Work: Civic Traditions in Modern Italy*. Princeton, NJ: Princeton University Press.

Putnam, R. (2000) *Bowling Alone: The Collapse and Revival of American Community*. New York: Simon & Schuster.

Rothstein, B. (2011) *The Quality of Government: Corruption, Social Trust and Inequality in International Perspective*. Chicago, IL: University of Chicago Press.

Rowan, M. (2012), 'Democracy and punishment: a radical view', *Theoretical Criminology* 16 (1): 43–62.

Savelsberg, J. (1994) 'Knowledge, domination and criminal punishment', *American Journal of Sociology* 99(4): 911–943.

Scott, D. (ed.) (2013) *Why Prison?* Cambridge: Cambridge University Press.

Scharff Smith, P. (2012) 'A critical look at Scandinavian exceptionalism: welfare state theories, penal populism and prison conditions in Denmark and Scandinavia', in T. Ugelvik and J. Dullum (eds) *Penal Exceptionalism? Nordic Prison Policy and Practice*. London: Routledge, 38–57.

Simon, J. (2007) *Governing Through Crime: How the War on Crime Transformed American Democracy and Created a Culture of Fear*. New York: Oxford University Press.

Simon, J. (2014) *Mass Incarceration on Trial: A Remarkable Court Decision and the Future of Prisons in America*. New York: The New Press.

Skocpol, T. (2002) *Diminished Democracy: From Membership to Management in American Civic Life*. Norman, OK: University of Oklahoma Press.

Sunshine, J. and Tyler, T. (2003) 'The role of procedural justice and legitimacy in shaping public support for policing', *Law & Society Review* 17: 513–547.

Sutton, J. (2013) 'The transformation of prison regimes in late capitalist societies', *American Journal of Sociology*, 119(3): 715–746.

Sztompka, P. (1999) *Trust: A Sociological Theory*. Cambridge: Cambridge University Press.

Taslitz, A. (2012) 'The criminal republic: democratic breakdown as a cause of mass incarceration', *Ohio State Journal of Criminal Law*, 9(1): 133–193.

Tonry, M. (2007) 'Determinants of penal policies', in M. Tonry (ed.) *Crime, Punishment and Politics in Comparative Perspective*. London: University of Chicago Press, 1–48.

Trägårdh, L. (2013) 'The historical incubators of trust in Sweden: from the rule of blood to the rule of law', in M. Reuter, F. Wijkström and B. K. Uggla (eds) *Trust and Organizations: Confidence across Borders*. New York: Palgrave Macmillan.

Travis, J., B. Western and S. Redburn (eds) (2014) *The Growth of Incarceration in the United States: Exploring Causes and Consequences*. Washington, DC: National Academies Press.

Turkle, S. (2011) *Alone Together: Why We Expect More from Technology and Less from Each Other*. New York: Basic Books.

Tyler, T. (2006) *Why People Obey the Law*. Princeton, NJ: Princeton University Press.

Uggen, C., Manza, J. and Thompson, M. (2006) 'Citizenship, democracy and the civic reintegration of criminal offenders', *Annals of the American Academy of Political and Social Science* 605: 281–310.

Uslaner, E. U. (2002) *The Moral Foundations of Trust*. Cambridge: Cambridge University Press.

Van Craen, M. and Skogan, W. G. (2014) 'Trust in the Belgian police: the importance of responsiveness', *European Journal of Criminology*, August: 1–22.

Wacquant, L. (2009) *Punishing the Poor: The Neo-Liberal Government of Social Insecurity*. Durham, NC: Duke University Press.

Wallman Lundåsen, S. and Wollebaek, D. (2013) 'Diversity and community trust in Swedish local communities', *Journal of Elections, Public Opinion and Parties*, 23(3): 299–321.

Weaver, V. and Lerman, A. (2010) 'Political consequences of the carceral state', *American Political Science Review*, November: 1–17.

Weaver, V., Hacker, J. and Wildeman, C. (2014) 'Detaining democracy? Criminal justice and American civic life', *Annals of the American Academy of Political and Social Science* 651(1): 6–21.

Western, B. (2007) *Punishment and inequality in America*. New York: Russell Sage Foundation.

Zmerli, S. and Newton, K. (2008) 'Social trust and attitudes toward democracy', *Public Opinion Quarterly*, 72(4): 706–724.

6

CRIME, JUSTICE AND 'THE MAN QUESTION'

Ann Oakley

Most discussions of justice and penal policy take place in a context that does not query the location of the penal system in a particular set of social and economic structures organized around commodity capitalism and the systematic domination by men of women and other men, technically known as 'patriarchy'. Yet the task of reimagining penal policy must engage with the impact both the social relations of capitalism and those of patriarchy have on shaping antisocial behaviour and sociolegal responses to it. This task is hampered by the ways in which penal policy and theory have traditionally been conducted; the former drawing uncritically on the constructions of official statistics, the latter engaging in forms of discourse that ignore the empirical world of actual crime and actual penal outcomes (Hudson, 2002).

Most crime, especially violent crime, is committed by men, who also participate disproportionately in other forms of antisocial behaviour. As the social scientist and public servant Barbara Wootton famously noted in her groundbreaking *Social Science and Social Pathology* more than fifty years ago, 'if men behaved like women, the courts would be idle and the prisons empty'. With respect to the reasons for this abiding gender difference, Wootton observed that, 'No one seems to have any idea why; but hardly anyone seems to have thought it worthwhile to try to find out' (Wootton, 1959a: 32). This chapter reviews developments in understandings about gender and antisocial behaviour, the relationship between these and public policy, and the relevance of such issues to questions of fairness and justice as marks of a democratic society. The argument is that a general failure to confront 'the man question' has weakened criminological theory and empirical work, has impaired the application of effective prevention and treatment policies, and has offered only a limited telescopic vision of the whole landscape connecting socioeconomic structures, antisocial behaviour and masculinity.

Questions of gender

The original invitation to contribute a chapter to this book (and a paper to the conference that preceded it) requested a text on 'justice and women'. This is the conventional framing of questions about gender in many areas of social life: gender is about women, and women are added in as an afterthought and/or special case. The rest of the subject is about men, although this is rarely explicitly stated. Thus, as Jeff Hearn has observed, the conjunction of the terms 'men' and 'social policy' sounds odd: what is social policy about, if it is not about men (Hearn, 2010)? In criminology, the treatment of women as a separate issue allows men and masculinity untrammelled freedom to constitute the subject without being seen to do so (Brown, 1986); another way to put this is to say, as the historian Linda Gordon has done of work on the welfare state, that what is gender-blind is also gender-obscuring (Gordon, 1990). 'Gender' as an analytic term did not exist when Wootton made her original observations about the savings to be made in penal system costs were men to behave like women. The historical lack of separation between biological sex and cultural treatment encouraged biological explanations of behaviour, which flourished in criminology for many years, from the pre-occupation with brain size and chromosome constitution to Otto Pollak's inventive description of women specializing in easily concealed crime such as shoplifting because they are good at pretending to have orgasms during intercourse with men (Pollak, 1950).

'Naturalizing' is a perpetually useful technique for hiding the social nature of problems in and with social relations (Romito, 2008). A more helpful sense of how sex and gender interact to produce differential patterns of antisocial behaviour arrived in the late 1960s and 1970s, most notably with Frances Heidensohn's 'The deviance of women: a critique and an enquiry' (1968) and Carol Smart's *Women, Crime and Criminology* (1977) – although both of these followed the habit of the time in settling on 'the woman question' rather than 'the man question'. These texts were part of a general invasion of feminist scholarship into the academy which launched a multidisciplinary interrogation of hidden bias and more obvious omissions. Heidensohn's 1968 paper (sparked by her reading of Barbara Wootton) reminded us that sex/gender differences in antisocial behaviour had been observed for well over a hundred years and displayed the regularity and uniformity that normally attract social science attention. But very little had happened. Policy, too, had shied away from confronting the puzzle of why it is mainly men who offend; when it came across an example of women's deviance, for instance prostitution, the response was to hide it from the public and professional gaze. Heidensohn's observations drew strength from her own qualitative interviews with and about female 'deviants'; looking back in 2010 on the frustrations of trying to analyse and understand these, she recalled giving a paper based on 'The deviance of women' at the London School of Economics staff seminar in 1967, where she met 'polite incomprehension' from people who did not regard the themes she raised as either important or particularly challenging (Heidensohn, 2010).

Masculinities are a matter of situational accomplishment, and crime is a means of 'doing gender' (Messerschmidt, 1993). The study of masculinity/masculinities as a criminological topic – its conceptualization as a phenomenon demanding attention – came later, largely as a by-product of the feminist enterprise (Connell, 1993; Dowd, 2010; Newburn and Stanko, 1994). Masculinity studies in the area of crime and penal policy focus on the question that the 'and women' approach never asked: why *do* men behave badly? Criminologists saw the intellectual mystery as, instead, the *lack* of criminality in women. This is 'a classic illustration of the way patriarchal ideology takes men as the norm and understands women as departing from it' (Connell, 1993: x). Nonetheless (or perhaps therefore), exploring the relationship between cultures of masculinity and men's antisocial behaviour has itself come to be regarded as a 'specialist, even eccentric, pursuit within criminology': 'Go to a criminology conference and it is unlikely that "the man question" will be at the top of the agenda' (Naffine, 2003: 11). Or, as Heidensohn put it (2003: 6), it is doubtful that criminology has been shaken to its core by any of these more recent intellectual advances.

Violent masculinities: the 'facts' of men and crime

The disproportionate share of antisocial behaviour contributed by men is 'the first fact that any theory of crime should fit' (Braithwaite, 1989: 44). Figure 6.1 shows the gender distribution for major categories of crime in England and Wales in 2011/12. The male percentages exceed 80 per cent in every category except for

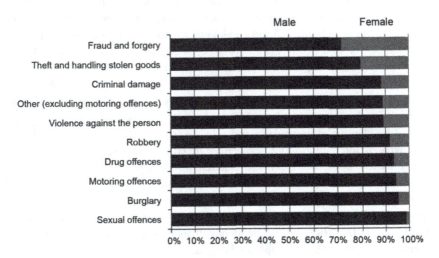

FIGURE 6.1 Gender of offenders: offenders found guilty at all courts in England and Wales in the 12 months ending September 2012

Source: Ministry of Justice criminal justice statistics September 2012, conviction tables, Table Q4.2.

fraud and forgery and theft and handling stolen goods, where they are slightly lower. Motoring offences, burglary and sexual offences are the most masculine crimes: men commit well over 90 per cent. In addition to the categories shown in Figure 6.1, men form 78 per cent of people receiving Penalty Notices for Disorder, 85 per cent of those arrested and 95 per cent of prisoners (Ministry of Justice, 2014a, 2014b). This statistical association between crime and masculinity is of the order that in many other fields would have attracted concentrated attention; epidemiologists, for example, studying disease patterns would surely have concluded that something toxic is involved in the correlation between the 'disease' of crime and masculinity. Yet not only is the pattern of antisocial masculinity rarely commented on, it is extremely hard even to collate the data. In England and Wales, Ministry of Justice/Home Office/Office of National Statistics figures relating to crime, justice and penal policy pay less attention to sex/gender than to ethnicity and socioeconomic circumstances as 'offender characteristics'. The sex/gender of people who offend is overwhelmingly hidden, or is mentioned casually, with no accompanying comment. For instance, the Office of National Statistics Bulletin on *Violent Crime and Sexual Offences* gives information about sex of victim and age of offender, but there is only a single reference to, and no comment on, offender sex − 86 per cent male (ONS, 2014). The Home Office Statistical Bulletin (2012) *Homicides, Firearm Offences and Intimate Violence* makes no mention of offender sex in any of its 61 tables: a casual one-liner in the text observes that 90 per cent of those convicted of homicide are male. Another concealment device is illustrated by the latest European Union report on violence against women, which refers to the male perpetrators in gender-neutral language, as 'partners' (FRA, 2014). Official analyses of episodes such as the riots of 2011 in Britain provide information about age, ethnicity, neighbourhood and employment status, but do not comment on the fact that 92 per cent of defendants are male, as are 100 per cent of those charged with offences involving violence (Cockburn and Oakley, 2011).

Official statistics do not simply report what happens; they 'are not *collected*, but *produced*' in a social process which affects the picture of 'reality' they give us (Irvine et al., 1979: 3). Decisions about which tables and which variables to 'produce' are shaped by ideological frameworks and values − where the taken-for-granted view that what is interesting about sex/gender in crime and justice is not that men commit crime but that women and children are victims of it. The relative silence about masculine antisociality explains why a google search on 'violent crime and gender' yields 9,130,000 results when 'victim' is added, but only 346,000 for 'perpetrator'. Scientific and popular articles on male violence mention victim gender over three times more frequently than perpetrator gender (Phillips and Henderson, 1999). The main focus relating to gender in the production of official statistics about crime and justice is on *women* as *victims* as crime, rather than on *men* as *perpetrators*. Thus the annual Ministry of Justice reports *Statistics on Women and the Criminal Justice System* have chapters on 'victims', 'police activity' and 'defendants'; the chapters on 'offender characteristics', 'offence analysis' and 'offender management' all focus on the small proportions of women who offend rather than the large proportions of men who do. These reports are produced to meet the 'equality' provision of the 1991 Criminal Justice Act. Comparable reports on men and the criminal justice system are not apparently part of the equality agenda.

Had this chapter been about 'Crime, justice and the woman question', women's role as victims of domestic, sexual and interpersonal violence would have made an early entry. There is plenty of evidence. Between 20 per cent and 50 per cent of women globally are affected by such violence at some stage in their lives (Heise et al., 1999; Jewkes, 2002). A study conducted for the World Health Organization involving 24,000 women in ten countries showed that 'intimate partner violence' is the most common form of violence in women's lives, with pregnancy being a particularly vulnerable time; such violence is an important but usually hidden cause of miscarriage, stillbirth and maternal deaths (Lewis and Drife, 2005; Mezey, 1997; WHO, 2005). In England and Wales one in four women experiences domestic abuse and one in five sexual assault in their lifetimes (Home Office, 2011). Many discussions of domestic violence are keen to make the point that men are victims as well, but the scale is very different; for example, partner violence accounts for 40–70 per cent of female homicides internationally, whereas the comparable figure for men is 4–8 per cent (Krug et al., 2002).

Masculine violence occupies a continuum from the intimate to the impersonal, from the local to the global scene. As Figure 6.1 shows, men also specialize in motoring offences, which often cause injury and death: 94 per cent of motoring offences are committed by men (Ministry of Justice, 2014a). Notably, such offences, despite being crimes in every reasonable sense (Wootton, 1957), are not seen in law as acts of personal violence. The precedent for treating motoring crimes less seriously than other crimes causing injury and death was set by the coroner at the inquest in 1896 on the first pedestrian in Britain to die on the roads: her death, the coroner declared, was an 'accident' (Porter, 1998). Motoring crimes account for far more homicides than personal acts of violence: 23 per cent of deaths from injury globally, compared with 11 per cent caused by other violence and 3 per cent caused by war (Dyer, 2004). Carnage on the roads is, indeed, akin to war: 3000 deaths a day, the same figure *every day* as those killed in the attack in the World Trade Center, which launched President Bush and Prime Minister Blair's 'war on terror' (Roberts, 2004).

Cars emerged from a masculine world of engineers, manufacturers and entrepreneurs: they were made for men by men within the 'rough-hewn, masculine self-image' of the automobile industry (O'Connell, 1998: 5; see Scharff, 1991). The legacy of this today is a technological culture aimed at men, with women less likely to drive (their lack of access to cars both reflecting and causing their confinement to the home). Women's much lower involvement in accidents and speeding and other such offences does not prevent the continued proliferation of jokes about their driving abilities (Select Committee on European Union, 2004). Until recently, gender differences in motoring offences were reflected in lower insurance premiums for women, but when the European Court of Justice, in another strange interpretation of the principle of equality, decreed that men and women must be treated the same, women started to pay the costs of men's more hazardous motoring behaviour (Cockburn and Oakley, 2013).

Our cultural dependence on cars entails injury not only to people but also to the environment through pollution, politically hazardous over-dependence on oil, and road-building destruction of land. As I argued some years ago (Oakley, 2002), a systemic analysis of gender implicates processes, activities, systems and values that are normally disconnected and assumed to operate more or less autonomously. This separation between different forms of the same thing is a societal strategy for hiding a social problem: thus different expressions of masculine violence are seen as different phenomena (as child abuse, domestic violence, rape, homicide, killing in armed conflict, dangerous driving, etc.), and this disaggregation prevents their analysis as a single category or a *continuum of violence* (see Cockburn, 2004; Romito, 2008). Discrimination against women, interpersonal violence, the deployment of masculine technologies such as cars and guns, and the destruction of the environment all threaten public and planetary welfare, and all are associated through their shared dependence on a culture of hegemonic masculinity. 'Hegemonic masculinity' in the 'world gender order' is defined as 'the masculinity associated with those who control its dominant institutions: the business executives who operate in global markets, and the political executives who interact (and in many contexts, merge) with them' (Connell, 2005: 16). It exemplifies an 'ethos that privileges what have traditionally been seen as natural male traits' (Whitehead, 1999: 58). Since masculinity, like femininity, is a matter of performance in social contexts, there are different masculinities (associated with, for example, heterosexuality, toughness, power, authority, competition). Importantly, men as well as women can be victims of hegemonic masculinity (Schippers, 2007).

Corporate crime is another category of behaviour that usually escapes attention in the crime statistics. Its association with hegemonic masculinity is clear: men hold a virtual monopoly on syndicated corporate and political crime (Beirne and Messerschmidt, 2007). 'The men who guide the modern corporation and the outlying financial, legal, legislative, technical, advertising and other sacerdotal services of corporate function are the most responsible, affluent and prestigious members of the national community. They are the Establishment,' wrote the renowned economist J. K. Galbraith (Galbraith, 1980: 361). Global economic power is concentrated in the hands of transnational corporations, run mainly by men, which produce a vast range of goods and services, and export to the Third World the environmental costs of resource-hungry and pollution-intensive industries, thus promoting both climate instability and the unhealthy lifestyles of the West (Madeley, 1999; Pearce and Tombs, 1998; Shiva, 2000). This 'structural violence' is strongly related to hegemonic masculinity (Scott-Samuel, 2009).

Other prime consequences of hegemonic masculinity are military conflict and warfare. 'It is not that "masculinity" generates war … but rather that the process of militarization both draws on and exaggerates the bipolarization of gender identities *in extremis*. Mustering troops is all about the mobilization of men into aggressive expressions of hypermasculinity' (Mama, 2013). As the writer Virginia Woolf noted in her remarkable *Three Guineas*, written on the eve of the Second World War, masculinity as a socially produced category and the pursuit of war, violence and political authoritarianism are tied up with one another and with the institution of the patriarchal state. Most of the people subjected to war violence are civilian women and children; this includes those who are sexually assaulted, raped and/or forced to flee their homes (Amnesty International, 2004). Rape is deployed as 'a weapon of war' in countries throughout the world: it is a deliberate military strategy used as a reward for victory in battle, to boost troop morale, incite revenge, eliminate religious or political groups and destabilize entire communities (Amnesty International, 2004; Kivlahan and Ewigman, 2010). Pregnant women are, again, a particular target: in Syrian war zones in 2013 snipers used the abdomens of pregnant women as target practice, winning packets of cigarettes for 'successful' results (*The Times*, 2013).

Most of the 390 million privately owned small arms in the world today belong to men. Although men are the major casualties of gun violence, women suffer disproportionately from firearms violence, 'given that they are almost never the buyers, owners or users of such weapons' (Amnesty International, 2005: 2). The risk of homicide is increased three times and that of suicide five times for people living in homes with guns; for every stranger killed in self-defence by a handgun, 109 lives are lost in homicides, suicides and unintentional shootings (Kellerman and Reay, 1986; Sugarmann, 2000). These statistics undermine the argument of those who defend the personal right to own firearms on the grounds that having a gun protects the vulnerable. On the contrary, the availability of firearms is directly associated with rates of women killed (Hemenway et al., 2002); access to a gun increases the risk fivefold of a woman's chances of being killed by her male partner (Campbell et al., 2003).

'The man question': a threat to personal and public health?

Although the antisocial and violent behaviours produced by masculinity hide in the official statistics of crime and justice, gender-linked concepts of harm have been receiving increasing attention in one sector, that of health care. Here masculine gender-based violence has been reconceptualized as a threat to both personal and public health.

As James Gilligan (2001) argues, shifting violence from the category of a moral/legal problem into that of a public health issue alters the lens through which its causes and prevention are seen. For example, the definition of violence against women by male intimate partners as 'domestic' enabled it to escape serious policy attention for many years. Its redefinition by health agencies (in some parts of the policy landscape at least) as 'a serious human rights and public health problem' has highlighted the fact this kind of violence often has a profound impact on physical and mental health, causing injuries, suicide and other 'excess mortality' (Jewkes, 2002: 253). It is now recognized that no other major public health problem has been 'so widely ignored and so little understood' (WHO, 2005: 1, 22). On another, related, front, Nicholas Freudenberg (2014) has argued that the (male–run) food, alcohol, tobacco, automobile, pharmaceutical and gun industries are now the main sources of damage to public health. These industries pack regulatory systems with people who defend their interests in the face of massive evidence of harm – from obesity, drunkenness, smoking-related disease, prescription drugs, and gun-associated injury – at the same time as evading corporate tax to the tune of an amount that far exceeds all international development aid (Shaxson, 2011). A relevant factor here is the harm caused by income inequality itself, leading as it does to status anxiety and competitive behaviours (Bricker et al., 2014). The often-quoted association between poverty and crime is better conceptualized as an inequality effect, for, as Wootton remarked, if poverty caused crime, then most criminals would be poor old women (Wootton, 1959b).

Hegemonic masculinity helps to shape unequal political and social relations, a relationship often elided in academic commentaries, which tend to focus separately on class or gender or ethnicity as axes of social differentiation. The inequalities of patriarchy, of which masculine crime and antisocial behaviours are a part, are a health problem for men too. In developed countries, men have a higher mortality rate than women at all ages, and on average they die nearly seven years earlier. A multivariate analysis of data from 51 countries suggests that male mortality is highest in the most patriarchal countries (Stanistreet et al., 2005). States with greater gender equality also use less violence during international crises, prompting questions about what happens to policy when the traditional gender affiliations of policy-makers are disturbed (Caprioli and Boyer, 2001).

Policy, crime processing and 'the man question'

The most striking aspect of crime, justice and 'the man question' is its almost total neglect by policy-makers. Most policy responses echo the framing of the statistical reports in focusing on what can be done to lessen the victimization of women caused by antisocial masculinity rather than how to prevent antisocial masculinity itself (MacDonald, 2000). They do not comment on the extraordinary absence of statistics about the masculine perpetration of violence. The Home Office's 2011 'strategic vision' for ending 'violence against women and girls' contains no refer-ence to the problem of violent masculinity. There are no social programmes that aim to undo the ideological associations between masculinity and antisociality. Boys at school are not taught how to curb their imitations of aggressive masculinity in the interests of a more altruistic and pacifist citizenship. Celebrity men and others with power who commit crimes against women and children are not asked by the justice system to confront their gender-based failures to use power respon-sibly. Gender is particularly invisible to men, and thus to many male policy-makers: 'As the Chinese proverb has it, the fish are the last to discover the ocean' (Kimmel, 2004: 6). Relevant here is the fact that three-quarters of staff in the police service and the judiciary are men. In both these sectors, women are particularly scarce at senior levels (Ministry of Justice, 2014a). Women police officers internationally report experiences of working in 'a macho cop culture, manifested in sexual discrimination and sexual harassment' (Heidensohn and Silvestri, 2012: 347).

What Joanne Belknap (1998: 3) has called the 'crime processing' system does not offer equal treatment to men and women (whether it should do so is an important question). Magistrate court decisions are biased towards remands in custody and more medicalized interventions for women (Edwards, 1984; Heidensohn, 1981; Steward, 2006). Perhaps in part because criminality among women is low, the treatment of those women who are involved in it may contain an element of punishment for the transgression of gender norms. From the 1990s on, the number of women sentenced to immediate imprisonment has grown far faster than the comparable male figure (1997–2008, up 68 per cent for women and 35 per cent for men (Hedderman, 2010)), a development that has attracted surprisingly little attention from policy-makers (Carlen and Tombs, 2006; Player, 2005). Evidence on how crime processing works demonstrates that women's sentencing is explained more by their social characteristics and particularly by their perception 'as caring or neglectful mothers, faithful partners or promiscuous sluts' than it is by their actual crimes (Hudson, 2002: 28). Justice for women is more about who they are than what they have done.

The Corston Report on 'women with particular vulnerabilities in the criminal justice system', published in 2007, drew attention to many such anomalies and contradictions resulting from gender-blindness on the policy front. The report made 43 recommendations addressing the need for 'a distinct, radically different, visibly led, strategic, proportionate, holistic, woman-centred, integrated' approach – a formidable list of adjectives reflecting the multiple failures flowing from the historical treatment of women's offending as an 'add-on' to the treatment of male offending. Corston called 'unacceptable' the normal approach of, 'This is how we do it for men, how can we tweak it to accommodate women?' (Corston, 2007: 21). One of Corston's themes returns us to the focus on women as victims: she points out that twice as many imprisoned women as men report the experience of domestic violence and three times as many sexual abuse: thus, many women in prison have a double role as victim and offender. In view also of the less serious crimes they commit, prison is a costly and ineffective method of processing many women offenders who pose no risk to public safety.

Although the government accepted 41 of the Corston Report's recommendations, this acceptance has not yet been translated into the kind of cross-departmental ministerially led strategies needed for their implementation (House of Commons Justice Committee, 2013). Women's offending is seen as a gender problem and subject to the usual marginalization meted out to 'women's issues', whereas the links between men's offending and *their* gender continue to escape attention. Violence towards women in intimate relationships, for instance, has been labelled 'gender-based violence' 'because it evolves in part from women's subordinate status in society' (Population Information Program, 1999: 1). But male-perpetrated violence associated with men's superordinate status is not seen as gender-based. Academic research and study in the area of masculinity is treated as belonging to gender studies, not to policy studies. The study of policy for the most part closes its eyes to 'the man question'.

Perhaps partly for this reason, the social sciences have not contributed a great deal to the theorization of male violence and antisociality, or to understandings of its absence from policy discourse. When Cynthia Cockburn and I published an article in *The Guardian* called 'The culture of masculinity costs all too much to ignore', the comments we received were striking for their trivialization and/or repetition of familiar themes about 'man-hating' and 'man-baiting' (Cockburn and Oakley, 2011). What we argued was that the facts of crime and antisocial behaviour point to the culture of masculinity as an important and ignored policy problem, a problem with enormous economic and social costs. Following Wootton's logic, we pointed out that, were men to commit crimes leading to custodial sentences at the same rate as women, the saving to the exchequer (on a quick calculation) would be around £3.4b a year. If men's crime rate equalled women's, there would be an annual saving of some £42b. The social sciences have mostly followed the policy-makers and the media in singling out the protection of victims as the main issue: better child protection; enhanced support in domestic violence cases; exposure of paedophile rings; tighter gun control. Celebrity revelations such as the Jimmy Saville case in the UK are treated as shocking new isolated incidents, not as manifestations of a masculine culture in which the power to misbehave is taken for granted (Cockburn and Oakley, 2013). Men's absence from the debate about the harms of masculinity is also striking. As Jack O'Sullivan asked in a recent *Guardian* column, 'Can there be any group that is subject to so much debate and accusation, and is so apparently powerful – yet remains so utterly speechless?' Men tend to operate in their personal worlds of change, with no social movement akin to the women's movement connecting these worlds (O'Sullivan, 2013).

What should be done?

Warfare, interpersonal conflict and masculine violence are not inevitable aspects of human society (Gilligan, 2001; Moore, 1994). The two most significant aspects of antisocial behaviour and its treatment in law and society in many nation-states today are its gender patterning and the fragile, mostly non-existent, relationship between efforts to prevent, manage and control it, on the one hand, and evidence about which strategies are effective and which are not, on the other. Of course, an evidence-based approach to criminal justice would also mean taking account of the evidence about gender.

Many recommendations for reducing the burden of death, disease and distress caused by masculine antisocial behaviour concentrate on reducing women's vulnerability as victims by raising their socioeconomic status, widening their access to education and employment, and increasing gender equality (WHO, 2005). Exposure to violence in the home predicts youth crime: parental support, quality day-care for pre-school children, and school programmes to promote better interpersonal skills and reduce bullying have all been shown to have positive effects in reducing antisocial behaviour in youth and adulthood (Hall and Lynch, 1998; Piquero et al., 2009; Zoritch et al., 1998). These, however, have not so far directly addressed the problem of masculinity. Education that exposes and interrogates beliefs about gender can play a role: Romito and colleagues, implementing a 15-hour course on violence against women for first-year medical students, found some positive effects – increased knowledge, less prejudice and less trivialization of the topic – although some students protested against the 'feminism' of the course (Romito et al., 2014). This dubbing as 'feminist' of any attempt to examine masculinity repeats the error of equating 'gender' with 'women', and is a real barrier to progress on the policy front.

Educational programmes have to compete against the enormous impact from childhood of a culture in which aggressive antisocial masculinity is an admired quality; the subject of games, even, and thus of role play, and thus of roles in adult life. In her introduction to the revised (2002) edition of her *Boys Will be Boys: Breaking the Link between Masculinity and Violence*, Myriam Miedzian notes the increase in military toys and games in toy stores since the book's original publication in 1991: 'A major section of the boys' toy section is ... devoted to killing, kicking, shooting, destroying, and blowing up' (Miedzian, 2002: lxvi). *Advanced Warfare* is the latest in the series of video games, *Call of Duty*. The gamer chooses, holds and fires a weapon and scores by wounding and killing opponents. Although the gamer can theoretically be female, the game is profoundly gendered and designed to appeal to men and boys. In its rival game, *Grand Theft Auto*, it is possible to choose to have sex with a prostitute and then shoot her instead of paying (Cockburn, 2014). Young people need to have access to role models not based on equating masculinity with armed violence (Amnesty International, 2005), or indeed, with an activity as apparently innocuous as sport, where male violence is applauded as 'virile' (Naffine, 2003; Williams and Taylor, 1994).

Taking these two points together, the gender differences in crime and antisociality, and the need for robust evidence as to effective prevention and treatment approaches, we need well-designed studies of interventions that test plausible strategies based on understandings of the interactions between gender and antisocial behaviour. Anthony Petrosino's famous example of how well-designed studies may reveal popular approaches as ineffective or harmful is relevant here. Examining evaluations of a fashionable approach to youth crime prevention in the USA, Petrosino found that introducing young men at risk of criminal activity to 'real' criminals (an approach known as 'Scared Straight') actually made them more and not less liable to offend (Petrosino et al., 2003). There are two methodological points here. The first is the difference between the types of evidence yielded by policy/practice interventions that are poorly evaluated (for example, by comparing pre- and post-intervention behaviours or studying dissimilar intervention and 'control' groups, or reporting 'stakeholder' enthusiasms) and those produced by randomized control group designs. The former often overestimate positive effects and underestimate harms (Weisburd and Lum, 2001).

The most reliable evidence about what works is gained by well-designed studies, and by collecting the findings of these together in systematic reviews. Since 2000, the Campbell Collaboration, an international research network following the model of the Cochrane Collaboration in health care, has been producing systematic reviews of the effects of social interventions. There are currently 38 systematic reviews in the crime and justice area available on the Campbell Collaboration website as a guide to policy-makers, practitioners, academics and the lay public (www.campbellcollaboration.org/). However, and significantly, none of these reviews takes as their subject approaches for reducing antisocial masculinity. Even if they did, the crime policy and justice system agenda, driven mainly by anecdotal evidence, programme 'favourites of the month' and political ideology, has not generally accepted the need for effective policy based on reliable evidence, which now informs other public sectors, notably health care (Sherman et al., 2002). A critical and evidence-based approach to 'the man question' in crime and justice would raise those central and often-debated issues about whether 'the therapunitive prison' is possible, especially when incarceration provides a concentrated breeding ground for masculine antisocial behaviours, and separates women in unhelpful ways from their caring responsibilities. The detrimental effects of prison for most prisoners outweigh any impact of in-prison therapies: what happens outside prison in terms of housing, jobs and personal relationships is much more likely to facilitate law-abiding lives (Carlen and Tombs, 2006; Farrall, 2002; Maruna, 2000).

The second methodological point is about the desirability of designing and testing approaches to policy and practice that are based on plausible theories about human behaviour. The need for theory-based strategies is increasingly acknowledged in health care and health promotion (see e.g. Glanz and Bishop, 2010), but remains rare in the crime and justice sector. In the case of Scared Straight, for instance, meeting real prisoners probably encouraged imitative behaviours in young men already 'at risk' of antisocial behaviour, because antisociality is an acceptable and even desirable aspect of adult masculinity in a social context that valorizes this link. Any strategy to reduce antisocial behaviour will not get very far unless it recognizes the psychological pull of this link.

Conclusion

When Wootton revisited her original observation about the effect on the criminal justice system of men behaving more like women twenty years later, her observation, she realized, was still 'substantially true'; in terms of advances in understanding, the sex difference in crime had been 'explained away' rather than 'explained' (Wootton, 1978: 240–1). Ratios of male to female crime have changed very little (Heidensohn and Silvestri, 2012: 344).

As Susan Miller observed of her edited volume *Crime Control and Women* (1998: xv), the text in this chapter is one 'I wish did not have to be written'. My chapter reads, and some will inevitably interpret it as, a litany of complaints about men. It is not about men as individuals; it is about a culture of masculinity that is a problem for all of us, and which connects a web of policy issues, not just in crime and justice, but across all sectors, including welfare, education and health. Violent crime, overwhelmingly a male activity, is both a problem and a consequence of masculinity. State interventions to control violence and other forms of antisociality are no less gendered: 'structures of response, from arrest through imprisonment, glorify tough cops, celebrate adversarial relations and construct a virtuous "protective" state by incarcerating or, in some countries, killing the "bad guys"' (Braithwaite and Daly, 1998: 151).

Masculine violence is a preventable disease. A public debate about this needs to happen; perhaps also there should be, as Scott-Samuel (2009) suggests, a global commission on masculinities. Ending male violence and other forms of antisocial behaviour connected to hegemonic masculinity will require 'profound social changes ... especially in the power relationships between genders, and between adults and children. ... Opposing male violence is a formidable task: it is not just a question of changing the law and behaviour, but of bringing into question a structured and deep-seated system of control and privilege. It is not conceivable, and in fact does not happen, that those benefitting from this system will let it be dismantled or limited without opposition' (Romito, 2008: 22–4). Social scientists have an important role to play in urging this dismantling, in providing convincing and trustworthy analyses of social processes, and in helping to construct an evidence base for policy theorists and policy-makers which is true to, and insightful about, the real world of human experience. Justice is not about forms of divided masculinity/femininity, or about hegemonic masculinity and subordinated femininity. It is, or should be, about the right of all human beings to safe, healthy, peaceful, free and respected lives on a planet that is itself not under threat from harmful human behaviour.

Acknowledgement

Thanks to Cynthia Cockburn, Graham Crow and Robin Oakley for their helpful comments on this chapter.

References

Amnesty International (2004) *Lives Blown Apart. Crimes against Women in Times of Conflict.* London: Amnesty International Publication.

Amnesty International, the International Action Network on Small Arms and Oxfam International (2005) *The Impact of Guns on Women's Lives.* Oxford: The Alden Press.

Beirne, P. and Messerschmidt, J. (2007) *Criminology*, 4th edition. Oxford: Oxford University Press.

Belknap, J. (1998) *The Invisible Woman: Gender, Crime and Justice.* Belmont, CA: Wordsworth Publishing.

Braithwaite, J. (1989) *Crime, Shame and Reintegration.* Cambridge: Cambridge University Press.

Braithwaite, J. and Daly, K. (1998) 'Masculinities, violence and communitarian control'. In Miller, S. L. (ed.) *Crime Control and Women.* Thousand Oaks, CA: Sage, 152–180.

Bricker, J., Ramacharan, R. and Krimmel, J. (2014) 'Signaling status: the impact of relative income on household consumption and financial decisions', *Finance and Economics Discussion Series (FEDS) Working Paper*, Federal Reserve Board.

Brown, B. (1986) 'Women and crime: the dark figures of criminology', *Economy & Society*, 15(3).

Campbell, J. C., Webster, D., Koziol-McLain, J., Block, C. and Campbell, D. (2003) 'Risk factors for femicide in abusive relationships: results from a multisite case control study', *American Journal of Public Health*, 93: 1089–1097.

Caprioli, M. and Boyer, M. (2001) 'Gender, violence, and international crisis', *Journal of Conflict Resolution*, 45(4): 503–518.

Carlen, P. and Tombs, J. (2006) 'Reconfigurations of penality', *Theoretical Criminology*, 10(3): 337–360.

Cockburn, C. (2004) 'The continuum of violence: a gender perspective on war and peace'. In Giles, W. and Hyndman, J. (eds) *Sites of Violence: Gender and Conflict Zones*. Berkeley, Los Angeles, London: University of California Press.

Cockburn, C. (2014) 'Masculine violence: call of duty, or call for change?', *OpenDemocracy*, 27 November.

Cockburn, C. and Oakley, A. (2011) 'The culture of masculinity costs all too much to ignore', *The Guardian*, 25 November.

Cockburn, C. and Oakley, A. (2013) 'The cost of masculine crime', *OpenDemocracy*, 8 March.

Connell, R. W. (1993) 'Foreword'. In Messerschmidt, J. W. *Masculinities and Crime*. Lanham, MD: Rowman and Littlefield Publishers, vii–xv.

Connell, R. W. (2005) *Masculinities*, 2nd edition. Cambridge: Polity Press.

Corston, J. (2007) *The Corston Report: A Review of Women with Particular Vulnerabilities in the Criminal Justice System*. London: Home Office.

Dowd, N. E. (2010) *The Man Question: Male Subordination and Privilege*. New York: New York University Press.

Dyer, O. (2004) 'One million people die on world's roads every year', *British Medical Journal*, 328: 851.

Edwards, S. (1984) *Women on Trial*. Manchester: Manchester University Press.

Farrall, S. (2002) *Rethinking What Works with Offenders*. Cullompton: Willan Publishing.

European Union Agency for Fundamental Rights (FRA) (2014) *Violence Against Women: An EU-wide Survey*. Luxembourg: Publications Office of the European Union.

Freudenberg, N. (2014) *Lethal but Legal*. Oxford: Oxford University Press.

Galbraith, J. K. (1980) *Annals of an Abiding Liberal*. London: André Deutsch.

Gilligan, J. (2001) *Preventing Violence*. London: Thames & Hudson.

Glanz, K. and Bishop, D. B. (2010) 'The role of behavioural science theory in development and implementation of public health interventions', *Annual Review of Public Health*, 31: 399–418.

Gordon, L. (1990) 'What is gender blind is gender obscuring: the new feminist scholarship on the welfare state'. In Gordon, L. (ed.) *Women, the State and Welfare*. Madison: University of Wisconsin Press, 9–35.

Hall, D. and Lynch, M. A. (1998) 'Violence begins at home', *British Medical Journal*, 316: 1551.

Hearn, J. (2010) 'Reflecting on men and social policy: contemporary critical debates and implications for social policy', *Critical Social Policy*, 30(2):165–188.

Hedderman, C. (2010) 'Government policy on women offenders: Labour's legacy and the Coalition's challenge', *Punishment and Society*, 12(4): 485–500.

Heidensohn, F. (1968) 'The deviance of women: a critique and an enquiry', *British Journal of Sociology*, 19(2): 160–175.

Heidensohn, F. (1981) 'Women and the penal system'. In Morris, A. and Gelsthorpe, L. (eds) *Women and Crime*. Cropwood Conference Series 13. Cambridge: Institute of Criminology.

Heidensohn, F. (2003) 'Changing the core of criminology', *Criminal Justice Matters*, 53: 5–6.

Heidensohn, F. (2010) 'On writing "The deviance of women": observations and analysis', *British Journal of Sociology*, 61 (Supplement s1): 127–132.

Heidensohn, F. and Silvestri, M. (2012) 'Gender and Crime'. In Maguire, M., Morgan, R. and Reiner, R. (eds.) *Oxford Handbook of Criminology*. Oxford: Oxford University Press: 336–369.

Heise, I., Ellsberg, M. and Gottemoeller, M. (1999) *Ending Violence Against Women*. Baltimore, MD: Center for Communication Programs, Johns Hopkins School of Public Health.

Hemenway, D., Shinoda-Tagawa, T. and Miller, M. (2002) 'Firearm availability and female homicide victimization rates among 25 populous high-income countries', *Journal of the American Medical Women's Association*, 57(2): 100–104.

Home Office (2011) *Violence against Women and Girls*. London: Home Office. Available at: www.homeoffice.gov.uk/crime/violence-against-women-girls/.

Home Office (2012) '*Homicides, Firearm Offences and Intimate Violence*'. Statistical Bulletin. London: Home Office.

House of Commons Justice Committee (2013) *Women Offenders: After the Corston Report. Second Report of Session 2013–14*. London: HMSO.

Hudson, B. (2002) 'Gender issues in penal policy and penal theory'. In Carlen, P. (ed.) *Women and Punishment*. Cullompton: Willan Publishing, 21–46.

Irvine, J, Miles, I. and Evans, J. (1979) 'Introduction: demystifying social statistics'. In Irvine J., Miles I. and Evans J. (eds) *Demystifying Social Statistics*. London: Pluto Press, 1–8.

Jewkes, R. (2002) 'Intimate partner violence: causation and primary prevention', *Lancet*, 359 (20 April): 1423–1429.

Kellerman, A .L. and Reay, D. T. (1986) 'Protection or peril? An analysis of firearm-related deaths in the home', *New England Journal of Medicine*, 314(24): 1557–1560.

Kimmel, M. S. (2004) *The Gendered Society*. New York: Oxford University Press.

Kivlahan, C. and Ewigman, N. (2010) 'Rape as a weapon of war in modern conflicts', *British Medical Journal*, 340: c3270.

Krug, E. G., Dahlberg, L. L., Mercy, J. A., Zwi, A. B. and Lozano, R. (eds) (2002) *World Report on Violence and Health*. Geneva: WHO.

Lewis, G. and Drife, J. (2005) *Why Mothers Die 2000–2002: Report on Confidential Enquiries into Maternal Deaths in the United Kingdom*. London: RCOG Press.

MacDonald, R. (2000) 'Time to talk about rape', *British Medical Journal*, 321: 1034–1035.

Madeley, J. (1999) *Big Business, Poor Peoples*. London: Zed Books.

Mama, A. (2013) 'Challenging militarized masculinities'. *OpenDemocracy*, 29 May.

Maruna, S. (2000) 'Desistance from crime and offender rehabilitation: a tale of two research literatures'. *Offender Programs Report*, 4(1): 1–13.

Messerschmidt, J. (1993) *Masculinities and Crime: Critique and Reconceptualisation of Theory*. Lanham, MD: Rowman and Littlefield.

Mezey, G. (1997) 'Domestic violence in pregnancy'. In Bewley, S., Friend, J. and Mezey, G. (eds) *Violence against Women*. London: RCOG.

Miedzian, M. (2002) *Boys Will be Boys: Breaking the Link between Masculinity and Violence*. New York: Lantern Books.

Miller, S. L. (1998) 'Introduction'. In Miller, S. L. (ed.) *Crime Control and Women*. Thousand Oaks, CA: Sage, xv–xxiv.

Ministry of Justice (2014a) *Statistics on Women and the Criminal Justice System: 2013*, National Statistics, November (www.gov.uk/government/uploads/system/uploads/attachment_da ta/file/380090/women-cjs-2013.pdf).

Ministry of Justice (2014b) *Prison Population Figures: 2013* (www.gov.uk/government/statis tics/prison-population-figures-2014).

Moore, H. (1994) 'The problem of explaining violence in the social sciences'. In Harvey, P. and Gow, P. (eds) *Sex and Violence*. London: Routledge, 138–155.

Naffine, N. (2003) 'The "man question" of crime, criminology and criminal law', *Criminal Justice Matters*, 53(1): 10–11.

Newburn, T. and Stanko, E. (eds) (1994) *Just Boys Doing Business: Men, Masculinities and Crime*. London: Routledge.

Oakley, A. (2002) *Gender on Planet Earth*. Cambridge: Polity Press.

O'Connell, S. (1998) *The Car in British Society: Class, Gender and Motoring 1896–1939*. Manchester: Manchester University Press.

Office of National Statistics (2014) *Focus on Violent Crime and Sexual Offences 2012/13* (www.ons.gov.uk/ons/dcp171776_352548.pdf).

O'Sullivan, J. (2013) 'A man walks out of a room', *The Guardian*, 21 May.

Pearce, F. and Tombs, S. (1998) *Toxic Capitalism: Corporate Crime and the Chemical Industry*. Aldershot: Dartmouth Publishing.

Petrosino, A., Turpin-Petrosino, C. and Buehler, J. (2003) 'Scared Straight and other juvenile awareness programs for preventing juvenile delinquency: a systematic review of the randomized experimental evidence', *Annals of the American Academy of Political and Social Science*, 589: 41–62.

Phillips, L. and Henderson, M. (1999) '"Patient was hit in the face by a fist": a discourse analysis of male violence against women', *American Journal of Orthopsychiatry*, 69(1): 116–121.

Piquero, A. R., Farrington, D. P., Welsh, B. C., Tremblay, R. and Jennings, W. G. (2009) 'Effects of early family/parent training programs on antisocial behavior and delinquency', *Journal of Experimental Criminology*, 5(2): 83–120.

Player, E. (2005) 'The reduction of women's imprisonment in England and Wales', *Punishment and Society*, 7(4): 419–439.

Pollak, O. (1950) *The Criminality of Women*. Baltimore, MD: University of Pennsylvania Press.

Population Information Program and Center for Health and Gender Equity (1999) *Ending Violence Against Women*, Issues in World Health Series L, no. 11. Baltimore, MD: Center for Communication Programs, Johns Hopkins University School of Public Health.

Porter, A. (1998) 'First fatal car crash in Britain occurred in 1896', letter, *British Medical Journal*, 317: 212.

Roberts, I. (2004) 'War on the roads: two years on', *British Medical Journal*, 328: 845.

Romito, P. (2008) *A Deafening Silence: Hidden Violence against Women and Children*. Bristol: Policy Press.

Romito, P., Grassi, M. and Beltramini, L. (2014) 'Educating medical students on violence against women: a quasi experiment in the real world'. In K. Smedslund and D. Risse (eds) *Violences envers les femmes: responsabilités individuelles et collectives*. Montreal: Presses de l'Université du Québec.

Schippers, M. (2007) 'Recovering the feminine other: masculinity, femininity, and gender hegemony', *Theory and Society*, 36: 85–102.

Scharff, V. (1991) *Taking the Wheel: Women and the Coming of the Motor Age*. New York: Free Press.

Scott-Samuel, A. (2009) 'Patriarchy, masculinities and health inequalities', *Gaceta Sanitaria*, 23(2).

Select Committee on European Union (2014) *Twenty-Seventh Report*. London: Select Committee on European Union.

Shaxson, N. (2011) *Treasure Islands: Tax Havens and the Men who Stole the World*. London: Bodley Head.

Sherman, L. W., Farrington, D. P., Welsh, B. C. and MacKenzie, D. L. (2002) 'Preventing crime'. In Sherman, L. W., Farrington, D. P. and Welsh, B. C. (eds) *Evidence-based Crime Prevention*. Abingdon: Routledge, 1–12.

Shiva, A. (2000) 'The world on the edge'. In: Hutton, W. and Giddens, A. *Global Capitalism*. New York: Pantheon.

Smart, C. (1977) *Women, Crime and Criminology: A Feminist Critique*. London: Routledge.

Stanistreet, D., Bambra, C. and Scott-Samuel, A. (2005) 'Is patriarchy the source of men's higher mortality?' *Journal of Epidemiology and Public Health*, 59(10): 873–876.

Steward, K. (2006) 'Gender considerations in remand decision-making'. In Heidensohn, F. (ed.) *Gender and Justice: New Concepts and Approaches*. Cullompton: Willan Publishing.

Sugarmann, J. (2000) *Every Handgun is Aimed at You*. New York: New Press.

The Times (2013) 'Assad's snipers target unborn babies in wombs', 19 October.

Walby, S. (2004) *The Cost of Domestic Violence*. London: Women and Equality Unit.

Weisburd, D. and Lum, C. M. (2001) 'Does research design affect study outcomes in criminal justice?' *Annals of the American Academy of Political and Social Science*, 578: 50–70.

Whitehead, S. (1999) 'Hegemonic masculinity revisited', *Gender, Work and Organisation*, 6: 58–62.

Williams, J. and Taylor, R. (1994) 'Boys keep swinging: masculinity and football culture in England'. In Newburn and Stanko (eds), 214–233.

Woolf, V. (1938) *Three Guineas*. London: Hogarth Press.

Wootton, B. (1957) 'Who are the criminals?' *Twentieth Century*, August: 138–148.

Wootton, B. (1959a) *Social Science and Social Pathology*. London: George Allen and Unwin.

Wootton, B. (1959b) *Contemporary Trends in Crime and its Treatment*, The Nineteenth Clarke Hall Lecture. Bedford: The Sidney Press.

Wootton, B. (1978) *Crime and Penal Policy*. London: George Allen & Unwin.

WHO (2005) *WHO Multicountry Study on Women's Health and Domestic Violence against Women*. Geneva: WHO.

Zoritch, B., Roberts, I. and Oakley, A. (1998) 'The health and welfare effects of day-care: a systematic review of randomised controlled trials', *Social Science and Medicine*, 47(3): 317–327.

7

RIGHTS, JUSTICE AND SINGLE-MINDEDNESS

Thérèse Murphy and Noel Whitty

This is a chapter about single-mindedness about rights. It accepts that the single-mindedness it examines is both inescapable and, in ways, hugely important. What prisoner, for instance, would not want to be represented by a lawyer who wasn't to some degree single-minded? And who would support a human rights organization (say, Amnesty International) that did not pursue its goals with zeal? Equally, given that single-mindedness can also take an anti-rights form, isn't it possible that it is one of the forces that keeps rights complacency, narcissism, or other similar excess, in check?

We are not averse then to a degree of single-mindedness about rights. We would not seek to strip it away, even if that were possible. We are, however, concerned about the collective effect of diverse strains of single-mindedness. These strains are generally polar opposites in their thinking and practices, yet in combination they seem to be limiting how both human rights in general and prisoners' rights in particular are seen. The chapter that follows describes these different strains of single-mindedness – aversion, aspiration and avoidance – and documents the danger of their collective effect. It also looks at how that effect might be countered. In doing so, it makes the following claim: there is a pressing need to engage empirically and conceptually with human rights practices on the ground – and to do so not just for legal practices but for non-legal ones too. It is through this engagement, complex though it will be, that there is the best chance of *socializing* both single-mindedness about rights and also rights themselves.

Socializing rights, drawing out both rights as they manifest in law and rights as a broader idiom of justice, won't solve political or normative questions or technical legal ones. But it will nurture an open-minded sociology of rights that should make it harder to cleave to extremes or, indeed, to apathy. It will, in other words, take the edge off aversion, aspiration and also avoidance of rights. It will also call for a commitment to the type of empirical enquiry that is everyday amongst those we identify as 'avoiders' – namely, sociologists, criminologists and anthropologists.

One final preliminary point: single-mindedness is, for us, a catch-all. We are not claiming that it is the only way of describing the stances on rights and human rights outlined below, or that it captures all possible positions (there are reasoned, reflective positions, both pro- and anti-rights, that fall outside our focus). We are also not saying that single-mindedness is exclusive to rights; other frames with kindred status (security, for instance) may well attract similar mindsets. Accuracy-wise, we do not see it as pinpoint-perfect either. Single-mindedness suggests a considered stance, and possibly a passionate or a blinkered one; at a minimum, it indicates motivation and a degree of deliberateness and also unswervingness. There will be considerable evidence of this sort of single-mindedness as we describe aversion, aspiration and avoidance. But there will also be ambiguity – in particular, instances where we are not able to point to motivation, and others where it seems likely that single-mindedness is a performance that is being deployed as camouflage or as a negotiating stance.

We are sticking with single-mindedness, however, even if it is problematic. Its appeal is that it *solidarizes*: it allows us to pull together a range of ways of speaking (and not speaking) about rights so that their collective effect comes into view. We believe that this effect is both distinctive and dangerous. The problem, above all, is that it misrepresents rights. And this in turn diminishes the chances of a fair and just measure of rights – a measure of what rights have and have not done, of what they can and cannot do, and of how they interact with other idioms of justice, and with considerations such as practicability and economic cost.

Three strains of single-mindedness

We turn now to the three principal strains of single-mindedness. We begin with aversion and aspiration, which are already well known and widely written about as duelling factions, though generally labelled as rights scepticism and rights evange-lism. By relabelling them as strains of single-mindedness the aim in part is to see them afresh. In part, too, this new attention to single-mindedness allows us to identify a hidden strain: avoidance. By bringing this into clear view, and exploring the reasons for it, we set the stage for the project we are calling 'socialization'.

Aversion to rights

The first of our three strains of single-mindedness is best seen as active, insistent and increasing in strength. It also has at least two sub-strains: first, the sustained critique of rights and human rights that can be found in the work of critical legal scholars from an array of countries; and second, the systematic aversion to the Human Rights Act and the European Court of Human Rights that is today asso-ciated with the Conservative Party in the United Kingdom. There are, to be fair, dissenting voices within each sub-strain. In the UK, for instance, the Conservatives are not unanimous (Grieve, 2014), and there are also politicians from other West-minster parties, as well as senior UK judges, who seem to have kindred aversions to 'European' human rights (Straw, 2013; Sumption, 2013). The most striking lines, however, are generally the avowedly aversive ones. Consider, for instance, the promise to 'scrap the Human Rights Act' (which is a priority for the Conservative government); the insistence that the European Court of Human Rights needs 'sorting out'; and the characterization of legal aid as a tool of 'pressure groups' and 'left-wing lawyers' (e.g. Grayling, 2014). What is also striking is how often such promises, claims and characterizations call upon *prisoner* or *detention* cases by way of supporting evidence. These cases are, it seems, the best of arguments against human rights – or at least against the practice of rights that stems, it is said, from the European Convention on Human Rights.

In October 2014, then justice secretary Chris Grayling published an eight-page strategy report, *Protecting Human Rights in the UK*, which used four such cases to accuse the Strasbourg Court of 'mission creep'. These were the blanket ban on prisoner voting; prisoner access to artificial insemination; foreign-national challenges to deportation orders upon release from prison; and the requirement to review life sentences after a period of 25 years. The report insisted that, in the circumstances, continuing with the Human Rights Act was not an option: 'fundamental changes' were needed 'to restore common sense and put Britain first'. The proposed replacement, described as a 'Bill of Rights and Responsibilities' (Conservative Central Office, 2014), would therefore be limited by a 'seriousness' threshold: in this way, its application would be restricted to cases involving 'criminal law and the liberty of an individual, the right to property and similar serious matters' (but excluding any application to British military operations abroad) (2014: 5–7).[1]

It seems then that there is a place within the Conservative Party for (some) fundamental rights – it is, however, a very particular, or restricted, place and very definitely anti-European.[2] Of course, as we said earlier, neither the Conservatives nor Westminster politicians more broadly exhaust this first strain of single-mindedness: legal writing, and critical legal writing in particular, are the source of a further sub-strain – one that is equally active and equally insistent, though a great deal less rhetorical and more reasoned than the politicians' variant. The scholars' aversion targets the international human rights movement, or national rights-based claims-making and adjudication, or both. Typically, its critique will allege one or more of the following: human rights are indeterminate; neo-colonial; likely to advantage the already-advantaged; skewed towards market capitalism and individualism so that the freedom they proffer is both limited and limiting; institutionalized, even narcissistic, in ways that block other vocabularies of justice; and finally, both rights and the rights movement are desperately apolitical, even anti-political. Several of the claims associated with these critiques have become well known and much cited in rights circles: are rights a hollow hope (Rosenberg, 2008) or perhaps a myth? Do they always have dark sides (Kennedy, 2004; O'Neill, 2005), and is paradox ever present (Brown, 2002)? Moreover, have we all just accepted that rights are now 'the most we can hope for', a moral idiom obsessed with pain and suffering, rather than a 'political discourse of comprehensive justice' (Brown 2004: 453)?

In part, this largely left-leaning critique is targeting what it sees as human rights' minimalism. There are, it alleges, no radical claims for social change coming from human rights. Thus, abuses are denounced, victims of violations are represented and may even have both a day in court and a win, but there are no revolutions; nothing, for instance, to reduce the prison population (in fact, today's international human rights movement, in its expanding commitment to the fight against impunity, seems ever more invested in criminal justice systems and the modes of punishment they can provide). Moreover, the left critics ask, why all the fuss with fancy legal moves when rights-based enhancement of, for example, prison conditions can have unwanted effects − above all, a strengthened capacity to control (Feeley and Swearingen, 2004)?

In part, too, the scholars' critiques are targeting maximalism, documenting a human rights industry that is overly focused on rights and 'rule of law' training for all and sundry, overly committed to universal values and overly expansionist. Hopgood (2010), for instance, has criticized Amnesty International for its maximal turn. Associated initially in the 1960s with letter-writing campaigns for the release of political prisoners and later in the 1970s with trial and detention conditions more generally, Amnesty is today a professional defender of *all* human rights. It is, as Hopgood points out, as likely to 'demand dignity' for 'prisoners of poverty' as it is to demand the release of prisoners of conscience (2010: 157, citing Amnesty International, 2009: 17). Hopgood sees this expansion (which could be viewed as part of a new human rights attentiveness to socio-economic rights) as a mistake. For him, Amnesty has wrong-footed itself: it risks 'vacating its niche', becoming 'the global NGO against all bad things' (2010: 157).

Aspiration for rights

Let us now turn to aspiration, the second strain of single-mindedness about rights. It is both the opposite of aversion and in other ways very similar to it. It is, for instance, just as programmatic and just as deliberate about its goals; its ambition is just as vaunting. It is also bound to aversion in that the scholar-critics discussed earlier are a direct response to the status of rights, and to the sense of self that is said to characterize aspiration.

So who are these aspirants? It is not easy to specify individual names: aspiration is more of a collective, perhaps even a bureaucratic, orientation. It doesn't encompass all those who are pro-rights; it involves a 'step up' to what we have been describing as single-mindedness. It is associated (fairly or not) with the United Nations and its agencies, most of all with the treaty-monitoring bodies and the special procedures (both draw heavily on the services of academics). It is also associated with regional human rights organizations and with non-governmental organizations and, to a degree, with individual scholar-activists.

Naming the goals of the aspirants is easier. The goals are totemic: respect, protection and fulfilment of human rights or, more broadly still, democracy, human rights and the rule of law. The principal techniques should be familiar too: they include naming and shaming, and remedies for violations, as well as advocacy and standard-setting. Proposals for new or newly strengthened mechanisms abound. As a general rule, law – from new constitutions to litigation and adjudication – features very heavily. Thus for some, the time has come for a World Court of Human Rights (Panel on Human Dignity, 2011; cf. Alston, 2014). Others have been encouraging national and regional courts to extend the reach and effect of rights via extra-territoriality (e.g. Maastricht Principles, 2011). Elsewhere the focus remains on powers of judicial review, which contributes to a sense that aspiration is all about human rights having the 'last word'.

Courts are not the only concern, however. Others focus on the promotion of rights-based approaches (to development, humanitarianism, and so on), or on the promotion of new rights. Still others look to move beyond the human rights movement's traditional focus on the state. This can be done, they say, by developing a better appreciation of how civil society engages with rights, or by refusing the logic of the public/private divide so that non-state actors (for example, transnational businesses) are brought within the realm of rights (e.g. Human Rights Watch, 2008).

As this list demonstrates, the range and depth of aspiration can seem limitless. There can be a sort of fierceness too: in part because there is always 'real work' to be done, which produces a pattern of working intensely on particular projects but then having to move on, or perhaps watching donors or the public move on. This is not easy to manage, of course, and often feelings of futility are not far from the surface. Even 'true believers' can find they need respite and many search for this in scepticism, critique or irony – provided these are channelled with care:

> [I]t seems perfectly appropriate for a human rights advocate to reflect critically on her work – in writing or in other ways – as long as it is done in an appropriate forum, one that does not interfere with the 'real' work on behalf of marginalized individuals and groups that needs to be accomplished.
>
> *(Engle, 2012: 49)*

Avoidance of rights

There is no such 'splitting' within avoidance, the third and final strain of single-mindedness. Here though we are on new ground: avoiders are not part of the familiar human rights story, which features only the clash of sceptics and evangelists. But not talking about rights – whether rights as law or rights more broadly – is also surely a position on rights. Some avoiders are definitely explicit; they explain their reasons (but with minimal evidence of the sort of stinging rebuke that would raise it to the level of aversion to rights). Elsewhere, avoidance is unexplained and thus apparently unmotivated. Here our best guess would be that it is the product of a sort of legal, or rights, *un*consciousness. It is the likely end result where, for instance, rights are never mentioned at all, or where they are just one part of a longer, undifferentiated list of idioms of justice. It is also the likely end result where rights are treated as abstract standards or as relevant only to 'activist' lawyering, bombastic politicking and lofty judicial pronouncements.

So how might avoidance be explained? We think it arises in part because 'rights talk' combines so often with 'law talk'.[3] It is, in other words, the *legal* character of human rights that is to blame – the fact that rights play out mostly or, at least, most publicly in the key of law. For many avoiders, this signals a surfeit of legal institutions, legal actors, legal doctrines and legal forms of subjectivity. And crucially it isn't just excess that is the problem: whether applied to institutions, actors, doctrines or forms of subjectivity, for many avoiders the adjective 'legal' is a synonym for irritating, exclusionary, and limited and limiting.

The fact that courts seem to be to the fore, or an inevitable fallback, is part of the problem. There is a strong sense that, democracy-wise, this is not a good thing. It is seen to carry the threat of a politicized judiciary and a judicialized politics. Judges, it is argued, can be deferential or they can be usurping; there are, apparently, no other options. There is also, at least in some jurisdictions, the problem of adversarialism (which may not fit, for instance, with the way that NGOs want to work at solving problems). Courtroom conventions more generally can be seen as frustrating too. There are reports that, at the recent international criminal tribunals, some expert witnesses with backgrounds in history and the social sciences felt hemmed in by the demands of 'legal truth'; it seems they wanted to counter-claim, 'It is more complex than that' (Wilson, 2011: 218). There is also a sense that court judgments generally do not reach the problems that matter, or that they do so in ways that do not matter for the long term. Moreover, as many point out, even the most promising judgments can fall short in implementation as either policy or practice.

For some avoiders, human rights reporting is part of the problem too. Such reporting is of course the stock-in-trade of human rights NGOs: activists collect stories or testimony from victims and witnesses about what happened, when it happened and who was involved; they check and cross-check their facts; and then they produce a report and do their best to gain publicity. In so doing, the core aim is to bear witness. There can also be a desire to lay the groundwork for accountability in judicial or quasi-judicial fora. More generally, by documenting human rights violations in this way, the aim is to prevent similar behaviour in the future. Thus, as Stanley Cohen pointed out some time back, human rights reports are a means to an end (1996: 517). But, as Cohen also pointed out, where NGOs focus excessively on the production process, neglecting dissemination and impact, a report can become an end in itself (ibid.).

There has also been concern that human rights reports tell the story of violations, and victims, in very particular ways – ways that surface particular root causes, particular violators and particular victims, whilst rendering others less visible or even invisible (Moon, 2012; cf. Dudai, 2009). Some complain that human rights advocates play with people by playing with words: what is important in telling one's own story and what is seen as crucial in testimony for prosecution purposes are, of course, not necessarily the same. There are problems outside the courtroom too: for an individual rights claimant – an asylum seeker, for instance – there can be a near-impossible pressure to tell the 'right' story, the story that fits the rules, precedents and priorities (Sandvik, 2009).

Another complaint concerns the limited reach or power of law. In making this complaint, the avoider draws out the ways in which ostensibly legal institutions continually ignore, subvert or manage 'the law' in their organizational and occupational cultures and associated working practices. This subversion isn't necessarily secret: it may be widely reported and analysed, and it may even have prompted promise after promise of change and a slew of legal and other interventions. The problem, as the avoider points out, is that cultures and practices often seem stronger than the law or, at least, slow to shift. What, the avoider asks, does it say about law that, out in the open, there are legal institutions that are not 'legally proper'?

Antipathy towards the language of law seems to be a further reason for avoidance of rights. 'Law talk' typically raises two opposing complaints: most of the time, the complaint is that law talk is hair-splitting, arcane, artificial and thoroughly lacking in 'common sense'. But there are times when the complaint is that law talk is not robust or distinctive enough; that it is all just politics, money or some other raw sort of power (Sarat, Douglas and Merrill Umphrey, 2007). There are related complaints concerning the way in which lawyers generally instrumentalize everything and, connected to this, their apparent predisposition towards either strong optimism or deep pessimism, allied with a total lack of curiosity about the broader details of social contexts. This point is nicely illustrated by the contrast between legal scholars' accounts of cases concerning prisoners' rights and the prison ethnographies produced by sociologists and criminologists: whether optimistic or pessimistic, the lawyers' accounts are, by and large, radically distant from the mundane realities and pains of imprisonment that come through very clearly in the ethnographers' work (Crewe, 2009; Carlen, 2011; Phillips, 2012) (the legal scholars might of course point out that neither law nor rights features in much prison ethnography[4]). There is also a sense that the tone of some legal scholarship is not quite right, that it goes against the grain of most other writing about prisons:

> No small proportion of books and other writings about prisons flow from positions that are in one way or another embattled: the practitioner's memoir, the prisoner's autobiography, the social movement pamphlet, and often enough the party manifesto.
>
> *(Sparks, 2010: 522)*

There is one final clutch of reasons we want to mention that might explain avoidance. We sense, in some circles, a feeling that rights and the human rights movement are too normative or too activist, or both. To engage with human rights might therefore put what David Garland calls the role of the 'dispassionate observer' (2007: 163) at risk. There could be other risks too, ranging from threats to specialization or, indeed, autonomy within the academic field (would engaging with rights be akin to an invitation to law to choke off sociology or criminology?), to harm to one's standing with powerful external clienteles who prioritize policy-relevant or 'serviceable' knowledge (Loader and Sparks, 2012: 15). Prison ethnography, for instance, requires access to prisons and prisoners, and the willing co-operation of all parties: even in the most favourable political climate, it is not hard to imagine why a request to prioritize research on *rights* might be perceived by some as a challenge too far. The 'safest' option, in the circumstances, may be to black-box rights – and typically this will extend not just to rights 'as law' but also to rights consciousness and rights cultures.

The costs of single-mindedness

It is time to take stock. We have suggested that there are diverse strains of single-mindedness about rights, and we named these as aversion, aspiration and avoidance. Our three strains do not exhaust thinking and practice on rights. However, in combination, they seem to constrain how both rights in general and prisoners' rights in particular are seen. Specifically, they cast human rights and the human rights movement as too minimalist but also too maximalist, too political but also not political enough, and too law-focused but also not law-focused enough. Contradictions abound here, but not in a way that has a quelling or calming effect. Changes of heart (or mind) have not generally had a cooling effect either. Thus, the acknowledgement made by former Treasury Counsel, Lord Brown, during a 2014 House of Lords debate on proposed restrictions to legal aid for prisoners, that he was speaking out in part 'to atone for [his] own part as Treasury Counsel 30 years or more ago, when [he] did all that [he] could to obstruct the recognition of prisoners' rights' (Hansard, 2014) did not prompt other similar admissions.

The different strains of single-mindedness cannot be wished away, however. And to be honest, even if we could make it happen, we wouldn't want them to disappear totally. There are, we believe, times when prison lawyering demands single-mindedness (Denbeaux and Hafetz, 2011; Pierce, 2012). We think the same is true of NGO practice. Single-mindedness has merit more generally too: there is always a risk of enchantment when dealing with human rights and human rights law, and one potential benefit of some strains of single-mindedness is that their constant, trenchant criticism makes this risk more remote. Single-mindedness also helps to ensure that the gaps between the promise and the fulfilment of legal rights, and the limits of law more generally, are not forgotten. It can help to expose other gaps too. The 'evaluation gap' is one of the most obvious of these: whilst there is rapidly growing interest (some of it donor-driven) in human rights circles in questions about 'what works', 'how' and 'why', evaluation continues to be 'the least well developed dimension of human rights practice and scholarship' (Alston, introducing Salazar Volkmann, 2012: 396). Moreover, as this dimension develops, and human rights practice grapples with the challenges of measurement, certain strains of single-mindedness might be useful in averting the excesses of any 'turn to numbers'.

However, single-mindedness about rights is also 'off' in lots of ways. Some of the allegations levelled against rights can be applied far more widely: unintended, unexpected and unwanted consequences, for instance, are not unique to rights practices. Other allegations are wrong and unfair in that they miss (or perhaps actively misrepresent) what rights 'as law' actually say. We think that insisting on accuracy might be the best antidote to this. It would for instance help to drive home the point that, as regards UK prisoners' rights cases, most judgments are modest and limited. Apparently contentious judgments (notably the Strasbourg Court's ruling against the current UK position on prisoner voting) also need to be placed in context: only three (out of 28) other European Union states have a position similar to the UK, and the Strasbourg Court has ruled that UK prisoners will not be entitled to any monetary compensation as a result of the current delay in reforming UK electoral law (*McHugh* v *United Kingdom*).

Single-mindedness also carries the risk that what matters about rights is neglected. Human rights are not everything of course, but they are not nothing either – they can make a difference; they have made a difference. Human rights law is an important part of the story here (though by no means the only part). Take the array of human rights treaties that states have agreed: there is, and will continue to be, a great deal of contestation around these treaties, but this should not distract us from why and how they matter. They matter because they offer legal authority (states have agreed and ratified the obligations they contain), because they say certain values have to be taken account of and cannot be dismissed or traded away, because they provide a framework for debate and decision-making, and because they offer an extraordinary resource via the decades-long and ongoing elaboration of their meaning by treaty bodies, courts, scholars, NGOs and others. More broadly, and crucially, human rights law foregrounds the dignity and agency of individuals: being able to name something as a right, and to see oneself and others as rights-holders, can be transformative.

Single-mindedness about rights has other blocking effects too. In the UK, there is still very little critical examination of what rights can achieve, and what it takes to produce and to sustain any such achievement (Halliday and Schmidt, 2004). For instance, do we know if rights adoption is likely to be more successful and more secure over time where it merges with other views and idioms of justice? Looking specifically at prisons, what do we really know about how the growth of prisoners' rights has affected the rest of the prison–justice 'mix' – notably, decency, legitimacy, rehabilitation, and latterly 'tough justice'?[5] And turning to specific prison-justice actors, whilst we might expect rights to be at the core of the work of the UN Sub-Committee on Prevention of Torture and the European Committee for the Prevention of Torture,[6] what do we know about the part they play in the 'healthy prisons' tests used by HM Inspectorate of Prisons (HMIP)? True, we know that successive chief inspectors have framed HMIP's purpose partly in light of the UK's obligations under the Optional Protocol to the UN Convention against Torture (HMIP, 2014: paras 2.1–2.2). We also know that the Inspectorate's reports are informed by publicly available standards, called 'Expectations' (HMIP, 2012), and that these draw upon a range of international human rights instruments. But how precisely is translation achieved, on paper and in practice? For instance, do the backgrounds of individual inspectors have an impact on translation? Some inspectors are prison managers on secondment, others are experts in fields such as probation, psychology and health. Relatedly, has translation differed with different chief inspectors? And how has it been affected by other modes of monitoring and control within prisons, including key performance targets and audits (Bennett, 2014)?

The lack of interest with respect to when, how and why rights matter has left other gaps too. Insisting on rights is important, but overselling and under-evaluating them are naïve choices (Loader, 2007). To protect and promote rights, we also need to know what *cannot* be said in the language of rights. And we need to know if and how rights discourses disempower other discourses of justice. We also need to know about the role of courts in precise contexts: general 'democracy' discussions (those that revolve around the question 'are courts inevitably anti-democratic or not?') do not draw out when, and where, the equalizing or levelling power of strong courts has been crucial. Real-world examples – and not just familiar 'developed world' ones – are vital here. Examples that focus, for instance, on when courts have opened a path for legitimate confrontation that could not be forged by means of 'local' or internal problem-solving. Furthermore, when and why this has been particularly important for those, like prisoners, who do not enjoy broad public support? Also, do courts in such cases interweave international and domestic norms, and when and how, in turn, do their judgments feed new norms and practices elsewhere? Equally, where and how precisely have individual courts engaged fully with structural litigation?[7] Knowing about the latter category of cases could be especially useful in dislodging the motif of the 'selfish prisoner' that runs through much aversion to prisoners' rights, and also the general complaint that rights claims are all about aggrieved, relatively powerful individuals and never reach structural questions. Other stereotypes might take a hammering too – including those that treat court decisions as invariably democracy-damaging, or as somehow self-enforcing or self-implementing.

The important question is, of course, 'what now?' We do not have a primer (which may be a good thing given the plethora of handbooks, manuals and pocket-sized guides in the human rights world), but we do have two pointers. First, the strain of single-mindedness that we labelled 'aspiration for rights' should not be relied upon to address the blocking effects just outlined. This strain veers at times towards the evangelical, which means that explanation is not its strong point. It is also dominated by conventional lawyerly preoccupations, and while such preoccupations with intricate and detailed questions of 'the law' have a vital part to play, there is more both to law and to rights. Some scholars already work with the technicalities (and in creative ways) *and* with more than the technicalities (e.g. Lazarus, 2004; Simon, 2014), but more are needed.

Second, single-mindedness has to be addressed both directly and indirectly. In the next part of the chapter we shall be concentrating on the former but here we can make some brief comments about the indirect route. One possibility would be to deepen the strand of scholarly and policy work (e.g. Armstrong and McAra, 2006; Goold and Lazarus, 2007; Loader and Walker, 2007) that aims to expand how we think about 'basics' such as security and punishment. This work would function as a counterpoint to the 'common sense' that security and punishment, on the one hand, and rights, on the other, are always opposed. Another possibility is to resist the pressure to treat the legal field as a lumpen mass. The expression 'the law is the law' captures a particular truth, but it has masking effects too. Thus it is important to look at the interplay between bodies of law – between international, national and local norms, and also between public and private law. It is also important to think about how the end-goals of human rights law can be achieved, or blocked, by other bodies of law: is public procurement law, for instance, a mechanism for securing human rights compliance? A further option for tackling single-mindedness indirectly would be to excavate the hidden or under-discussed history of rights within the field of criminology (Murphy and Whitty, 2007; 2013).

Addressing single-mindedness *directly* requires us to address what is, for the most part, missing at present. We have seen that aversion and aspiration are strong on sweeping scepticism and on 'sunny' claims. Each of these, albeit to differing degrees, gains part of its strength from the absence of context. Delving into this missing context offers, we think, the best chance of *socializing* today's single-mindedness about rights.

Socializing single-mindedness

So the next question is: *how* is such socialization to be achieved? We suggest that, in the prison context, and especially in that context in England and Wales, it means broadening and deepening 'law and society' approaches to scholarship. We are not interested, however, in 'turf wars', so, if it is easier, this broader and deeper engagement can be described as qualitative or empirical, socio-legal or ethnographic in nature; or even as engagement with the 'thick present', or a 'nitty-gritty perspective' (Hornberger, 2011: 179). What is really of interest is the end result: precise, finely grained descriptions of rights and of law (and, of course, of rights 'as law') – descriptions that will challenge the sweeping statements of some of those who are single-minded about rights, and hopefully make 'law talk' and 'rights talk' more interesting to those who have been single-minded in avoiding rights. Some of the latter will engage fully, and those who do not will surely have to be more open about why law, rights and rights 'as law' remain 'unmentionable' in their writings on prisons and prisoners.

Dealing with the 'nitty-gritty' is, in large part, about taking seriously a claim that Amartya Sen made some time back: rights should never be cabined within a 'juridical cage' (2004: 319). The legal field is not unimportant, of course, and much more work could and should be done in following up what happens *after* court decisions (both important and apparently unimportant ones), and in learning how rights as law intersect with other bodies of law. But rights as law cannot exist or succeed without social processes, and rights practices are not simply the practices of courts and treaty bodies, legislators and lawyers. As some will be aware, these points have been made in a broader manner in the 'legal consciousness' scholarship associated with the socio-legal tradition, especially in the United States (Silbey and Ewick, 1998; Sarat and Kearns, 1995; see also Halliday and Morgan, 2013). What that scholarship points out is that, in order to study law, one has to study not just formal environments (such as courts or parliaments) but also attitudes to law in everyday life. These attitudes to law (and within that to rights as law) are more than just attitudes: they are constitutive of law, and of other justice idioms too. We are not, of course, discounting the legal field: it can be a weighty constraint – rights claimants are often turned away, told that their claims just don't 'fit'. Nonetheless, the basic point is sound: the juridical cage has to be broken open – everyday (non-law) accounts of law are part of law too.

There is a further layer to this with respect to rights: rights consciousness and legal consciousness are *not* synonymous. Consciousness of rights, in other words, may or may not combine with legal consciousness and the operation of the legal field (e.g. contacting a lawyer; having one's day in court; going all the way to Strasbourg). Rights consciousness can percolate up by means of other (non-law) justice strategies and languages. Moreover, when rights consciousness does combine with legal consciousness, it is not inevitable that making a claim always ends up in litigation, actual or threatened: rights talk as 'law talk' has far more than one register.

In socializing single-mindedness in the *prisoners' rights context*, getting to the 'thick present' or the 'nitty-gritty', we believe that legal consciousness and rights consciousness could usefully be explored by looking at NGOs, at prison management and personnel, and at prisoners themselves. Looking at prison NGOs (and also at their more broad-based human rights counterparts) would, for instance, bring to the surface the multiple ways in which rights talk can combine with law talk. NGOs' theories of change – their views, perceptions and assumptions about the ways in which social change can or will be achieved – encompass a multitude of attitudes towards law, lawyers and the state. Thus one NGO might have little faith in state law but still pursue a gaming attitude towards it, whereas another might focus its 'law' efforts on legality above or beyond the state. Still other NGOs will look to redeem, or develop, the potential of extant law. And others again will not see law as a lever at all – even perhaps when they are pursuing goals that seem to fit perfectly with those of human rights law.

Inside any individual NGO we should also expect shifts in attitude: perhaps because of changes in personnel or donors; because of evidence concerning the effects of reform projects in particular settings; because the state (typically a key interlocutor for NGOs) moves the goalposts; or because the NGO itself has been changed in the process of engaging with a particular prison (Jefferson, 2013; Jefferson and Gaborit, 2015). We should also be prepared for an overlapping but also discrete set of issues concerning how NGOs construe rights. Where and why are these constructions an outgrowth from moral, religious and local norms, rather than from human rights law? Why do some NGOs describe themselves as human rights NGOs, when others do not? What does it mean – for, say, the NGO's culture and practices – when an NGO describes itself in this way? And is it hard to live up to the description?

Broadening out, it would also be worth asking if and how *anti*-NGO stances can be productive. Lori Allen, in a study that is not about prisons but is still pertinent to the general point, offers a vivid ethnographic account of the Palestinian 'human rights industry', in particular the cynicism that industry generates amongst Palestinians in the face of its failures to end the Israeli occupation, prevent rights violations or generate forms of governance free of corruption. But paradoxically this cynicism – about rights rhetoric, international institutions and donor-driven NGOs – has generative capacities too:

> [Palestinians] may be cynical, insofar as they do not have huge hopes for the future or in the efficacy of [human rights organizations]. Yet they persist within the human rights system because they think it is a channel for being politically engaged, for doing something useful, for making a living, for articulating ideals of proper social relations and state forms.
>
> *(Allen, 2013: 188)*

NGOs do not, of course, exhaust the field of interest: prison staff, prison governors and managers, and prisoners themselves are also very obviously of interest in any project to socialize single-mindedness about rights. There are numerous studies of prison cultures, and particularly staff–prisoner relations, yet remarkably few of these have ever considered the nature and range of either rights consciousness or legal consciousness within different prison environments. How much rights talk and 'rights as law' talk is there in particular prisons? How have human rights norms actually affected prison management, staff and prisoner identities and practices, and the quality of different aspects of prison life? Is the impact different where prisons, and prisoners, have been participants in (threatened or actual) rights litigation – involving the presence of lawyers and legal documents in prison spaces, such as the visiting room, and perhaps the consequences of court judgments? What management strategies are adopted by prison staff when faced with rights-aware prisoners? And throughout the prison estate what have been the effects of the explicit anti-prisoners' rights rhetoric from successive justice secretaries (and prime ministers)?

In research conducted in one English prison in 2002, David Scott described a majority of the 38 prison officers he interviewed as 'disciplinarian' or authoritarian in their outlook (Scott, 2009). This outlook was strongly correlated with aversion to the notion of prisoners' rights; as one officer put it, 'The prisoners have got more rights than the staff at the moment, I think. When they introduce new rights for prisoners, they make it more difficult for us' (ibid.: 118). 'Do-gooder' court-mandated changes were considered an irritant, altering standard or traditional prison practices (e.g. by removing the disciplinary power to add additional days to sentences). We believe that understanding more about such sensibilities – how they are constituted, how they manifest in practice and what challenges them – would help us to gauge the power of human rights as a change agent in prison life. In describing the impact of rights on prisoner–officer culture in the Ugandan Prison Service, Tomas Max Martin has noted that 'human rights do not necessarily have as much top-down power as is both hoped for (and feared)'; rather '[t]he effect is messy and needs to be understood – and sought after – from the bottom up' (2014: 51):

> Human rights ... do not have imperative effects of success or failure as formally prescribed. They rather have ambiguous, accumulative and contingent effects and it is in the mix between different repertoires of norms that reform effects manifest themselves in practice.
>
> *(2014: 48)*[8]

Updated accounts of the effects of human rights on prison life in England and Wales, Scotland and Northern Ireland would allow us to see if what is true in Uganda is also true in the UK. It would also allow comparisons with 'living up' to rights in other criminal justice sites. One recent study of the effects of the Human Rights Act on policing in England and Wales suggests that rights-compliance cultures and practices amongst police officers are mostly about formalities, rather than substance. As one police officer explained:

> A lot of my job involves impinging on people's private lives and I have to be justifying this all of the time in terms of legality, necessity and proportionality. I am always signing forms saying 'I have considered human rights' but I'm not sure we understand what we are signing off (Officer 16).
>
> *(Bullock and Johnson, 2012: 614)*

The officer's comment about 'not [being] sure [officers] understand' speaks to the crucial question of translation. Legal change – the introduction, for instance, of new human rights legislation – typically sparks a spate of training, manuals or guides and circulars. But this material is often formal and abstract, falling short in terms of applied character. Interestingly, Karen Bullock and Paul Johnson observed that many of the police officers they interviewed were open about their lack of human rights knowledge. The officers brought in 'copies of a pocket-sized book that, having been issued soon after the [Human Rights Act] came into force, they had retrieved from their office drawers and bookshelves in order to "revise" for their interview with us' (2012: 616). The question is: would prison officers and governors make comments akin to those of these police officers? Has there been an equivalent 'bureaucratization of justice' (Jacobs and Riles, 2007) in the prison field, amidst ever more compliance paperwork and procedures, especially in the context of legally mandated risk assessments and dominant security considerations? How, more broadly, does management affect prison-officer culture as regards rights awareness and compliance? Which levels of management are most influential? Also, are known differences between public and private prisons duplicated as regards human rights standards?

There are other reasons too for updating and extending Scott's research on prison officers and human rights. Since that time there has been considerable 'heating up' of the criminal question (Loader and Sparks, 2010) and also, as we have seen, considerable growth in single-mindedness about rights (including a promise to repeal the Human Rights Act and dilute the influence of the 'foreign' court in Strasbourg). Austerity, and associated practices such as efficiency savings and further privatization, will have had an impact too. We can therefore anticipate changes in staff cultures and management priorities vis-à-vis rights since 2002, driven by an array of internal and external factors, and also perhaps a range of new issues concerning different types of prison, prisoner and human rights controversy (for example, the heightened tensions around Islamic religious practices (Liebling, Arnold and Straub, 2011; Earle and Phillips, 2012)).

This brings us to prisoners themselves. The headline-catching quality of *anti-*prisoners' rights rhetoric has undoubtedly created a sense that all of us know a lot – or at least, more than enough – about prisoners, rights and law (notably, in relation to the alleged need to end 'soft' prison life). In fact, practically nothing detailed is known about either the rights consciousness or the legal consciousness of prisoners, whether as individuals or as distinctive prisoner-populations. True, where prisoners' rights' litigation has resulted in a court decision, the 'facts' outlined in the written judgment will provide a biographical narrative of sorts. Yet no more than a fraction of claims proceed to judgment, and as a general rule the narratives that are found in judgments will be no more than truncated and technical descriptions of the prisoner at the heart of the case and of prison life. Thus, while the permeability of 'the prison's boundaries ... to juridical norms' (Jacobs, 1977: 105) is revealed by court judgments, that revelation is limited and formal, falling short on both depth and dimension.

What remains absent from the prison ethnography tradition today are detailed accounts of when and why particular prisoners, or groups of prisoners, exhibit rights consciousness, and relatedly make use of rights talk and, where possible, 'rights as law' talk. Are there, for instance, stages in the translation of grievances into rights claims and into 'rights as law' claims? Do pathways differ between familiar 'repeat' claims (e.g. requesting family contact), and rarer, or perhaps more politically contested, claims? Where choices present themselves in terms of discontinuing, settling or pursuing claims, how do prisoners negotiate those choices?[9] The distinctive political cultures of Scotland and Northern Ireland are, moreover, an important further dimension that must be taken into account (albeit that prisoner litigation emerging from these jurisdictions sometimes finds its resolution in the UK Supreme Court in London or, exceptionally, in Strasbourg).[10]

There are undoubtedly many reasons why rights and law might not, and do not, register in the inner life of prisons – reasons that include the broader legal and political culture, but also the imperative to 'manage' human rights risks at senior organizational levels (Whitty, 2011; see also Crewe and Liebling, 2012), the disempowering effects of imprisonment and the vulnerability of particular prisoners, and the pragmatic lack of interest in confronting penal authorities that prevails amongst (mostly short-term) prisoners. Sometimes, however, prisoners' rights do register, and it is these prisoners – their circumstances, motivations and so on – about whom we need to know more. It would of course also be useful to know more about unconsciousness concerning rights and rights 'as law' amongst prisoners; and the same is true concerning any deliberate discounting of rights by prisoners or by particular prison populations. Ben Crewe, for instance, has described how in some ways 'the prison experience is considerably less heavy than in the past':

> Power is exercised more softly, in a way that is less authoritarian. Yet in other ways, the prison experience has become 'deeper' and more burdensome. Movements are more restricted, security has been tightened, and risk has become the trump-card of the system. Prisons are materially more comfortable, but they remain psychologically damaging: in the words of one prisoner, 'it's cushier, but it hurts you in other ways'. For long-term prisoners in particular, once conditions reach a certain standard, they cause less consternation than the difficulties of progressing through the system.
>
> *(2011: 524)*

'The carceral experience', he concludes, is 'less directly oppressive, but more gripping – lighter but tighter' (ibid.). But what remains unknown is how, if at all, new types of environments are influencing rights, and rights 'as law', consciousness amongst prisoners.

Conclusion

Even prisoners have their moments of perceived merit. The case that turned the law around had begun when an assistant governor at Parkhurst imprudently chose the ablest barrack-room lawyer in the prison system on whom to practise a denial of due process at a hearing that, thanks to the labour-intensive traditions of prison bureaucracy, was recorded verbatim in longhand by a prison officer.

> The accusing officer recounted how he had found secreted in the prisoner's cell a biro adapted for smoking cannabis. The assistant governor thereupon announced that he found the case proved.
>   'Excuse me,' said the prisoner. 'Don't you want to hear my defence?'
>   'I'm not interested in your defence,' said the assistant governor. 'I find you guilty.'
>
> *(Sedley, 2011: 207–8)*

So writes Stephen Sedley, the former barrister (and later judge) who represented the prisoner in this judicial review action before the Law Lords in 1988. The case established that governors' adjudications were no longer immune from legal scrutiny (*Leech* v *Deputy Governor, Parkhurst Prison*). Earlier, in 1975, the European Court of Human Rights had ruled that a British prisoner's right to consult a solicitor could not be dependent on the permission of prison authorities (*Golder* v *United Kingdom*). As we write this 40 years later, it is a priority of the Conservative government both to limit the jurisdiction of the Strasbourg Court, making it the exception amongst 46 other member states in the Council of Europe, and also to introduce a new, distinctively 'British' Bill of Rights, the interpretation of which will rest with the UK Supreme Court.

The Conservatives' desire to repackage rights will, of course, raise both technical questions of law and, relatedly, serious political risks, not least because it stands alongside surging Scottish nationalism, on the one hand, and Northern Irish opposition to unpicking the core of the peace settlement on the other.[11] We can also expect any repackaging to bolster misrepresentations of both law and prison life, and also the demonization of prisoners. Harder forms of aversion to rights are admittedly producing new, more explicit defences of rights by politicians, such as the First Minister of Scotland, Nicola Sturgeon, and others too. But these defences will need to be allied with what we have been advocating: the socialization of single-mindedness about rights.

Both direct and indirect approaches to the task will be required. The latter must counter 'common sense' on security, punishment, risk and the like: reimagining punishment, for example, is an essential component in reimagining rights. Indirect approaches must also dilute the sense of law as a lumpen mass. They should follow up the 'before and after' of court decisions, and draw out the interplay between bodies of law – between international, national and local norms, and between public and private law. They should also ask: when are the goals of human rights law achieved, and when are they blocked, by other bodies of law? And when are these goals achieved or blocked by non-law decisions and norms, such as efficiency?

Mostly though we emphasize direct modes of socializing single-mindedness about rights. These will focus, above all, on the missing context: the gaps that reinforce the unarguable quality of both aversion and aspiration, the gaps that compromise a fair and just measure of rights. Context alone won't be enough, of course; there will also be persistent normative and political questions that need to be addressed. But it should curb aversion and aspiration by providing detail that will compromise their one-dimensional accounts of rights. Producing this context is, furthermore, an opportunity for those we described as unmotivated avoiders: the sociologists, criminologists and anthropologists who don't appear to think much at all about rights, law and rights 'as law', but who belong to fields noted for a commitment to open-minded enquiry that is entirely apt here. And, to be clear, producing context is not about making rights or law the last word on justice. It is about the missing detail; the detail of what rights have and have not done, and what they can and cannot do.

This detail is one obvious way to temper the accounts of rights, both hollowed out and overblown, that have become so prevalent. It will need to look in particular at NGOs, at prison managers, governors and officers, and of course at prisoners themselves. But for this detail to be retrieved, specified and inventoried, scholarship on imprisonment has to evolve and braid together more effectively than in the past.

Acknowledgement

Our thanks to the editors for very helpful comments.

Cases cited

Golder v *United Kingdom* (1975) 1 EHRR 524
Leech v *Deputy Governor, Parkhurst Prison* [1988] AC 533
Sentencia T-847 (2000), Constitutional Court of Colombia
Verbitsky, Horacio s/habeas corpus (2005), Supreme Court of Argentina
Donaldson v *United Kingdom* [2011] ECHR 2010
Moohan v *Lord Advocate* [2014] UKSC 67
McHugh v *United Kingdom* [2015] ECHR 155

Notes

1 The Conservative Party Manifesto 2015 promised to 'break the formal link between British courts and the European Court of Human Rights, and make our own Supreme Court the ultimate arbiter of human rights matters in the UK' (2015: 60).
2 The Queen's Speech 2015 contained no proposals on the Human Rights Act 1998, but the new Secretary of State for Justice, Michael Gove, has been tasked with finding a replacement – or modification – of it.
3 By contrasting 'rights talk' and 'law talk', and also rights and rights 'as law', we aim to capture a crucial point: although rights can have a legal form and this form has a social influence that needs to be acknowledged and specified, rights are not bound exclusively to law.
4 There are exceptions, notably Jacobs (1977); Ludlow (2015).
5 For accounts of the prison–justice mix over three decades, see e.g. King and McDermott (1995); Liebling (2004); HMCIP (2014).
6 Both are non-judicial preventive mechanisms, undertaking visits to detention sites in individual states and producing reports thereon.
7 See e.g. *Verbitsky* (2005) decided by the Supreme Court of Argentina; *Sentencia* (2000) decided by the Constitutional Court of Colombia.
8 Piacentini (2004) examines perceptions of human rights among prison staff in Russia.
9 Studies of political prisoners in Northern Ireland have analysed prisoner litigation strategies: see McEvoy (2001); Corcoran (2006).
10 See e.g. *Donaldson* (2011) (challenge by Northern Irish prisoner to ban on wearing emblems); *Moohan* (2014) (challenge by Scottish prisoners to their exclusion from voting in the Scottish Independence Referendum).
11 The promise to 'scrap' the Human Rights Act obscures the legal and political obstacles ahead and likely timeframe. Neither a majority in the House of Commons nor in the House of Lords can be assumed. If new legislation is eventually passed, the Scottish or Northern Irish governments, or other interested parties, may initiate legal action on the grounds of incompatibility with the terms (and referenda processes) of the Scotland Act 1998, Northern Ireland Act 1998 or the Belfast (Anglo-Irish) Agreement 1998. The UK Supreme Court would be the final domestic court of appeal (providing it with the

opportunity to clarify the limits of parliamentary sovereignty) and, ultimately, litigation before international courts is a possibility. For general discussion, see JUSTICE (2010); O'Cinneide (2012).

References

Allen, L. (2013) *The Rise and Fall of Human Rights*. Stanford, CA: Stanford University Press.

Alston, P. introducing Salazar Volkmann, C. (2012) 'Evaluating the Impact of Human Rights Work: The Office of the High Commissioner for Human Rights and the Reduction of Extrajudicial Executions in Colombia', *Journal of Human Rights Practice*, 4(3): 396–460.

Alston, P. (2014) 'Against a World Court for Human Rights', *Ethics & International Affairs*, 28(2): 197–212.

Armstrong, S. and McAra, L. (eds) (2006) *Perspectives on Punishment: The Contours of Control*. Oxford: Oxford University Press.

Bennett, J. (2014) 'Resisting the Audit Explosion: The Art of Prison Inspection', *Howard Journal of Criminal Justice*, 53(5): 449–467.

Brown, W. (2002) 'Suffering the Paradoxes of Rights', in W. Brown and J. Halley (eds) *Left Legalism/Left Critique*. Durham, NC: Duke University Press, 420–434.

Brown, W. (2004) 'Human Rights and the Politics of Fatalism', *South Atlantic Quarterly*, 103 (2): 451–463.

Bullock, K. and Johnson, P. (2012) 'The Impact of the Human Rights Act 1998 on Policing in England and Wales', *British Journal of Criminology*, 52(3): 630–650.

Carlen, P. (ed.) (2011) *Women and Punishment*. Cullompton: Willan Publishing.

Cohen, S. (1996) 'Government Responses to Human Rights Reports: Claims, Denials, and Counterclaims', *Human Rights Quarterly*, 18(3): 517–543.

Conservative Central Office (2014) *Protecting Human Rights in the UK*. London: Conservative Central Office.

Conservative Central Office (2015) *The Conservative Party Manifesto 2015*. London: Conservative Central Office.

Corcoran, M. (2006) *Out of Order: The Political Imprisonment of Women in Northern Ireland 1972–1998*. Cullompton: Willan Publishing.

Crewe, B. (2009) *The Prisoner Society*. Oxford: Oxford University Press.

Crewe, B. (2011) 'Depth, Weight and Tightness: Revisiting the Pains of Imprisonment', *Punishment & Society*, 13(5): 509–529.

Crewe, B. and Liebling, A. (2012) 'Are Liberal-Humanitarian Penal Values and Practices Exceptional?', in T. Ugelvik and J. Dullum (eds) *Penal Exceptionalism? Nordic Prison Policy and Practice*. London: Routledge, 175–198.

Denbeaux, M. P. and Hafetz, J. (eds) (2011) *The Guantanamo Lawyers: Inside a Prison Outside the Law*. New York: New York University Press.

Dudai, R. (2009) '"Can You Describe This?" Human Rights Reports and What They Tell Us about the Human Rights Movement', in R. A. Wilson and R. D. Brown (eds) *Humanitarianism and Suffering: The Mobilization of Empathy*. New York: Cambridge University Press, 245–264.

Earle, R. and Phillips, C. (2012) 'Digesting Men? Ethnicity, Gender and Food: Perspectives from a "Prison Ethnography"', *Theoretical Criminology*, 16(2): 141–156.

Engle, K. (2012) 'Self-critique, (Anti) politics and Criminalization: Reflections on the History and Trajectory of the Human Rights Movement', in J. M. Beneyto and D. Kennedy (eds) *New Approaches to International Law*. The Hague: TMC Asser Press, 41–73.

Feeley, M. and Swearingen, V. (2004) 'The Prison Conditions Cases and the Bureaucratization of American Corrections: Influences, Impacts and Implications', *Pace Law
Review*, 24(2): 433–475.

Garland, D. (2007) 'Beyond the Culture of Control', *Critical Review of International Social and
Political Philosophy*, 7(2): 160–189.

Goold, B. and Lazarus, L. (eds) (2007) *Security and Human Rights*. Oxford: Hart Publishing.

Grayling, C. (2014) 'We must stop the legal aid abusers tarnishing Britain's justice system',
Daily Telegraph, 20 April.

Grieve, D. (2014) *Why Human Rights Should Matter to Conservatives*, available at: www.ucl.ac.
uk/constitution-unit/ [accessed: 30 April 2015].

Halliday, S. and Morgan, B. (2013) '"I Fought the Law and the Law Won": Legal
Consciousness and the Critical Imagination', *Current Legal Problems*, 66(1): 1–32.

Halliday, S. and Schmidt, P. (eds) (2004) *Human Rights Brought Home: Socio-Legal Perspectives
on Human Rights in the National Context*. Oxford: Hart Publishing.

Hansard HL Deb 29 January2014, vol. 750, col. 1278.

HM Chief Inspector of Prisons for England and Wales (2014) *Annual Report 2013–14*.
London: Her Majesty's Stationery Office.

HM Inspectorate of Prisons (2012) *Expectations: Criteria for Assessing the Treatment of Prisoners
and Conditions in Prisons*. London: Her Majesty's Inspectorate of Prisons.

HM Inspectorate of Prisons (2014) *Inspection Framework*. London: Her Majesty's Inspectorate
of Prisons.

Hopgood, S. (2010) 'Review Essay: Dignity and Ennui', *Journal of Human Rights Practice*, 2(1):
151–165.

Hornberger, J. (2011) *Policing and Human Rights: The Meaning of Violence and Justice in the
Everyday Policing of Johannesburg*. London: Routledge.

Human Rights Watch and Center for Human Rights and Global Justice (2008) 'On the
Margins of Profit: Rights at Risk in the Global Economy', available at: www.hrw.org/
sites/default/files/reports/bhr0208webwcover.pdf [accessed: 16 October 2015].

Jacob, M.-A. and Riles, A. (2007) 'The New Bureaucracies of Virtue: Introduction', *Political
and Legal Anthropology Review*, 30(2): 181–191.

Jacobs, J. B. (1977) *Stateville: The Penitentiary in Mass Society*. Chicago, IL: University of
Chicago Press.

Jefferson, A. M. (2013) 'The Situated Production of Legitimacy: Perspectives from the
Global South', in J. Tankebe and A. Liebling (eds) *Legitimacy and Criminal Justice: An
International Exploration*. Oxford: Oxford University Press, 248–266.

Jefferson, A. M. and Gaborit, L. S. (2015) *Human Rights in Prisons: Comparing Institutional
Encounters in Kosovo, Sierra Leone and the Philippines*. London: Palgrave Macmillan.

JUSTICE (2010) *Devolution and Human Rights*. London: JUSTICE.

Kennedy, D. (2004) *The Dark Sides of Virtue: Reassessing International Humanitarianism*.
Princeton: Princeton University Press.

King, R. D. and McDermott, K. (1995) *The State of our Prisons*, Oxford: Clarendon Press.

Lazarus, L. (2004) *Contrasting Prisoners' Rights: A Comparative Examination of England and
Germany*. Oxford: Oxford University Press.

Liebling, A. (2004) *Prisons and their Moral Performance: A Study of Values, Quality and Prison
Life*. Oxford: Clarendon Press.

Liebling, A., Arnold, H. and Straub, C. (2011) *An Exploration of Staff–Prisoner Relationships at
HMP Whitemoor: 12 Years On*. London: Ministry of Justice National Offender Management
Service.

Loader, I. (2007) 'The Cultural Lives of Security and Rights', in B. Goold and L. Lazarus
(eds) *Security and Human Rights*. Oxford: Hart Publishing, 27–44.

Loader, I. and Sparks, R. (2010) *Public Criminology?* London: Routledge.

Loader, I. and Sparks, R. (2012) 'Situating Criminology: On the Production and Consumption of Knowledge about Crime and Justice', in M. Maguire, R. Morgan and R. Reiner (eds) *Oxford Handbook of Criminology*, 5th edition. Oxford: Oxford University Press, 3–38.

Loader, I. and Walker, N. (2007) *Civilizing Security*. Cambridge: Cambridge University Press.

Ludlow, A. (2015) *Privatising Public Prisons: Labour Law and the Public Procurement Process*. Oxford: Hart Publishing.

'Maastricht Principles on Extraterritorial Obligations of States in the Area of Economic, Social and Cultural Rights' (2011), reprinted in *Netherlands Quarterly of Human Rights*, 29(4): 578–590.

Martin, T. M. (2014) 'The Importation of Human Rights by Ugandan Prison Staff', *Prison Service Journal*, 212 (March): 45–50.

McEvoy, K. (2001) *Paramilitary Imprisonment in Northern Ireland: Resistance, Management and Release*. Oxford: Oxford University Press.

Moon, C. (2012) 'What One Sees and How One Files Seeing: Reporting Atrocity and Suffering', *Sociology*, 46(5): 876–890.

Murphy, T. and Whitty, N. (2007) 'Risk and Human Rights in UK Prison Governance', *British Journal of Criminology*, 47(5): 798–816.

Murphy, T. and Whitty, N. (2013) 'Making History: Academic Criminology and Human Rights', *British Journal of Criminology*, 53(4): 568–587.

O'Cinneide, C. (2012) *Human Rights and the UK Constitution*, London: British Academy Policy Centre.

O'Neill, O. (2005) 'The Dark Side of Human Rights', *International Affairs*, 81(2): 427–439.

Panel on Human Dignity (2011) *Protecting Dignity: An Agenda for Human Rights, 2011 Report*, available at: www.udhr60.ch/docs/PanelhumanDignity_rapport2011.pdf [accessed 30 April 2015].

Phillips, C. (2012) *The Multicultural Prison*, Oxford: Oxford University Press.

Pierce, G. (2012) *Dispatches from the Dark Side*, London: Verso.

Piacentini, L. (2004) *Surviving Russian Prisons: Punishment, Politics and Economy in Transition*, Cullompton: Willan Publishing.

Rosenberg, G. (2008) *The Hollow Hope: Can Courts Bring about Social Change?*, 2nd edition. Chicago, IL: Chicago University Press.

Sandvik, K. B. (2009) 'The Physicality of Legal Consciousness: Suffering and the Production of Credibility in Refugee Resettlement', in R. A. Wilson and R. D. Brown (eds) *Humanitarianism and Suffering: The Mobilization of Empathy*. New York: Cambridge University Press, 223–244.

Sarat, A. and Kearns, T. (eds) (1995) *Law in Everyday Life*. Ann Arbor: University of Michigan Press.

Sarat, A., Douglas, L. and Merrill Umphrey, M. (2007) 'Complexity, Contingency and Change in Law's Knowledge Practices: An Introduction', in A. Sarat, L. Douglas and M. Merrill Umphrey (eds) *How Law Knows*. Stanford, CA: Stanford University Press, 1–24.

Scott, D. (2009) *Ghosts Beyond Our Realm: A Neo-abolitionist Analysis of Prisoner Human Rights and Prison Officer Culture*. Milton Keynes: VDM Verlag.

Sedley, S. (2011) *Ashes and Sparks: Essays on Law and Justice*. Cambridge: Cambridge University Press.

Sen, A. (2004) 'Elements of a Theory of Human Rights', *Philosophy and Public Affairs*, 32(4): 315–356.

Silbey, S. and Ewick, P. (1998) *The Common Place of Law: Stories from Everyday Life*. Chicago, IL: University of Chicago Press.

Simon, J. (2014) *Mass Incarceration on Trial: A Remarkable Court Decision and the Future of Prisons in America*. New York: New Press.

Sparks, R. (2010) 'Review of D. van Zyl Smit and S. Snacken, *Principles of European Prison Law and* Policy (OUP, 2009)', *Edinburgh Law Review*, 14(3): 520–522.

Straw, J. (2013) 'Oral Evidence to Joint Committee on the draft Voting Eligibility (Prisoners) Bill', House of Commons (QQ 93–109).

Sumption, J. (2013) *The Limits of Law*, available at: www.supremecourt.uk/docs/speech-131120.pdf [accessed: 30 April 2015].

Whitty, N. (2011) 'Human Rights as Risk: UK Prisons and the Management of Risk and Rights', *Punishment and Society*, 13(2): 123–148.

Wilson, R. A. (2011) *Writing History in International Criminal Trials*. New York: Cambridge University Press.

8

EXAMINING IMPRISONMENT THROUGH A SOCIAL JUSTICE LENS

Ruth Armstrong and Shadd Maruna

> We need to reconstitute sources of knowledge that can make prison social order more visible to a public whose infatuation with incarceration depends on deep ignorance as to its fundamental effects.
>
> *(Simon, 2000: 303)*

> The penal crisis is in essence a moral crisis ... the penal system is ... the source of very substantial injustice, and the crisis is unlikely to be solved unless this injustice is mitigated.
>
> *(Cavadino, Dignan and Mair, 2013: 31)*

> Without consideration of 'justice for all', issues of morality rarely arise.
>
> *(Hegtvedt and Scheuerman, 2010: 354)*

Introduction

Prisons represent an enormously costly investment and intrusion into the lives of citizens, yet rarely is this investment questioned and examined. What are prisons for? What do they do for society that could possibly justify their extremity in terms not just of expense but also the infringement on the most fundamental liberties enshrined in liberal democracies? The answers to these questions need not be based in what Tasioulas (2006: 283) calls 'top-down' penal theory: the theoretical purposes of punishment (deterrence, retribution, reform, etc.) that are well known from introductory textbooks but may bear little relation to 'the values implicit in our practice of punishment' (ibid.: 283). After all, the prison is not the only institution that could achieve the often conflicting aims of penal theory, and indeed it may be uniquely unsuited to the achievement of most of them.

With over a half-century of sustained research on the effects of imprisonment following the pioneering research of Sykes (1958/2007), Haney, Banks and

Zimbardo (1973) and others, it is beyond disingenuous to pretend we still do not know what the impact of prisons are on prisoners, prison employees and prisoners' families (see for example Liebling and Maruna, 2005; Travis, Western and Redburn, 2014). The vast majority of this research demonstrates the considerable damage that prisons can cause at the individual level. Less attention has been paid to prisons as social institutions, in terms both of their place in and their implications for wider society (although see the important work of Clear, 2007; Clear and Frost, 2013; DeFina and Hannon, 2013; Travis and Waul, 2003; Wacquant, 2007; 2009a; 2009b). This chapter is an attempt to address this gap in the literature by exploring existing research through a social justice lens. We are minded to do so in light of Halsey's claim that 'Incarceration is the medium for the exacerbation of deprivation rather than the means of deprivation per se' (2007: 361), which caused us to wonder whether prisons could ever be agents of social justice.

We begin the chapter by outlining three different understandings of social justice: minimalist, mutual and egalitarian. Next, we present research evidence on the nature and effects of imprisonment. We consider this evidence in light of the different models of social justice and describe perceived deficits. Recognition of the social injustices of incarceration, particularly for neighbourhoods suffering from high rates of incarceration, has underpinned recent steps towards reform through 'justice reinvestment' (JR). This movement aims to reduce the *resort to* imprisonment and the *impact of* imprisonment through reinvesting some of the money spent on sending people to prison back into communities that suffer from high imprisonment rates. We argue that, while this may reduce the overall amount of harm caused by incarceration, it does little to challenge the 'corrupt version of retributivism' that Matravers (2012: 37) argues characterizes the tone of contemporary penal policy. We describe how the philosophy underpinning the JR movement risks being narrowed into a money-saving endeavour, and argue that economic reinvestment alone is unlikely to address the social justice deficits of imprisonment. In the final part of the chapter we employ a social justice imagination to consider what prison might look like if it were redesigned under a penal policy that aimed to maximize civic inclusion rather than to facilitate social exclusion. Our thesis is that, if prisons could facilitate prisoners' expression and experience of citizenship while incarcerated, this would enhance their potential to be agents of social justice, but that any attempt to move in this direction will necessitate a more deliberate and more strategic movement towards a theory of individual punishment that is grounded in notions of social justice.

Examining social justice

So what is social justice? Heffernan (2000) outlines three concepts of social justice that he argues coincide in part, but also conflict in part. The first of these is what he calls a 'minimalist' version of social justice, which purports that 'the sole purpose for which society can impose burdens on its members is to insure public safety' (ibid.: 50). The second is a 'mutuality' version of social justice. Heffernan calls it a 'welfare-state conception of social justice', which is grounded in the idea of social life as a mutual enterprise, and therefore the need for social justice to be about extending this mutuality as much as possible, especially through sharing of basic goods and services. The third version is an 'egalitarian' model of social justice, focused on the equal distribution of wealth in a society among its members through social organization and collective efforts that produce both services and commodities. The 'egalitarian' model moves beyond the 'mutuality model' to address the social structures that might facilitate equal access to and distribution of wealth as 'a matter of entitlement and not ... an act of grace' (ibid.: 51).

Heffernan focuses on areas where these three conceptions of social justice conflict when applied to aspects of procedural criminal justice and ideas of who deserves punishment and why. We, however, use his tripartite structure in terms of its commonalities. He argues that these three understandings of social justice intersect in their approach to maximization of a common life; their focus on defending the community; and the social nature of the outputs of commercial exchange. In this sense, our understanding of the term 'social justice' is Platonic – we think of the ideal of social justice as a version of justice that holds society together, which makes us more, rather than less, intermingled. We believe that each of the three strands identified by Heffernan – minimalist public safety, maximizing mutuality and economic egalitarianism – can work together to help to hold individuals in society closer together. This is how we will operationalize 'social justice' in this analysis.

Our understanding of social justice, then, necessitates a movement beyond individualized, abstracted notions of equality and just deserts. It involves asking ourselves what it might mean for how we 'do' imprisonment if our overriding aim was for prison to be an agent of equitably rendering what was due to individuals in a way that maximized mutuality and egalitarianism without compromising public safety? Hence, we want to know whether imprisonment is fair, not just individually (for prisoners or their family members), but also socially. In a Lockean sense, our question is whether imprisonment could ever make social existence more, rather than less, possible? By this, we mean does it limit mutual interactions only to the extent necessary in order to protect, punish and reform? If this is not possible (and it may not be), then our concern is that prisons damage social existence through a misconceived notion of promoting social safety through individual exclusion. Underpinning all of these questions of whether prisons are, or can be, agents of social justice, is the fundamental question of whether the exchange of individual liberties for communal liberties inherent in imprisonment is worthwhile, socially. In an attempt to answer this question, below we look at evidence of who gets imprisoned and what the effects of imprisonment are. We then consider this evidence using a 'social justice lens' to ask whether prison could be a social institution that promotes the common good through simultaneously making society safer, more mutual and more egalitarian. Implicit in asking such a question is the follow-up: If not, then what accounts for the enormous societal investment in such an institution.

The effects of imprisonment

Research suggests that, in nearly every jurisdiction where they are utilized, prisons detain those who have been disadvantaged from early on in life and continue to be at the margins socially whether through racial isolation, victimization, abuse or poverty. In England and Wales, for instance, a study of over 6000 children who were detained in custody over a six-month period in 2008 found that 39 per cent of the children had been on the child protection register and around 70 per cent were known to social services prior to their incarceration (Jacobson et al., 2010; see also Goldson, 2015). Additionally, experiences of neglect and early bereavement were common among the sample, as were mental health problems and learning difficulties. The statistics for the adult population are no less sobering. In 2014, in England and Wales over half of the women in prison and nearly a third of all the men in prison reported being abused as children. A quarter of all people in prison were taken into care as a child – whereas only 2 per cent of the general population were cared for by social services (Prison Reform Trust, 2014).

The people whom the state incarcerates then are disproportionately likely to be vulnerable members of our society. Compounding this disadvantage, there is consistent evidence to show that imprisonment has negative consequences not only for the vulnerable individuals we incarcerate but also for their families (Murray et al., 2014; Wakefield and Wildeman, 2013), their communities (Clear, 2007; Coyle, 2010), and for society more broadly (DeFina and Hannon, 2013). These disadvantages relate to the fact of imprisonment per se rather than pre-existing social vulnerability and disadvantage (see esp. Travis et al., 2014). Murray et al. (2014) disentangled the effects of imprisonment on the children of prisoners from the effects of having a parent involved in crime and from other disadvantages such as poverty, social class and low educational achievement. They found that the harmful effects of parental imprisonment on children were not predicted by the arrest and conviction of a parent without imprisonment (see also Murray et al., 2012). These negative effects of parental incarceration were also found to be much higher in England than in Sweden or Holland (Besemer et al., 2011). This led to suggestions that higher levels of welfare support, or less punitive penal policies, might reduce the harmful effects of imprisonment on the children of prisoners. The finding also suggests that the elements of social justice outlined above may work together in both positive and negative directions. Where penal policies are less focused on punishment and exclusion and more focused on social policies that aim to make society more egalitarian (through the provision of welfare to those in need and through aiming towards integration rather than simply exclusion or containment), some of the recognized negative effects of incarceration may be ameliorated (Murray et al., 2012).

Not only does the state disproportionately incarcerate the socially vulnerable but by so doing it increases these vulnerabilities and makes it more likely these individuals will be repeatedly criminalized. Jacobs (2006: 387) examined the role of mass incarceration in the proliferation of criminal records and boldly opened his findings with the statement 'the criminal justice system feeds on itself'. His research shows how having a criminal record contributes to what he calls 'the growth of an ex-offender and ex-prison-inmate underclass' (ibid.: 420). The well-established criminogenic effects of embroilment in the criminal justice system makes the consequences for those who are imprisoned, and for their families and their communities, a self-perpetuating and ever deepening and broadening injustice (for further evidence see Brenburg and Krohn, 2003; Davies and Tanner, 2003; and Chiricos et al., 2007). Prison plays a major part in the criminal justice system's insatiable appetite for perpetual cannibalization. For instance, adolescent incarceration is one of the strongest predictors of continued adult criminality (Tracy and Kempf-Leonard, 1996; Goldson, 2015). Prison is also more criminogenic than other forms of sanction (Bales and Piquero, 2012; Jolliffe and Hedderman, 2015). While prisons have been shown to have a minimal effect on reducing crime rates, ever-increasing imprisonment rates dissolve this gain through increasing the ripple effect of the social costs of imprisonment (Public Safety Performance Project, 2007). The more incarceration is used, the less effective it is (Roeder et al., 2015). Prisons therefore do not just ensure an illusion of social separateness through keeping people locked up; increasing resort to imprisonment helps to create, maintain and increase this illusion through exacerbating the likelihood of reconviction and exaggerating social vulnerabilities and powerlessness on an individual and a communal basis.

As social institutions, it is therefore difficult to argue that prisons are minimalizing harm and ensuring public safety because they are contributing to increased risk of reoffending and reconviction. Similarly, because prisons disproportionately house the vulnerable in society, and then make it more difficult for them to access the goods essential to a decent life on the same footing as people who have not been convicted of criminal offences and incarcerated, it is difficult to argue that they are maximizing mutuality. Instead, they help to deepen and broaden these disadvantages within vulnerable groups of the population. It therefore appears inescapable that prisons are failing to promote social justice on the 'minimalist' and 'mutualist' definitions of the term – but what about the egalitarian approach to social justice? How does prison work in terms of its impact on the provision of equal access to and distribution of wealth and the social structures that support this?

Research on the geography of imprisonment, of who goes to prison, makes clear that prisoners are not randomly distributed; they come from geographical clusters, from certain communities and social strata. In the US, special mapping techniques have now been used to map the migration flow of people to prison, back to their community and back to prison again for the nation's major cities.[1] The map in Figure 8.1 below depicts what this looks like in practice for Brooklyn, New York. The grey spots shown are prisoner homes. There are clusters, and then there are blank spots. The clusters are 'million-dollar blocks' – so called because it costs a million dollars a year to incarcerate the prisoners taken from that single city block. The public investment in mass incarceration significantly reduces the economic resources necessary to maintain the infrastructure of civic society in these areas. It reduces the public money available for housing, for education, for health care and for families in need (see Cadora, Swartz and Gordon, 2003).

The lines in Figure 8.2 below show where all of the prisoners identified in Figure 8.1 are going to serve their prison sentences. It makes for intriguing art but remarkably poor social policy. Prisons fracture communities not simply because of the inherently exclusionary nature of the institution but also because new prisons are built in excluded rural areas far from prisoners' homes. It is now well established and largely uncontested that the ability to stay connected with one's community through visitation from family and friends reduces some of the pains and negative impacts of incarceration (Holt and Miller, 1972; Bales and Mears, 2008; Mears et al., 2012) and can support efforts to desist from crime (Maruna and Toch, 2005, but see Kirk, 2009). Yet such evidence has borne little weight against a

FIGURE 8.1 Migration flow of people to prison, back to their community and back to prison again in Brooklyn, New York

Source: Images courtesy of Spatial Information Design Lab, GSAPP, Columbia University. Architecture and Justice, Million Dollar Blocks, 2006.

FIGURE 8.2 Map showing where all of the prisoners identified in Figure 8.1 are going to serve their prison sentences

Source: Images courtesy of Spatial Information Design Lab, GSAPP, Columbia University. Architecture and Justice, Million Dollar Blocks, 2006.

flawed response to social disorganization theory that believes, if a problem exists in our inner cities, the solution is in relocating individuals to remote rural areas (Moran, 2015). It is a flaw that runs through much penal policy, which responds to the individual and their location as the nexus of criminality, and deftly blindsides the role and implications of broader social structures. Prisoners live in socially deprived areas with little investment, but rather than investing in these communities with acknowledged social deprivation, vast amounts of money are spent investing in faraway rural communities where prisons can be crucial employers.

Prisons do not encourage egalitarianism through engineering social organization for a more equal distribution of wealth in society. Instead of making social structures more egalitarian, criminal justice spending has become the primary public investment in many high-incarceration areas, deviating funds and thereby gutting socially deprived areas of both human and public infrastructure (Wacquant, 2010).

Synchronically, prisons act as 'urban exostructures' through displacing investments to rural locations far from the communities prisoners return to (Spatial Information Design Lab, 2009: 7).

While this massive spatial displacement has been mapped in the US, the problem is not isolated to America. The UK is following suit, forging ahead with plans to build a 'Titan Prison' housing 2000 prisoners in North Wales. Popular press coverage of these plans highlights how penal policy is increasingly crafted in primarily economic terms – with headlines announcing privately run '£250m super prison to create 1,000 jobs in North Wales' (BBC, 2013). The forecast 'economic boost' to the local area of housing this new privately owned profit-making prison trumps any attention paid to the broader social costs of displacing the majority of the prisoners who will make up the 2000 people confined in the £250 million investment.[2] It overlooks the fact that research on the economic effects of 'rescuing' small rural industrial towns through expanding the incarceration industry suggests building prisons does not bring the expected economic benefits because 'simple job growth is an inaccurate measure of a prison as a tool of economic growth' (King et al., 2003: 19). Neither does it pay attention to reports that a prison with a population of 400 prisoners is four times more likely to perform 'well' than one housing 800 prisoners (Hussain, Capel and Jeffery, 2008), nor to the possibility that increased employment may not benefit the immediate local community, and that there can be economic downsides in relation to other avenues of inward investment for communities that become renowned as 'prison towns' (King et al., 2003).

Yet while the UK is still looking to build more and bigger prisons, some of the highest-incarcerating states of the US are desperately trying to claw their way out of their incarceration crisis through capping the amount of public money invested in building prisons and, in some cases, reinvesting this money into the provision of public services in high-incarceration communities. For example, in 2007 Texas legislators allocated $241 million for treatment and incarceration diversion programmes during 2008/9 rather than spending $500 million on new prisons (Justice Centre, 2007). Below we discuss whether the political traction of the economic implications of mass imprisonment can provide hope that prison policy could be shaped by a social justice vision.

The hopes of 'justice reinvestment'

The last decade has seen the idea and practice of 'justice reinvestment' (JR) gain political support at record pace. The original essay that sparked all of this action made a simple statement:

> There is no logic to spending a million dollars a year to incarcerate people from one block in Brooklyn and return them, on average, in less than three years stigmatised, unskilled, and untrained to the same unchanged block.
>
> *(Tucker and Cadora, 2003: 2)*

As a result, Tucker and Cadora argued that some of the state funds used on incarceration should be redirected into communities impacted by high incarceration. JR aimed to achieve this through devolving power over local law-breakers to local communities. The aim was to make local communities responsible for local public safety through giving them the budget and freedom to respond to local residents who break the law in ways that would best decrease the risks of crime in that specific community (ibid., 2003: 5). By 2009 this idea had inspired the state of Michigan's bipartisan 'Justice Reinvestment Working Group' to make plans to channel $300 million saved by closing prisons into community improvement work. Parallel developments have mushroomed across a wide variety of states in the US and similar enthusiasm has spread internationally (for an overview of what has been done in the name of justice reinvestment and how, see Clear, 2011). In the United Kingdom, a House of Commons paper called 'Cutting Crime: The Case for Justice Reinvestment' (2009) was supported by all three major political parties and has led to initiatives such as the Social Impact Bonds, payable to private companies that invest in initiatives that reduce recidivism rates more than government-run programmes.

The JR movement has gained so much ground in the US, Australia and the UK in large part because of the times of 'austerity' that immediately followed its inception. The House of Commons Justice Committee's 'Case for Justice Reinvestment' begins by situating its aims within the realities of economic cutbacks – a Ministry of Justice that needed to save £1.3 billion in three years, alongside the inconsistencies of an ever-increasing imprisonment rate in a time of decreasing household violence and violent crime rates (Sivarajasingam et al., 2014). In the US the motive was similar. The Council of State Governments states that the purpose of JR is 'to manage and allocate criminal justice populations more *cost-effectively*, generating *savings* that can be reinvested in *evidence-based* strategies that increase public safety while holding individual offenders accountable' (Center for Effective Public Policy, 2013, emphasis added).

But in his overview of the work of JR thus far, Clear (2011) raises questions about the kind of strategies the JR approach has tended to promote. He highlights concerns with the way evidence-based fiscal incentives work towards reducing incarceration, citing the fact that, although 'policy makers widely believe them to be effective at reducing correctional costs and increasing correctional effectiveness, ... this confidence is based on a weak empirical foundation' (ibid.: 591). Moreover, Clear also describes his concern that, in JR initiatives, 'consensus-driven, evidence-based strategies' (ibid.: 593) are being used not to channel monies into local community initiatives but, rather, to fund other government-based social services, such as drug treatment capacities and housing initiatives. He calls this a 'service delivery agenda' rather than a 'community development agenda' (ibid.: 593).

This preference for 'action' based on 'evidence' when investing in local crime prevention strategies is not new to JR. Wikström (2007) described how local crime prevention strategies often prefer to invest in '*action*' that can be easily evidenced as effective, rather than '*content*' that draws on a sound criminological knowledge base. He argues that local crime reduction strategies need to ask both *why* a problem occurs and *how* it can be tackled (ibid.: 60). Without understanding both causes and the best ways to tackle problems, local schemes miss out on the 'social, situational and developmental processes in which intervention has the greatest potential for success' (ibid.: 62–63). In part, this is a problem of 'evidence-based commissioning' funding strategies, which one commentator on Social Impact Bonds described as 'seemingly innocuous but actually devilish problems ... which make it easier to pay for an ambulance at the bottom of the cliff than a fence at the top' (Ainsworth, 2014). But this preference could also be evidence of a deeper social justice enemy in the 'new governance of crime' agenda (see Loader and Sparks, 2002) that is reticent to engage with marginalized communities as a competent part of the body politic capable of designing, constructing and maintaining their own fences when the ambulances of the criminal justice machinery are a more politically expedient mechanism for those individuals on the outskirts who fall over the edge.

Towards justice reinvention?

Viewed through a social justice lens, the forms of JR that have emerged, hopeful as they may be, do not necessarily move prisons towards being more active in terms of promoting social justice. Arguably, in practice JR has focused on the minimalist and egalitarian aspects of social justice but neglected 'mutuality' through doing 'to' communities rather than 'through' communities. JR aims to increase public safety and reduce re-imprisonment through impacting on prisons' 'failure rates', and re-invest the money saved into the communities most impacted. While this may not rebalance the economic disadvantages of these areas, it is a genuflection to economic egalitarianism as 'entitlement' rather than 'grace' (Heffernan, 2000: 51). As Maruna (2011: 661) has previously argued, JR is no doubt a 'thing of beauty', but in practice it perhaps lacks some of the symmetry associated with definitions of beauty because it is dominated by a politically expedient economic discourse that is committed to *action* sometimes at the expense of *content*. As a result JR has not paid sufficient attention to knowledge of what might be the best way to produce the most common good – to make society safer, more mutual and more egalitarian.

Yet if we look back to JR at its inception, it was never designed as a merely economical approach to reducing the social harms of imprisonment. The need for a shift in the *content* of criminal justice practice and policy is not lost on its original proponents, it just seems to have been somewhat neglected in the implementation. The original article called for two things to facilitate justice reinvestment:

1. the reinvestment of some of the $20 million spent on incarceration into other ways to make communities safe, and
2. a 'fundamental shift in the way we think about public safety in America' and within this, 'a fundamental change in the nature of incarceration' (Tucker and Cadora, 2003: 2).

The JR movement could learn from past criminal justice panaceas that have similarly failed to achieve the change hoped for when single elements of their guiding philosophy have been abstracted and the rest discarded. While JR has done an excellent job of bringing the false economy of mass incarceration to the fore, its implementation has paid little attention to the concept of justice itself (Maruna, 2011). We know that ideas about justice, values and political orientations influence penal practice (Liebling and Crewe, 2012b). As a result, any effort at truly reshaping practices is likely to require more than merely rechannelling funds. If prisons are to be agents of social justice, the parameters of the conversation will need to move on from merely addressing the indices of their destructiveness (Toch, 2007). We think this will require a return to the original goals of the JR movement, which inextricably placed *justice reinvention* alongside *justice reinvestment*.

Changing the tone of penal policy

In the remaining part of this chapter we argue that for JR to move prisons towards being agents of social justice it will require a change in the tone of penal policy. We describe how reincorporating the second strand of social justice (mutuality) back into JR (alongside public safety and economic egalitarianism) could help to achieve this. The question we have set ourselves in this chapter is essentially an 'ought' question – as Duff (2001: 201) puts it: 'the task of justifying criminal punishment ... is the task of so transforming the content and context of criminal punishment that it can become what it ought to be.'

But before 'becoming' there is need for debate as to what this 'ought' might be – just as Wikström (2007) argued that before *action* there is a need to consider the *content* of that action, and while asking *why* a problem occurs we need to ask *how* the results we desire might be best achieved. The *action*-based justice reinvestment has seen an exponential growth over the last decade, while its sister concept, the *content*-based justice reinvention, has somewhat fallen by the wayside. The economic shift underpinning JR has been bolstered by the simple fact that many jurisdictions (like Texas and California, where the prison obsession has essentially bankrupted the states) have run out of funds to pay for their carceral addiction. There has been remarkable momentum towards investing in the criminal justice system *becoming* something different, something new, but there has been less political appetite for a conversation about what this change *ought* to be. Player (2014: 291) astutely identifies this challenge as underpinning the contradictions in penal policy for women, which she argues 'are not due to inadvertent human error but are the logical and coherent outcomes of a process in which reforms rooted in principles of social inclusion and social justice are pursued within a broader penal context grounded on principles of "less eligibility" and exclusion'.

What prisons are for and what they are trying to achieve can have important effects in the day-to-day nature of imprisonment – the moral context in which prisoners live (Liebling and Crewe, 2012a). As a result, we think that paying attention to the broader tone of penal policy in which imprisonment operates may alter the moral context of imprisonment, and make it more or less likely to be an agent of social justice. We are persuaded this is important because criminological scholarship has shown that social moral context influences criminal action (Wikström, 2010) and can strengthen or weaken the potential for desistance from crime (Bottoms and Shapland, 2011; Fox, 2014; Weaver and McNeill, 2014). Research on desistance has shown that increased perceptions of social stigma can increase the probability of recidivism (LeBel et al., 2008). In contrast, positive social connections are an important part of desistance (Weaver and McNeill, 2014) because they provide a context for 'moral engagement' in reciprocal obligations that ground social interactions, and the communal nature of the 'shared moral space' in which a sense of 'belonging' that underpins relational reciprocity can be forged (Fox, 2014). Arguably, this sense of moral belonging is the basis of the kind of 'lived citizenship' that characterizes the nature of social inclusion separating those who desist from crime from those who continue to offend (Farrall et al., 2014). This suggests that the moral context of prison – by which we mean both the day-to-day carceral experience and the broader social messages that both encase prisons and emit from prisons – could be an important factor in the prison's tendency to feed on itself and its ever-increasing appetite. Therefore, reducing the punitive tone of incarceration might be one important factor in reducing some of its harmful effects.

Despite the apparent moral vacuity in the pragmatic economic drivers for carceral reform in JR, we are idealistically inclined to be hopeful that JR reforms might eventually expose the need for, and herald a return to, this moral dialogue about the broader penal policy in England and Wales and elsewhere, of which prisons form an increasingly popular part. In a rather ironic twist, some of the policies resulting from austerity could provide part of the catalyst for this conversation (Goldson, 2015). In the US imprisonment moved to a more austere economic model in early 2000, well ahead of prisons in England and Wales. As a result of slashed budgets some states made specific efforts to recruit a free army of volunteers to deliver axed services. For example, Texas established a Volunteer Coordination Committee in 1994 and by 2013 there were 21,305 trained volunteers delivering services to prisoners and ex-prisoners, ranging from education and chaplaincy services, sex offender treatment programmes through to Alcoholics Anonymous classes and victim services (Texas Department of Criminal Justice, 2013: 42). This resort to volunteer efforts is beginning to forge its way slowly into England and Wales through the 'Transforming Rehabilitation' (TR) conservative coalition government agenda (see, for example, Ministry of Justice, 2013).

While we acknowledge the risks for 'social innovation' posed by the reforms of the 'rehabilitation revolution' (Fox and Grim, 2015), we retain an obstinate hope that policy initiatives seeking to involve local community groups in delivering a 'rehabilitation' agenda might help to ignite a conversation on the moral purposes of imprisonment, because research has shown that when people get to know prisoners and ex-prisoners this reduces punitive attitudes (Hirschfield and Piquero, 2010), just as vicarious ways of experiencing imprisonment predicts lower levels of punitiveness (Johnson, 2009). When people become familiar with stigmatized individuals, stigmatizing attitudes decrease (Dovidio et al., 2005). This 'normalization thesis' arising from intergroup contact can depend upon the context of the familiarity, but research has consistently shown that where people visit prisoners in a voluntary context their punitive attitudes decrease as their negative stereotypes are shattered (Wilson, et al., 2011; Ridley, 2014; Chui and Cheng, 2013; Cohen, 2012 and Hawker, 2014: 14–15). Allport originally proposed four 'conditions' under which intergroup contact would have a 'normalising' (de-stigmatizing) effect, these were: that the conditions created a sense of equal status between the groups; that the groups had common goals they could draw upon; that there were opportunities for intergroup cooperation; and that the contact took place within an environment that had the explicit support of authorities, social institutions, law or custom (Allport, 1954). Research has shown that these factors are important (although not always necessary) for positive de-stigmatizing effects from intergroup contact. Applied in this context, it means that *if* the TR agenda provides more opportunities for people in local communities to be directly involved with the people who have committed offences and been incarcerated, levels of punitiveness and stigma could decrease.

However, there is a circular element to this argument that can serve as a cautionary note to policy makers. If their hope is that ground-up, community-led responses to criminal offences and the rehabilitation of offenders will be more effective than government-led measures have proved to be, simply changing the method of rehabilitation delivery without changing the social and institutional message supporting these measures could limit their potential. In a meta-analysis of research on Allport's 'intergroup contact theory', Pettigrew and Tropp (2005) show that the distal societal conditions for reducing prejudice through intergroup contact are probably even more influential than Allport originally supposed. What this means is that, if perceptions of social stigma are important to the commission of offences and desistance from offending, and intergroup contact can reduce this stigma, especially when this contact is officially and socially supported, penal policy and the rhetoric about offenders could influence whether or not changing the method of 'rehabilitation' delivery proves to be effective. Within this, it is pertinent to note that the emotions of anxiety and threat negatively mediate the link between contact and prejudice (Blair et al., 2003; Stephan et al., 2002; Stephan and Stephan, 1992; Stephan and Stephan, 2005, Voci and Hewstone, 2003) – so that institutional conceptualizations of ex-prisoners in terms of the risks they pose rather than the potential they possess could sabotage positive opportunities they may otherwise encounter to feel and be a part of civic society despite being convicted of a crime.

Reviewing research on restorative justice, Braithwaite (2006) argued that part of its success in producing a more holistic version of justice is grounded in its move away from a punitive paradigm. He explains how this is achieved in restorative justice initiatives through crafting spaces whereby the power imbalances of legal justice institutions are upset through the inclusion of a broader spectrum of people – members of civil society – in criminal justice processes. What this does, he explains, is expose the myth that criminal action is merely a matter of individual culpability. As a result, he argues 'if justice is to be an accomplishment of our civilization, it will be more an accomplishment of civil society than the state' (ibid.: 407). If justice reinvestment is riding the wave of the current economic tone of incarceration, the renewed focus on voluntary civic engagement in prisons being dragged along with this wave could leave a welcome sediment in its wake. Making our prisons more porous – bringing civil society in – could be one way to reduce the punitive stigma of the carceral experience, create routes out of prison and herald a much needed shift in the moral context in which prisoners are forced to live. But more importantly, it could be a catalyst for a deeper, more social, more mutual, more egalitarian conversation about the moral purposes of imprisonment.

There are small seeds of evidence of this beginning to take place under the 'transforming rehabilitation' agenda in England and Wales. 'Through the Gate' social enterprise experiments are beginning to emerge involving prisoners and ex-prisoners in cleaning, grounds maintenance, catering and construction industries (Conaty, 2014). Initiatives such as 'Freedom Bakery', operating out of Low Moss Prison in Scotland,[3] draw on lessons from inspirational forms of mutuality through social co-operatives in Italy that exist with the explicit purpose and legislative support to benefit ex-prisoners and other excluded people. They provide training and purposeful activity to prisoners, and through capacitating them give them a route into employment post-release. In the case of 'Freedom Bakery' this is offered through a high street bakery that provides employment to trained prisoners post-release. These innovations to pilot co-operative solutions within the criminal justice system are a means through which prisoners and ex-prisoners can be empowered to 'co-produce' their own rehabilitation and change (Weaver and Nicholson, 2012). In this way, the 'transforming rehabilitation' agenda could provide an economic impetus for more than simply transforming the bodies responsible for delivering rehabilitative interventions. It could also help to move this second 'rehabilitation revolution' beyond the problems that C. S. Lewis associated with its predecessor of the 1950s, which he forewarned would result in depriving law-breakers of 'the rights of a human being' through making the 'criminal' an 'object to be cured' rather than a subject of rights who is being justly and respectfully punished (Lewis, 1949/1987: 148).

We are cautiously optimistic that the times of austerity underpinning the economic motivations and political support for JR, and a post-managerial era of contractualized criminal justice services in the transforming rehabilitation agenda, could have positive implications for social justice and for rehabilitative models. Our optimism is grounded in two ingredients that make the social and penal landscape fundamentally different to that facing C. S. Lewis in the 1950s. The first of these is the existence of a body of criminological research on desistance from crime that has grown up over the last thirty years, which establishes and explains the fact that most people do leave a life of crime behind them, and that many do so on their own initiative (Bottoms, 2013). A leading desistance scholar has memorably argued that if this body of work were taken seriously by policy makers it would change the face of rehabilitation:

> To the legendary visitor from Mars, these simple facts – and they are facts – might seem to offer huge hope to earth-bound criminal justice systems. Earthly politicians might therefore be expected to constantly reiterate their truth, while the forensic professions and the probation service might be expected to have forged strong links between 'indigenous' (offender-initiated) desistance and their own rehabilitation programmes and supervision practice. But, of course, in real life none of this has happened, at least until very recently.
>
> *(Bottoms, 2013: 251)*

The second ingredient is grounded in the current economic crisis itself. The near collapse of the financial markets underpinning the neo-liberal market economy model of social and economic life has led to a degree of disenchantment with 'cold-hearted bare-knuckled neo-liberalism' that emphasizes individuals as autonomous and responsible for their own success or failure (Hackworth, 2010). To some degree, this has opened the way not only for new economic thinking but also for opportunities to re-imagine and reshape 'what constitutes the good society' in a new political era (Hall et al., 2013). The small but important growth of 'through the gate' social enterprises, community interest companies and social co-operatives working with prisoners and ex-prisoners are especially encouraging in this time of change. They model a transformed notion of rehabilitation that manifests the learning from desistance research and attempt a more egalitarian economic model of social inclusion where individuals, companies and agencies join forces to provide a mutually supportive environment in which all parties cooperate to create viable economic structures that support the kind of society in which they want to live. Prisons that facilitate, fund and further work of this kind could in our opinion stake a claim to be acting as agents of social justice.

Being part of the conversation

In our commitment to the urgency of a more egalitarian conversation about imprisonment, we end this chapter by bringing our social justice imaginations to bear on the question of what imprisonment is *for* (content), and then tentatively suggesting how this might impact on what imprisonment is *like* (action). We began this chapter by referencing the theoretical purposes of punishment: deterrence, retribution, reform, etc. What we note about these ever-present aims of criminal sentences is that they are individual-centric. Prison is about protecting society from individuals, punishing them or reforming them. Taking a social justice imagination to the purposes of imprisonment necessitates a move towards viewing individuals as social beings and re-imagining what prisons would look like if they were designed for maximization of social safety, mutuality and egalitarianism. What if, in answer to the question 'what is prison for?', we moved away from thinking of it as a control mechanism for individuals who offend against social mores, and start thinking of it as a social institution through which those who struggle to access society safely, mutually and on equal footing with others can be supported to do so? Could prisons be agents of social justice if they operated as mechanisms of social inclusion rather than social exclusion?

Using our social justice imaginations, we wondered how prisons could became hubs of social and economic activity in disadvantaged communities? This re-imagination of justice led us beyond a mere redirection of some of the £4 million National Offender Management Service (NOMS) budget into neighbourhoods of high imprisonment through reinvestment, and towards the potential impact of relocating prisons *as* the economic boon in the communities where prisoners come from.

Of course, we are well aware this is no panacea for transforming the tone of incarceration. Harris County jail, situated in downtown Houston, Texas, provides ample evidence of this. The jail is comprised of four high-rise buildings that sit alongside each other and house around 10,000 people from the local community. Of course, there are some economic benefits for the local community. The jails are run by the Harris County Sheriff's office, which employs over 4000 local people and has an annual budget of close to $400 million for a district covering a population of 1.4 million people. Every day the prisons check in about 350 inmates and check out another 350, releasing them onto the streets in the middle of the night. More than 81 per cent of its prisoners have been in the jail before. While we remain convinced of the *potential* benefits of justice relocation, it is evident that merely resituating prisons into the communities from which their residents are drawn provides little guarantee that the economic benefits that can accrue to local areas from new prisons will actually translate into policies or practices within prisons that promote social justice. Instead, it might just create huge monuments to society's commitment to the illusion of separateness, and then find ways to fill them up with vulnerable local residents, contributing all of the ensuing criminogenic disadvantages for the local community.

But our 'normalized' instinct suggests to us it does not have to be this way. *If* the location of our prisons was grounded in a social justice 'ought', where the purpose of imprisonment is *re-imagined* as the maximization of safety, mutuality and egalitarianism, then a *relocation* of prisons could facilitate these purposes. In our justice relocation imaginations, local prisons not only bring employment opportunities into high-unemployment areas and much needed money to local businesses from an increased number of employees frequenting the area, they also bring the potential for staff and prisoners to share a sense of local identity, which can contribute to good staff–prisoner relationships. It could permit voluntary community groups to be involved in the prison. It could help prisoners to maintain or to forge anew some positive connections that may assist them when they leave prison. It would make it easier for prisoners to stay in touch with family and friends. It could make prisons more porous through providing opportunity for through the gate initiatives such as social co-operatives, or, as we are beginning to see in England,

and as is commonplace in the US, through local education institutions providing classes to prisoners and students together. Time in prison need not sever exposure to the values produced and reinforced through civic engagement (Jacobs, 2013). Instead, prioritizing the maximization of mutuality could actually increase public safety, because many of these elements are known to reduce recidivism and help people leave a life of crime (Farrall et al., 2014). Prisons located in the communities they serve could even employ some of the high numbers of convicted people living in the local area to gain from their expertise in exiting a life of crime (for more on the work of 'wounded healers' see LeBel et al., 2014). Is it really so outlandish to think of prisons repairing neighbourhoods and individuals from the inside-out? Such a feasible ideal version of imprisonment might maintain the dignity of communicating adequate social censure for wrong-doing while not losing sight of the legitimating value of a form of punishment guided in practice by the value of and need for redemption to be at the heart of punishment.

Beyond and beneath these idealistic imaginings lies a fundamental truth that underpins our thinking, and that is that people who are convicted of criminal offences are part of our community, as are the prisons in which we house (some of) them. However we design and redesign prisons, and wherever we locate them, while they remain places in which people are forced to spend time as a sign of social censure, they will necessarily involve a removal of autonomy and be experienced as punishment. They will also necessarily feed both from and into the society of which they form part. If, then, we want individuals we incarcerate to develop the virtues of civil dispositions, it is not only ethical (Jacobs, 2013) but also logical that we aim, as far as possible, to maximize the extent to which prisons form part of a civil society. As prisons and prisoners have been increasingly excluded from the social moral context, prisoners' experience of moral censure through spending time in prison has weakened (Schinkel, 2014). When prisons are agents of metanormative justice – when they are agents in society being structured as it ought to be structured – they may then have a chance to facilitate the kind of normative outcomes they hope to achieve in terms of shaping how individuals act.

Conclusions

In this chapter we have argued that working towards social justice means making society increasingly safe, increasingly mutual and increasingly egalitarian. Drawing on research on the effects of imprisonment, we have argued prisons fail to achieve these aims. The increasing popularity and presence of justice reinvestment suggests that movements are afoot to address some of the social ills that are the consequences of our imprisonment addiction. Our current form of imprisonment is becoming less popular because it is unfit for purpose and because this makes it very costly. We welcome these moves but suggest that the economic driver for reform alone will not impact sufficiently on the negative consequences of imprisonment that we describe. We suggest that if prisons are to move towards being agents of social justice it will require a broader and deeper conversation about the purposes of prison, about what it is *for*, without which it is unlikely there will be any real change in what it *does*. In our minds, this means starting with a social justice reappraisal through justice reinvention to set the tone for justice reinvestment, which we argue could include a focus on the social justice implications of justice relocation. In our current penal system society acts on transgressing individuals to exclude them from community through prison. We suggest that, if prisons are to be agents of social justice, they will be institutions that act on society, through individuals (both incarcerated and not) to promote community. If prisons are to be agents of social justice, are to be places of punishment that work for the common good, we believe this will involve the work of the common people. But we also believe that the moral tone of penal policy can shape the nature and potential of community-led initiatives that would seek to transform rehabilitation.

In their examination of 'social structures and desistance from crime' Farrall et al. (2010) draw on the work of Amartya Sen (2009) – an economist with a keen interest in philosophy and social inequality – and suggest a direction for social policy that would challenge the structural barriers to desistance that they describe. Within these barriers they include a description of a risk-based, public protection approach to criminal policy that categorizes high-risk offenders, those most in need of help to desist, as 'hopeless' – a penal policy 'tone' that sends important messages to convicts, criminal justice professionals and broader society that could inhibit the required and desired processes of support and opportunities for change that underpin desistance. In contrast, Sen's 'capability approach' argues that people develop capabilities when they have the freedom to *function* – that is, to achieve the things they value being and doing (Sen, 1999: 75). Thus, by expanding what Sen calls 'opportunity freedoms', by removing the 'social structural blockages' to *functioning* as desired, people can build their capabilities to become the people they want to be. In light of their research, which shows that 'desisting from crime is a common, not a rare occurrence, even among recidivist offenders' (2010: 546), Farrall et al. argue that 'The case for policies aimed at a careful expansion of "opportunity freedoms" looks, and is, strong' (ibid.: 562). They praise the strength of Sen's theoretical approach in his recognition of 'the importance of structures in sometimes blocking "opportunity freedoms" for individuals' (ibid.: 563) but also seek to expand his theory to recognize that 'structures can be not only constraining ... but also enabling (enabling individuals and communities to work towards a better social policy approach to the encouragement of desistance)' (ibid.: 564).

If an economic approach to criminal justice reform is required in these times of austerity, we would argue that taking Sen's economic 'capability approach' to penal policy has real potential to 'transform rehabilitation'. It is not, in our mind, incongruous for prisons to simultaneously be institutions of social censure and 'enabling' institutions that can and should expand the 'opportunity freedoms' of the individuals they hold and the communities they serve. If reducing recidivism is the policy aim, then expanding capabilities should be the means. Instead, recent political initiatives have sought to 'transform rehabilitation' through implementing structural reforms to the ways in which social goods in the criminal justice arena are procured, alongside a punitive turn in the tone of penal policy and the introduction of initiatives that, among other things, have sought to: limit prisoners' recourse to assert their rights through cuts to legal aid; coerce prisoners into rehabilitation through removing incentives including limits to family contact if they do not participate; and limit prisoners' access to personal development through restricting their access to books and slashing budgets for education. It seems unlikely that rehabilitation will be transformed if the rhetoric around penal policy and the aims of penal practice remain committed to limiting opportunities for prisoners to *function* as desired.

It is, of course, too early to tell at the time of writing whether the new justice secretary Michael Gove will continue or change this dangerous course. However, the language of his first policy speech gave cause to hope for a change in rhetoric and perhaps for new policies arising from this. It has not escaped Gove (2015) that conservative penal policy was once rooted in a rhetoric of social justice, and he quoted heavily from Winston Churchill's famous appeal to the power of civic virtues in criminal justice practice:

> We must not forget that when every material improvement has been effected in prisons, when the temperature has been rightly adjusted, when the proper food to maintain health and strength has been given, when the doctors, chaplains and prison visitors have come and gone, the convict stands deprived of everything that a free man calls life. We must not forget that all these improvements, which are sometimes salves to our consciences, do not change that position.
>
> The mood and temper of the public in regard to the treatment of crime and criminals is one of the most unfailing tests of the civilisation of any country. A calm and dispassionate recognition of the rights of the accused against the state, and even of convicted criminals against the state, a constant heart-searching by all charged with the duty of punishment, a desire and eagerness to rehabilitate in the world of industry all those who have paid their dues in the hard coinage of punishment, tireless efforts towards the discovery of curative and regenerating processes, and an unfaltering faith that there is a treasure, if you can only find it, in the heart of every man – these are the symbols which in the treatment of crime and criminals mark and measure the stored-up strength of a nation, and are the sign and proof of the living virtue in it.
>
> (*Churchill, 1910: col. 1354*)

Acknowledgement

With special thanks for helpful conversations and comments on previous drafts to Brian Lawrence, Thomas Hawker, Tony Bottoms, the students and supervisors on the 'Learning Together' course at HMP Grendon 2015 and the editors of this collection.

Notes

1 See www.spatialinformationdesignlab.org/projects.php%3Fid%3D16.
2 Instead, reference is made to providing prison spaces close to home for prisoners in North Wales, but local prisoners are only likely to make up about 25 per cent of the prisoners housed (Crook, 2013).
3 www.freedombakery.org/.

References

Ainsworth, D. (2014) 'Six issues with social impact bonds', *Civil Society News*. Available at: civilsociety.co.uk/finance/blogs/content/17532/six_issues_with_social_impact_bonds [accessed 23 December 2014].

Allport, G. (1954/1979) *The Nature of Prejudice*. Cambridge, MA: Perseus Books.

Bales, W. and Mears, D. (2008) 'Inmate social ties and the transition to society: does visitation reduce recidivism?', *Journal of Research in Crime and Delinquency*, 45(3): 287–321.

Bales, W. and Piquero, A. (2012) 'Assessing the impact of imprisonment on recidivism', *Journal of Experimental Criminology*, 8(1): 71–101.

BBC (2013) '£250m super prison to create 1,000 jobs in north Wales', 27 June. Available at: www.bbc.co.uk/news/uk-wales-north-east-wales-23077995 [accessed April 2015].

Besemer, S., Geest, V., Murray, J., Bijleveld, C., and Farrington, D. (2011) 'The relationship between parental imprisonment and offspring offending in England and the Netherlands', *British Journal of Criminology*, 51(2): 413–437.

Blair, I., Park, B., and Bachelor, J. (2003) 'Are some people more anxious than others?', *Group Processes and Intergroup Relations*, 6(2): 151–169.

Bottoms, A. (2013) 'Desistance from Crime'. In Zoë Ashmore and Richard Shuker, *Forensic Practice in the Community*. London: Routledge.

Bottoms, A. and Shapland, J. (2011) 'Steps Towards Desistance Among Male Young Adult Recidivists'. In Steven Farrall, Mike Hough, Shadd Maruna and Richard Sparks (eds) *Escape Routes: Contemporary Perspectives on Life After Punishment*. Abingdon: Routledge.

Braithwaite, J. (2006) 'Doing justice intelligently in civil society', *Journal of Social Issues*, 62(2): 393–409.

Brenburg, J. and Krohn, M. (2003) 'Labeling, life chances and adult crime: the direct and indirect effects of official intervention in adolescence on crime in early adulthood', *Criminology*, 41: 1287–1318.

Cadora, E., Swartz, C. and Gordon, M. (2003) 'Criminal Justice and Health and Human Services: An Exploration of Overlapping Needs, Resources, and Interests in Brooklyn Neighborhoods'. In Jeremy Travis and Michelle Waul (eds) *Prisoners Once Removed: The Impact of Incarceration and Reentry on Children, Families, and Communities*. Washington, DC: Urban Institute.

Cavadino, M., Dignan, J. and Mair, G. (2013) *The Penal System: An Introduction* (5th edn.). London: Sage.

Center for Effective Public Policy (2013) 'Justice Reinvestment'. Available at: http://cepp. com/justice-reinvestment [accessed July 2015].

Chiricos, T., Barrick, K., Bales, W. and Bontrager, S. (2007) 'The labelling of convicted felons and its Consequences for recidivism', *Criminology*, 45: 547–581.

Chui, W. and Cheng, K. (2013) 'Effects of volunteering experiences and motivations on attitudes towards prisoners: Evidence from Hong Kong', *Asian Criminology*, 8(2): 103–114.

Churchill, W. (1910) *Hansard HC Deb*, vol. 19, col. 1354, 20 July 1910.

Clear, T. (2007) *Imprisoning Communities: How Mass Incarceration Makes Disadvantaged Neighbourhoods Worse*. New York: Oxford University Press.

Clear, T. (2011) 'A private sector, incentives-based model for justice reinvestment', *Criminology and Public Policy* 10(3): 585–608.

Clear, T. and Frost, N. (2013) *The Punishment Imperative: The Rise and Failure of Mass Incarceration in America*. New York: NYU Press.

Cohen, M.L. (2012) 'Harmony within the walls: perceptions of worthiness and competence in a community prison choir', *International Journal of Music Education*, 30(1): 46–56.

Conaty, P. (2014) *Social Co-operatives: A Democratic Co-Production Agenda for Care Services in the UK*. Available at: www.uk.coop/sites/storage/public/downloads/social_co-operatives_report.pdf [accessed 8 May 2015].

Coyle, A. (2010) 'Imprisoning communities: how mass incarceration makes disadvantaged neighbourhoods worse', *British Journal of Criminology*, 50(5): 975–977.

Crook, F. (2013) 'Building the Wrexham prison would be a titanic mistake', Howard League for Penal Reform. Available at: www.howardleague.org/francescrookblog/building-the-wrexham-prison-would-be-a-titanic-mistake/ [accessed 29 April 2015].

Dovidio, J., Glick, P. and Rudman, L. (2005) *On the Nature of Prejudice: Fifty Years After Allport*. Oxford: Blackwell Publishing.

Davies, S. and Tanner, J. (2003) 'The long arm of the law: effects of labeling on employment', *The Sociological Quarterly*, 44(3): 385–404.

DeFina, R. and Hannon, L. (2013) 'The impact of mass incarceration on poverty', *Crime and Delinquency*, 59(4): 562–586.

Duff, A. (2001) *Punishment, Communication, and Community*. Oxford: Oxford University Press.

Farrall, S., Bottoms, A. and Shapland, J. (2010) 'Social structures and desistance from crime', *European Journal of Criminology*, 7(6): 546–570.

Farrall, S., Hunter, B., Sharpe, G. and Calverley, A. (2014) *Criminal Careers in Transition: The Social Context of Desistance from Crime*. Oxford: Oxford University Press

Fox, K. (2014) 'Theorizing community integration as desistance-promotion', *Criminal Justice and Behaviour*, 42(1): 82–94.

Fox, C. and Grimm, R. (2015) 'The role of social innovation in criminal justice reform and the risk posed by proposed reforms in England and Wales', *Criminology and Criminal Justice*, 15(1): 63–82.

Goldson, B. (2015) 'The Circular Motions of Penal Politics and the Pervasive Irrationalities of Child Imprisonment', in B. Goldson, and J. Muncie (eds) *Youth Crime and Justice*, 2nd edition. London: Sage.

Gove, M. (2015) 'The Treasure in the Heart of Man: Making Prisons Work'. Speech given at the Prisoners Learning Alliance. Available at: www.gov.uk/government/speeches/the-treasure-in-the-heart-of-man-making-prisons-work [accessed July 2015].

Hackworth, J. (2010) 'Faith, welfare, and the city: the mobilization of religious organizations for neoliberal ends', *Urban Geography*, 31: 750–773.

Hall, S., Massey, D. and Rustin, M. (2013) 'After neoliberalism: analysing the present', editorial, *Soundings* 53: 8–22. Available at: www.lwbooks.co.uk/journals/soundings/pdfs/s53hallmasseyrustin.pdf [accessed 19 April 2015].

Halsey, M. (2007) 'On confinement: resident and inmate perspectives of secure care and imprisonment', *Probation Journal*, 54(4): 338–367.

Haney, C., Banks, C. and Zimbardo, P. (1973) 'Interpersonal dynamics in a simulated prison', *International Journal of Criminology and Penology*, 1(1): 69–97.

Hawker, T. (2014) 'How Does Interaction with Prisoners Affect Punitiveness? A Study of a Student Choir Visiting Prison', unpublished thesis, University of Cambridge, Radzinowicz Library of Criminology.

Heffernan, W. C. (2000) 'Social Justice/Criminal Justice'. In William C. Heffernan and John Kleinig (eds), *From Social Justice to Criminal Justice: Poverty and the Administration of Criminal Law*. New York and Oxford: Oxford University Press.

Hegtvedt, K. and Scheuerman, H. (2010) 'The Justice/Morality Link: Implied, Then Ignored, Yet Inevitable'. In S. Hitlin and S. Vaisey (eds) *Handbook of the Sociology of Morality*. New York: Springer.

Hirschfield, P. and Piquero, A. (2010) 'Normalization and legitimation: modeling stigmatizing attitudes toward ex-offenders', *Criminology*, 48(1): 27–55.

Holt, N. and Miller, D. (1972) 'Explorations in Inmate-Family Relationships', Research Report no. 46. Sacramento, CA: California Department of Corrections.

Hussain, I., Capel, S. and Jeffery, N. (2008) 'Titan Prisons: A Gigantic Mistake', Prison Reform Trust. Available at: www.prisonreformtrust.org.uk/Portals/0/Documents/Titan% 20prisons%20-%20a%20gigantic%20mistake.pdf [accessed 29 April 2015].

Jacobs, J. (2006) 'Mass incarceration and the proliferation of criminal records', *University of St. Thomas Law Journal*, 3(3): 387–420.

Jacobs, J. (2013) 'The liberal polity, criminal sanction, and civil society', *Criminal Justice Ethics*, 32(3): 231–246.

Jacobson, J., Bhardwa, B., Gyateng, T., Hunter, G. and Hough, M. (2010) *Punishing Disadvantage: A Profile of Children in Custody*. London: Prison Reform Trust.

Jacobson, M. (2005) *Downsizing Prisons*. New York: New York University Press.

Johnson, D. (2009) 'Anger about crime and support for punitive criminal justice policies', *Punishment and Society*, 11(1): 51–66.

Jolliffe, D. and Hedderman, C. (2015) 'Investigating the impact of custody on reoffending using propensity score matching', *Crime and Delinquency*, 61(8): 1051–1077.

Justice Center (2007) *Justice Reinvestment State Brief: Texas*. Available at: www.pewtrusts.org/~/media/legacy/uploadedfiles/TX20State20Briefpdf.pdf [accessed: April 2015].

King, R., Mauer, M. and Huling, T. (2003) *Big Prisons, Small Towns: Prison Economies in Rural America*, a report by The Sentencing Project: Washington, DC. Available at: http://prison.ppjr.org/files/tracy%20huling%20prisons%20economy%20study.pdf [accessed 24 May 2015].

Kirk, D.S. (2009) 'A natural experiment on residential change and recidivism: lessons from Hurricane Katrina', *American Sociological Review*, 74(3): 484–505.

LeBel, T., Burnett, R., Maruna, S. and Bushway, S. (2008) 'The "chicken and egg" of subjective and social factors in desistance from crime', *European Journal of Criminology*, 5(2): 131–159.

LeBel, T., Richie, M. and Maruna, S. (2014) 'Helping others as a response to reconcile a criminal past: the role of the wounded healer in prisoner reentry programs', *Criminal Justice and Behavior*, 42(1): 108–120.

Lewis, C. S. (1949/1987) 'The humanitarian theory of punishment', *AMCAP Journal* 13(1): 147–153, reprinted from C. S. Lewis (1949) 'The humanitarian theory of punishment', *The Twentieth Century: An Australian Quarterly Review*, 3(3): 5–12.

Liebling, A. and Crewe, B. (2012a) 'Prison Life, Penal Power, and Prison Effects'. In M. Maguire, R. Morgan and R. Reiner (eds) *The Oxford Handbook of Criminology*. Oxford: Oxford University Press.

Liebling, A. and Crewe, B. (2012b) 'Prisons Beyond the New Penology: The Shifting Moral Foundations of Prison Management'. In J. Simon and R. Sparks (eds) *Handbook of Punishment and Society*. London: Sage.

Liebling, A. and Maruna, S. (2005) *The Effects of Imprisonment*. London: Routledge.

Loader, I. and Sparks, R. (2002) 'Contemporary Landscapes of Crime, Order, and Control: Governance, Risk and Globalization'. In M. Maguire, R. Morgan and R. Reiner (eds) *The Oxford Handbook of Criminology*, 3rd edition. Oxford: Oxford University Press.

Maruna, S. (2011) 'Lessons for justice reinvestment from restorative justice and the justice model experience: Some tips for an 8-year-old prodigy', *Criminology and Public Policy* 10(3): 661–669.

Maruna, S. and Toch, H. (2005). 'The Impact of Incarceration on the Desistance Process'. In Jeremy Travis and Christy Visher (eds) *Prisoner Reentry and Public Safety in America*. New York: Cambridge University Press.

Matravers, M. (2012), 'Is Twenty-first Century Punishment Post-desert?' In M. Tonry (ed.) *Retributivism has a Past: Has it a Future?* Oxford: Oxford University Press.

Mears, D., Cochran, J., Siennick, S. and Bales, W. (2012) 'Prison visitation and recidivism', *Justice Quarterly* 29(6): 888–918.

Ministry of Justice (2013) *Transforming Rehabilitation: A Strategy for Reform*. London: Ministry of Justice.

Moran, D. (2015) *Carceral Geography: Spaces and Practices of Incarceration*. Farnham, Kent: Ashgate.

Murray, J., Bijleveld, C., Farrington, D. and Loeber, R. (2014) *Effects of Parental Incarceration on Children: Cross-National Comparative Studies*. Washington, DC: American Psychological Association.

Murray, J., Loeber, R. and Pardini, D. (2012) 'Parental involvement in the criminal justice system and the development of youth theft, depression, marijuana use, and poor academic performance', *Criminology* 50(1): 255–302.

Pettigrew, T. and Tropp, L. (2005) 'Allport's Intergroup Contact Hypothesis: Its History and Influence'. In John F. Dovidio, Peter Glick and Laurie A. Rudman (eds) *On the Nature of Prejudice: Fifty Years After Allport*. Oxford: Blackwell Publishing.

Player, E. (2014) 'Women in the criminal justice system: the triumph of inertia', *Criminology & Criminal Justice* 14(3): 276–297.

Prison Reform Trust (2014) 'Bromley Briefings Prison Fact File'. Available at: www.prison reformtrust.org.uk/Portals/0/Documents/Bromley%20Briefings/Factfile%20Autumn%20 2014.pdf [accessed 5 December 2014].

Public Safety Performance Project (2007) 'Public Safety, Public Spending: Forecasting America's Prison Population, 2007–2011'. Available at: www.jfa-associates.com/publica tions/ [accessed: December 2014].

Ridley, L. (2014) 'No substitute for the real thing: the impact of prison-based work experience on students' thinking about imprisonment', *Howard Journal of Criminal Justice* 52(1): 16–30.

Roeder, O., Eisen, L. B. and Bowling, J. (2015) 'What Caused the Crime Decline?', Brennan Center for Justice, NYU School of Law. Available at: www.brennancenter.org/publica tion/what-caused-crime-decline [accessed 8 May 2015].

Schinkel, M. (2014), 'Punishment as moral communication: the experiences of long-term prisoners', *Punishment & Society* 16(5): 578–597.

Sen, A. (1999) *Development as Freedom*. New York: Knopf Press.

Sen, A. (2009) *The Idea of Justice*. London: Allen Lane.

Simon, J. (2000) 'The "society of captives" in the era of hyper-incarceration', *Theoretical Criminology* 4(3): 285–308.

Sivarajasingam, V., Page, N., Morgan, P., Matthews, K., Moor, S. and Shepherd, J. (2014) 'Trends in community violence in England and Wales 2005–2009', *Injury* 45(3): 592–598.

Spatial Information Design Lab (2009) *Justice Reinvestment New Orleans*. Available at: www. spatialinformationdesignlab.org/sites/default/files/publication_pdfs/JR_NewOrleans.pdf [accessed 29 April 2015].

Stephan, W., Boniecki, K., Ybarra, O., Bettencourt, A., Ervin, K., Jackson, L., McNatt, P. and Renfro, C. (2002) 'The role of threats in the racial attitudes of blacks and whites', *Personality and Social Psychology Bulletin*, 28: 1242–1254.

Stephan, C. and White Stephan, C. (1992) 'Reducing intercultural anxiety through intercultural contact', *International Journal of Intercultural Relations*, 16(1): 89–106.

Stephan, C. and White Stephan, C. (2005) 'Intergroup Relations Program Evaluation'. In John F. Dovidio, Peter Glick and Laurie A. Rudman (eds) *On the Nature of Prejudice: Fifty Years After Allport*. Oxford: Blackwell Publishing.

Sykes, G. (1958/2007) *The Society of Captives: A Study of a Maximum Security Prison*. Princeton, NJ: Princeton University Press.

Tasioulas, J. (2006) 'Punishment and repentance', *Philosophy*, 81(2): 279–322.

Texas Department of Criminal Justice (2013) *Annual Review, 2013*. Available at: www.tdcj.state.tx.us/documents/Annual_Review_2013.pdf [accessed on 29 December 2014].

Toch, H. (2007) *Men In Crisis*. Chicago, IL: Alidine Publishing Company.

Tracy, P. and Kempf-Leonard, K. (1996) *Continuity and Discontinuity in Criminal Careers*. New York: Plenum Press.

Travis, J. and Waul, M. (eds) (2003) 'Prisoners Once Removed: The Impact of Incarceration and Reentry on Children, Families, and Communities'. Washington, DC: The Urban Institute.

Travis, J., Western, B. and Redburn, S. (eds) (2014). *The Growth of Incarceration in the United States: Exploring Causes and Consequences*. Washington, DC: National Academies Press.

Tucker, S. and Cadora, E. (2003) 'Justice reinvestment', 'Ideas for an Open Society' Occasional Paper, *Open Society Institute*, 3(3): 1–5.

Voci, A. and Hewstone, M. (2003) 'Intergroup contact and prejudice toward immigrants in Italy: the meditational role of anxiety and the moderational role of group salience', *Group Processes and Intergroup Relations*, 6: 37–52.

Wacquant, L. (2007) *Urban Outcasts: A Comparative Sociology of Advanced Marginality*. Cambridge: Polity Press

Wacquant, L. (2009a) *Punishing the Poor: The Neoliberal Government of Social Insecurity*. Durham, NC: Duke University Press

Wacquant, L. (2009b) *Prisons of Poverty*. Twin Cities, MN: University of Minnesota Press.

Wacquant, L. (2010) 'Prisoner re-entry as myth and ceremony', *Dialectical Anthropology* 34: 605–620.

Wakefield, S. and Wildeman, C. (2013), *Children of the Prison Boom: Mass Incarceration and the Future of American Inequality*. New York and Oxford: Oxford University Press.

Weaver, B. and McNeill, F. (2014) 'Lifelines: desistance, social relations, and reciprocity', *Criminal Justice and Behavior*, 42(1): 95–107.

Weaver, B. and Nicholson, (2012) 'Co-producing change: resettlement as a mutual enterprise', *Prison Service Journal*, 204: 9–16.

Wikström, P. O. (2007) 'Doing without knowing: common pitfalls in crime prevention', *Crime Prevention Studies*, 21: 59–80.

Wikström, P. O. (2010) 'Explaining Crime as Moral Actions'. In S. Hitlin and S. Vaisey (eds) *Handbook of the Sociology of Morality*. New York: Springer.

Wilson, D., Spina, R. and Canaan, J. E. (2011) 'In praise of the carceral tour: learning from the Grendon experience', *Howard Journal of Criminal Justice*, 50(4): 343–355.

9

DEMOCRACY (RE)IMAGINED

Some proposals for democratic policing

Elizabeth Turner

Introduction

The first directly elected 'Police and Crime Commissioners' (PCCs) in England and Wales began work in November 2012. This change represented the most significant reform to the governance of police forces since the Police Act of 1964 (Jones, Newburn and Smith, 2012; Raine and Keasey, 2012; Lister, 2013). The government claimed that the change would ensure the police were held 'democratically' accountable to local communities rather than 'bureaucratically' accountable to Whitehall (Herbert, 2011). Inevitably this prompted comment from politicians, the media, campaign groups, academics and the police themselves. Much of the comment focused on the potential for the police to become increasingly 'politicized' and for PCCs to threaten key liberal safeguards such as the 'operational independence' of the police (e.g. see ACPO, 2010; Joyce, 2011; Farthing, 2012; Millen and Stephens, 2012; Lister, 2013), while the widely predicted poor turnout for ill-timed and underfunded elections became the focus of much subsequent criticism (see Garland and Terry, 2012). However, some cautiously welcomed the demise of the low-visibility, and often low-impact, oversight provided by the old police authorities, expressing an interest in whether the introduction of PCCs had the potential to nurture more creative experimentation in the area of public engagement (e.g. see Loader, 2014) and perhaps even allow more socially progressive approaches to policing to emerge (e.g. see Loader and Muir, 2011; Reiner, 2013).

The introduction of PCCs seemed initially to offer an opportunity to revisit and rework some classic debates from the 1980s about police governance and accountability. These debates took place against a backdrop of significant social and political divisions and social unrest that often fed into intense disagreement between police authorities and 'their' chief constables about the appropriate use of police resources (see Jefferson and Grimshaw, 1984; Spencer, 1985; Simey, 1988). However, rekindling and advancing the often rather incendiary debates of that era has not proven to be central to scholarly considerations of PCCs thus far. Instead, for the most part discussion and analysis of PCCs has focused on more prosaic matters, such as critiquing the conduct of the PCC elections (Berman, Coleman and Taylor, 2012; Garland and Terry, 2012); tracing the history and underlying rationales of reforms of police governance (Joyce, 2011; Newburn, 2012; Raine and Keasey, 2012; Davies, 2014; Gilling, 2014); considering whether Police and Crime Panels (PCPs) can effectively hold PCCs to account (Chambers, 2014; Lister, 2014); and examining whether PCCs will impinge upon 'operational independence' (Lister, 2013; Winsor, 2013). All of these matters are of course important when it comes to understanding aspects of the impact of this particular policy, but they do not and cannot amount to a meaningful engagement with the *politics* of policing or what we might mean when we refer to 'democratic policing'. Ironically, then, a policy that was allegedly problematic because it would 'politicize' policing has, thus far, attracted few explicitly *political* analyses.[1]

As Lister and Rowe (2014: 15) have observed:

> a troubling aspect of the new governance model is that it risks conflating appeals for 'democratic policing' with an unhelpfully narrow set of electoral arrangements. Whether enhanced local accountability of the Police is provided through a directly elected office is clearly an important consideration for those who wish to nurture democratic policing. It is not, however, the only criterion against which the democratic credentials of policing should be measured.

Responding to this conflation of election-based arrangements for the governance of local police with 'democratic policing' more generally, this chapter makes some proposals for a more ambitious and extensive (re)imagining of what we mean when we talk about 'democratic policing'.

The purpose of the chapter is to provoke reflection and debate on whether the aspiration towards 'democratic policing' requires an expansion and reorientation of the study of policing. The chapter is structured as follows. First, I outline the case for a social justice-based conception of 'democratic policing'. Second, I consider some definitions of policing, and identify a safety-based definition as most useful for thinking about 'democratic policing' as policing for social justice. Third, I make some proposals for reorientating the study of policing by including a broader range of scholarship and decentring the police organization by challenging key elements of police mythology. I conclude with proposals for further research in three areas: (i) identifying threats to social justice; (ii) addressing the forms of policing most appropriate for addressing these threats; and (iii) considering what the police's 'capacity for decisive action' makes them particularly good (and bad) for in contemporary society.

Beyond elections: for a social justice-based understanding of 'democratic policing'

What exactly we mean by 'democracy' has long been the subject of intense debate. While some politicians and citizens in the Western world have often adopted a fairly complacent stance, seeing 'democracy' as something that 'we' have achieved but which has yet to be achieved in other parts of the world (Arblaster, 1994), many campaign groups and political theorists are much less sanguine about the extent to which we should see extant social and political arrangements in Western societies as adequately democratic. As Reiner (2013) has pointed out in his own discussion of the introduction of PCCs there are good reasons for wondering whether we are currently experiencing a period of plutocratic rule 'of the rich, by the rich, for the rich'. Meanwhile, Crouch (2004) suggests that we are living in a time of 'post-democracy', where the traces of democracy remain in our ways of thinking and talking about our political system, but where in reality citizens have few opportunities and extremely limited power to shape the kinds of societies in which they are living.

To provide a convincing account of the kinds of principles, practices and institutional structures that might be appropriate for democracy it is useful first to reflect upon why it is that we think we ought to favour it. For some the answer might simply be that legitimate authority over people can only be exercised with the consent of those same people. We should favour democracy, then, because it is the most rational way to assign authority. However, others have suggested somewhat more positive reasons for valuing democracy. Young (2000) argues that we favour and value democracy because it is seen as the best means we have to promote the self-development and self-determination of peoples, both of which are essential to social justice. Democracy and justice then are seen to be mutually dependent, neither being possible without the presence of the other.

A view of democracy as inextricably entwined with justice is evident in some recent attempts to identify the characteristics of 'democratic policing'. For example, both Jones et al. (1994) and Manning (2010) argue that whether or not police officers act fairly and equitably in their dealings with the public and whether policing is supporting the production of socially just outcomes are as important, if not more important, for democratic policing than the kinds of mechanisms in place to ensure that the police are responsive to 'public opinion'. Indeed, one of the primary concerns articulated about the switch to PCCs has been a concern that police forces will have to respond to majoritarian pressures by adopting superficially appealing populist approaches that are detrimental to unpopular minorities and thus to social justice more broadly. Wood (2014) suggests that the potential for such a situation to occur demonstrates the existence of a clear tension between 'liberal' and 'democratic' values, and highlights the need to ensure that the balance between the two is carefully struck. However, as Wood acknowledges, this apparent tension rests on a rather narrow understanding of democracy as 'electoralism'. So the kind of 'democratic pressures' that Wood refers to might, perhaps, be better understood as pressures emanating from an electoral system that is only superficially democratic (and may even be, in Crouch's (2004) term, 'post-democratic').

If we adopt a conception of democracy that treats an orientation towards social justice as fundamental (as proposed by Young (2000)), then we can avoid at least some of the apparent tension between so-called 'liberal' and 'democratic' values pointed to by Wood (2014). In Young's (2000) theory of democracy, decision-making rests on the equal inclusion of all those affected by a decision in some form of discussion and deliberation about the matter at stake. The deliberation must, in Young's account, be free from domination and be carried out by participants who are orientated towards giving reasons for their views and preferences and taking into account the views and preferences of the other participants. Justice is 'built in' to this process because participants will inevitably have to appeal to some kind of 'principles of justice' in order to construct legitimate arguments about what should be done. For Young, the whole purpose of the process of democratic communication, then, is 'the transformation of private self-regarding desire into public appeals to justice' (Young, 2000: 51). Similarly, Dryzek (2000: 46–7) suggests that when participants in deliberation must publicly defend their positions they will know that they must do so with respect to the public interest, rather than their own self-interest, and therefore they must present themselves as 'public-spirited'. This may have the effect of making them become more 'public-spirited' in order to maintain their own sense of their integrity.

What Young and Dryzek's accounts of deliberative forms of democracy make available to us is a way of understanding democracy as not merely something that citizens have a right to expect but also as something that imposes responsibilities on them. There is no room in a democracy for the adoption of policies and practices that are unduly oppressive and clearly detrimental to the interests of unpopular or vulnerable minorities purely on the basis that such policies and practices reflect the self-interested (and frequently unreflective and under-informed) preferences of the majority. Under the more deeply democratic conditions of inclusive, non-dominated deliberation, the expression of self-interested preferences is considered to be an illegitimate form of political persuasion and the views and preferences of minorities and vulnerable groups must be taken into account. Democracy is identified with the pursuit via inclusive mechanisms of just solutions to the problems that arise under social and political conditions of diversity and pluralism, rather than with the aggregation of individualized, self-interested preferences. Social justice, in the sense of people having equal opportunities to thrive and develop and to play a part in determining the conditions of their own existence, is seen as an essential component of democracy (Young, 2000: 31–2).

The identification of democracy with social justice provides a useful starting point for thinking more imaginatively about what democratic policing might mean. It supports Manning's (2010) claim that policing should at the very least not exacerbate already existing inequalities or compound the disadvantages experienced by the most vulnerable. Furthermore, as observed by both Manning (2010) and

Jones et al. (1994), democratic policing must clearly be effective at combatting those social ills that damage both the life experiences of individuals and communities and the fabric of democracy itself. While responsiveness to citizens is an important aspect of 'democratic policing', then, so too are matters of fairness and practical efficacy in securing the necessities for social justice. To summarise, by drawing on radical deliberative theories of democracy we can arrive at a much broader and more ambitious conception of what 'democratic policing' might mean, and transcend the limitations of narrow election-centred approaches. Following this line of reasoning through to its conclusion, then, 'democratic policing' refers to policing that first and foremost provides effective support for social justice, a condition where citizens have equal opportunities to thrive and develop and to play a part in determining the circumstances of their own existence (Young, 2000). Next I identify a definition of 'policing', which will prove useful for thinking about 'democratic policing' as policing that is supportive of social justice.

Policing, police and the creation of public safety

Historically the word 'police' referred to something much more expansive than an organization for controlling crime and maintaining order. It was associated with the notion of a system for ordering and managing a well-run society (Reiner, 1992; Neocleous, 2000). The advent of modern police organizations has led to a narrowing of the meaning of the words police and policing, coupled with a chronic ambiguity in their usage. Some uses of the words policing and police encourage a frustrating circularity in definition, implying that 'policing' is simply whatever 'the police' do, and whatever 'the police' do is 'policing'.[2] In recent years sociologists working in this area have sought to make a clear theoretical distinction between the activity of 'policing' and the institution 'the Police' (e.g. see Rawlings, 2002; McLaughlin, 2007; Reiner, 2010) as it is increasingly suggested that there has been a 'transformation' or 'pluralization' of policing (see Bayley and Shearing, 1996; Loader, 2000; Jones and Newburn, 2002; White and Gill, 2013) with public police organizations described by some as having lost their 'monopoly' on policing (e.g. see Bayley and Shearing, 1996; Crawford, 2008). While there is an ongoing debate about the extent to which the apparent trends should be regarded as novel (and, indeed, threatening), what is not in dispute is that it is possible, and frequently theoretically desirable, to draw a distinction between the activity of 'policing' and the organization 'the Police'.

McLaughlin (2007: 113) suggests that, under the unstable, fragmented and fragmenting conditions of postmodernity, critical police scholars must recognize that '"[p]olicing" is a socially necessary function but a state-structured police bureaucracy is not'. In fact, it seems to me, when we reclaim the activity of 'policing' from the institution of 'the police' we can start to think more creatively about what we should, as citizens of a democracy, be able to expect from both the activity *and* the state institution. Reiner's (2010: 5) definition of the term 'policing' as referring to systems of surveillance and detection linked to the threat of sanction where deviant behaviour is discovered can potentially encompass a range of institutional arrangements for regulating conduct, including institutions outside of the state police organization. An even wider definition is provided by Bayley and Shearing (1996: 586), who refer to policing as 'the self-conscious process whereby societies designate and authorize people to create public safety'. Clearly this 'process' may well encompass the systems of surveillance referred to by Reiner, but what Bayley and Shearing's definition adds is that it explicitly aligns policing with the production of an identifiable 'good', which is to say the production of 'safety'. And it is in this broad definition of policing, as orientated towards safety, that I think we can start to find the means to reimagine 'democratic policing'.

I have argued above that we should understand democracy as intrinsically linked to social justice. As such, if we accept Bayley and Shearing's definition of 'policing', then we can identify '*democratic* policing' with the creation of 'safety' from the kinds of things that threaten individual self-development and/or the capacity of communities to determine their own destinies. This is, to be sure, a very far-reaching definition of safety, and one that overflows both the definition suggested by Bayley and Shearing (1996), and the more limited expectations people generally have of the public police.[3] However, if we are serious about reimagining democratic policing along social justice lines it seems to me that we must develop a more expansive conception of what Bayley and Shearing (ibid.: 593) refer to as 'the "bottom line" of safety'.

This more expansive definition resonates with the term 'human security' coined by the United Nations Development Programme to capture 'the legitimate concerns of ordinary people who sought security in their daily lives' (UNDP, 1994: 22). The concept of 'human security' has been criticized for, amongst other things, being 'extraordinarily expansive and vague' (Paris, 2001: 88). However, it does have the advantage of recognizing that harm can take many forms, and that the types of worries and travails that loom large in many people's everyday lives are frequently not associated with intentionally inflicted criminal harms, but rather with difficulties accessing, maintaining access to, and feeling secure in one's access to personal, material, social and political resources and rights (for example adequate incomes, paid work, shelter, food, healthcare, a healthy environment, basic human rights, freedom from state repression). Reimagining the '"bottom line" of safety' in 'human security' terms decouples 'safety' from 'crime', and also emphasizes that 'policing' (the creation of 'safety') can take place in the absence of 'the police'. In a way, then, this reverts to the broader understanding of policing evident in historical usage of the term. This links 'policing' through an expanded conception of 'safety' to the broad definition of 'democratic policing' (as orientated towards social justice) I outlined above. In the next part of this chapter I make some proposals for reorientating the study of policing in order to accommodate the expanded definition of policing proposed above.

(Re)imagining democratic policing: reorienting the study of policing

Research on policing and the police has embraced a range of approaches, which have been adopted for a variety of reasons, by researchers with very different intellectual and *political* objectives (Manning, 2005; McLaughlin, 2007; Reiner, 2010). In recent years, a great deal of research has been preoccupied with 'evidence-based policing' and in particular with identifying ways in which the police can be effective at 'crime control' (Reiner, 2010). This trend has seen 'critical and theoretical' research take a back seat to research that is 'pragmatic [and] policy-oriented' (Reiner, 1992: 55; 2010: 14). Yet, as Reiner (1992: 777) has noted, the recurring crises of legitimacy and identity experienced by the police from the latter part of the twentieth century onwards have come about as a result of 'deeply rooted structural trends', which require critical, sociological analysis. Under these conditions, McLaughlin (2007: ix, emphasis added) suggests, 'it has never been more important to forge a *critical police studies* ... capable of conceptualizing policing developments against socio-cultural, economic and political transformations'. This project seems all the more urgent if 'democratic policing' is to be successfully (re)imagined along the lines outlined above.

In this part of the chapter I argue that, to pursue 'democratic policing' in the sense of policing for social justice, the study of policing needs to be reorientated in at least two ways. First, a wider range of perspectives, topics and approaches need to be brought into mainstream discussions of policing. Second (and relatedly), the hierarchical, uniformed, state bureaucracies that we call 'police' need to be decentred from the study of policing, and the mythology that surrounds these organizations needs to be challenged more effectively

'Policing for a Better Britain'? Broadening the horizons of policing scholarship

Published in November 2013, *Policing for a Better Britain* (Stevens, 2013) was the final report of the 'Independent Commission on Policing' set up by the Labour party to 'examine the roles and responsibilities of the Police Service in England and Wales'.[4] Chaired by a former Commissioner of the Metropolitan Police (Lord Stevens of Kirkwhelpington), the Commission was, perhaps, always unlikely to deliver any major surprises or departures from the status quo in its findings or recommendations. Yet the final report did turn out to be rather striking in terms of the issues it left largely unexamined. The report made only rather limited reference to matters including police violence, routine weaponization (e.g. the increased use of tasers), deaths in police custody or following contact with the police, police manipulation of and apparent failures to investigate the media (e.g. historic revelations in relation to Hillsborough and more recent allegations in relation to the Metropolitan Police investigation of News International), the policing of protest events (e.g. student fees and anti-fracking protests), police involvement in the surveillance of peace and environmental campaigners, and the apparently close relationships between the police and various private business concerns and interest groups (e.g. see Ball, 2013; Lewis and Evans, 2013; the *The Guardian*, 2013; Whyte, 2015). These issues, and the structural political and organizational contexts within which they have arisen, all seem to be highly relevant for a thoroughgoing discussion of what 'democratic policing' should and should not involve.

One can speculate about a range of causes for the omissions in the final report of the Stevens Commission (2013), but what seems clear is that those who contributed to the Commission's final report were not minded to make explicit reference to the structural context within which the inquiry took place. As a result, the deep social divisions and inequalities of wealth and power, which place limits on the extent to which ordinary citizens are able to exert any meaningful influence over the broad ideological and material conditions under which they must live their lives, are rendered largely invisible. Furthermore, the police-centric focus of the work of the Commission meant that those who contributed to its final form avoided any overt challenge to the notion that state police organizations in roughly their current form are necessary, and that their myriad objectives (the so-called 'omnibus role') are, broadly speaking, legitimate.

Ensuring that policing is 'democratic' is treated in the Commission's report (Stevens, 2013, and in the companion volume of academic papers (Brown, 2014) that helped inform its production) as a matter of implementing the most appropriate legal frameworks for governance and accountability.[5] This approach indicates the broadly 'liberal constitutionalist' (cf. Kinsey, Lea and Young, 1986: 164) orientations underpinning the report, which include a consensus view of society, a commitment to a view of both the police and the law as politically impartial, and an assumption that the state police organization as currently constituted is an essential and legitimate institution and should form the starting point for studying policing. The liberal orientations described above combine to produce a number of quite significant blind spots (or perhaps more accurately 'dark corners') in the mainstream of policing scholarship.

To avoid being accused of using a broad brush to paint a straw man I should clarify that I am not suggesting that liberal policing scholarship has not provided and cannot provide genuinely important and interesting insights into contemporary policing and police organizations, including criticisms of aspects of police activity and of the institutional structure of policing. Indeed, quite the opposite: some research falling within this tradition has provided important conceptual resources and empirical insights that enable us to move towards a more fully developed conceptualization of 'democratic policing' (and examples have been referred to above). Rather, what I wish to suggest is that the criticisms of the police that emerge from the liberal tradition of policing scholarship are, conspicuously, not placed in the context of the structural conditions of neo-liberal capitalism that create and maintain the injustices, harms, inequalities and social divisions that render policing an intensely and inherently political activity. Thus, while it has yielded significant and useful empirical and conceptual gains, the overall product of liberal policing scholarship as a tradition remains, I suggest, on its own inadequate to the task of (re)imagining 'democratic policing' in the manner that I have proposed.

However, while the broadly liberal orientations described above characterize many of the dominant voices raised in mainstream British policing scholarship, this is not to say that *nobody* is challenging the picture they paint, or attempting to shine a light into the dark corners of policing to which they give only a rather cursory glance. Indeed, some academics (as well as campaign groups and journalists) have long sought to point out the significant harms and humiliations caused to some vulnerable and marginalized groups by police activity (and inactivity) (e.g. see Scraton, 1982; Choongh, 1998; Pemberton, 2005; Tombs and Whyte, 2007; Tombs, 2008); to highlight repressive and intrusive police interventions in political protest movements (e.g. see Power, 2012; Evans and Lewis, 2013; Jackson and Monk, 2014); and to reveal the extent to which the police, and policing more broadly conceived, have been involved in serving the interests of powerful establishment groups as opposed to the wider public (e.g. see Whyte, 2015).

The problem, then, is not that critical research is not taking place or that critical insights are not coming to light; rather it is that these are not being adequately taken into account by the mainstream of policing scholarship. There are, it seems to me, two ways in which this occurs. First, where critical research focuses on things the police do that we might think they should not be doing (for example causing the deaths of citizens or protecting corporate interests by spying on trade unionists and environmental activists), mainstream liberal policing scholars have shown a tendency to carry on regardless, without engaging with the ways in which police violence and subversion of democratic rights undermine the institution's putative legitimacy and impartiality (a tendency that pervades the report of the Stevens Commission (2013), and the accompanying academic volume (Brown, 2014)). Second, some scholars providing critical insights *of relevance to* policing but which may concern aspects of policing in which the police are not directly concerned are not actually seen (sometimes even by themselves) as 'policing' scholars. As a result of both these tendencies, it seems, research that could pose a robust evidence-based challenge to liberal assumptions about the necessity and general righteousness of the state police in roughly their current form, or about the health of our democracy, is permitted to languish in a critical (or, as some have called it, 'Left-Idealist' (Kinsey, Lea and Young, 1986: 164)) ghetto. This is to the significant detriment of discussions about 'democratic policing'.

One salient example of the second way in which mainstream policing scholarship neglects relevant research can be seen with reference to the work of Steve Tombs and Dave Whyte, who have written extensively on the death and damage caused by 'safety crimes' (see Tombs and Whyte, 2007; Tombs, 2008). These crimes are, they note, treated as a 'sub–category' of criminal offences which are usually dealt with through regulatory agencies, rather than by the police. As such they tend not to be seen as 'real crime' (Tombs and Whyte, 2007: 93). Correspondingly, it seems, the empirical and theoretical insights provided by Tombs and Whyte tend not to be seen as insights that are specifically about policing or the police, and neither of these researchers would, I suspect, consider themselves to be policing scholars *per se*. However, if, as I have proposed above, the primary objective of 'democratic policing' should be the creation of forms of safety, which enable human development and self-determination, then the insights provided by research such as that carried out by Tombs and Whyte most certainly are relevant for a thorough reimagining of what 'democratic policing' might mean.

Acknowledging the breadth and variety of research both on, *and of relevance to*, policing and the police, even where that research may chip away at treasured liberal assumptions about society, democracy and the police, is an essential starting point for thinking deeply and critically about 'democratic policing'. However, broadening the horizons of policing research in the way outlined here requires a quite fundamental adjustment to the current position of the police in relation to policing research. It requires nothing less than decentring the police by cracking open the mythological carapace that has kept them centre stage for so long.

Decentring the police: counteracting police mythology

The symbolic importance of the police is premised upon an assemblage of myths, which provide cover for both their inadequacies and their excesses and limit the influence of the kind of radical criticism needed to (re)imagine both *their* role, and policing more generally. Preeminent amongst these myths is the characterization of the police as having been established in order to deal with rising crime, and as having been primarily concerned with this task throughout their history and right up to the present day. Along with this preeminent mythological cloak come various additional mythological accoutrements, including the notion that the police are politically impartial because their activity is shaped by the law rather than by special interests, and the belief that the police can control crime effectively without generating undesirable side-effects in the shape of repressive and discriminatory practices with the potential to criminalize, alienate and otherwise injure already vulnerable and socially excluded groups.

The historical and contemporary accuracy of these myths has been repeatedly questioned in the policing research literature (Reiner, 2010; Loader, 2014). Revisionist historical accounts of the emergence of the 'new' police in nineteenth-century England (for example see Storch, 1976) suggest that, rather than dealing with 'crime' *per se*, police activities were frequently concerned with curtailing those activities of the labouring classes that were regarded as disruptive to good order, good taste and good working habits as viewed from the perspective of the middle and upper classes. Sociologists working in the twentieth century, meanwhile, argued that in their day-to-day work the police are not first and foremost either law enforcers or 'crime-fighters' (e.g. see Banton, 1964; Manning, 1977; Bayley, 1994; Bittner, 2005 [1974]; Dixon, 2005; Westley, 2005 [1970]; Loader, 2014).[6]

Bayley (1994: 20) argues that uniformed 'patrol officers' are primarily engaged in responding to calls for assistance from the public, using the threat of law enforcement to 'interrupt or pacify situations of potential or ongoing conflict'. The fact that the police *can* invoke the law, and that their legal powers facilitate the use of force in order to gain compliance with their instructions, means that they have what Bittner (2005 [1974]: 164–5) calls 'a unique and powerful capacity to cope with all kinds of emergencies'. The law, then, is not something that provides a specific direction for police work, rather it provides the police with certain capacities that shape public demand for their services. As Westley (2005 [1970]: 138) notes the police is 'a group who can be assigned that which no other group can perform', namely intervening in situations where 'decisive action' is required (Bittner, 2005 [1974]).

Even a report by Her Majesty's Inspectorate of Constabulary (HMIC, 2012), for all that it gamely represents itself as contradicting sociological orthodoxy in order (presumably) to bolster the home secretary's promise 'to turn police into real crime fighters' (May, 2011), indicates that police officers in England and Wales still spend a good deal of their time attending incidents at which no crime has in fact occurred. Indeed, one of the report's 'key findings' is that police overwhelmingly spend their time 'on crime or *stopping things that the public feel are dangerous or wrong and should cease immediately*' (HMIC, 2012). Whether or not this is a deliberate echo of Bittner's (2005 [1974]: 161) famous claim that police attend incidents that involve 'something-that-ought-not-to-be-happening-and-about-which-someone-had-better-do-something-right-now!' is not clear, though the similarity is striking.

What we know about the *effectiveness* of police activity at reducing crime is also less than convincing, with a recent review suggesting that there is no conclusive evidence that 'traditional' tactics of random patrol, stop and search and rapid response have any effect at all on crime (Karn, 2013). Attempts to develop and test approaches that will allow the police to be more effective at reducing crime (for example targeting 'hotspots', intelligence-led and problem-orientated policing and partnership working) are argued to have shown some potential (Karn, 2013), but one might wonder whether the resources currently being expended on 'evidence-based policing' are better understood as a welcome and rational development, or as a desperate bid to find a way in which the police can finally live up to their own mythology. Certainly it seems likely that the enthusiastic championing of evidence-based policing by police leaders, politicians and academics will do little to dissuade the public from what Loader (1997: 11) refers to as their 'affective attachment to the "policing solution"'. Indulging this attachment keeps the police at the centre of debates about policing, crime and safety, their enduring 'symbolic power' stifling attempts to find alternate 'ways of speaking and acting vis-á-vis crime and social order' (ibid.).

But if the police are not effective at reducing crime and are not primarily engaged in upholding the law or fighting crime, then we might well ask what are they doing and why does the mythology surrounding them suggest they are doing something else? One plausible response to these questions can be found in the fact that portraying the police as crime fighters casts a veil over the inherently political nature of police work, which, in the end, always involves decisions about what, where, who and how to police. Resource constraints dictate that the suppression of crime and enforcement of law is always selective and 'incomplete' (Jefferson and Grimshaw, 1984). Thus, the law does not determine police action, but rather is used by police officers as a resource for pursuing objectives that they can, within limits, define for themselves (Bayley, 1994; Bittner, 2005 [1974]). Choongh (1998: 625) notes that these objectives can and often do include extracting what officers consider to be due deference from 'subordinate sections of society viewed as anti-police and innately criminal', in particular the poor, homeless people, unemployed people, ethnic minorities, gypsies and travellers. In fact, studies of police behaviour indicate that officers often use their own informal tests to determine which individuals require and deserve coercive attention. Their judgements are frequently based less on specific criminal behaviours than on visible markers of social status, or the failure of individuals to display sufficient respect towards officers' authority (see Loftus, 2010). In other words, in their normal day-to-day routines the police act most frequently and visibly against some of the most disadvantaged, vulnerable and marginalized sections of society, often in connection with quite trivial offences, or indeed no specific criminal offences at all.[7]

Meanwhile, the police are neither commonly expected nor regularly seen to act against the individuals and organizations responsible for causing some of the most far-reaching and catastrophic harms of everyday life in twenty-first century Britain, including companies that allow their workers to be seriously injured and killed, or the environment to be seriously degraded, by failing to adopt safe working practices (see Tombs, 2008); and the architects of the global financial crisis, which has precipitated catastrophic cuts to vital social services in the UK (prosecution of the odd criminally errant banker notwithstanding). At the same time the police *do* act against those who seek to mount effective political campaigns highlighting social divisions, inequalities and environmental concerns. Recent examples of police activity in this area have included aggressive public order police responses to a succession of protests by student, anti-austerity and environmental campaigners,[8] the ongoing series of revelations about close relationships between the police and private corporations,[9] and the involvement of the police in extensive surveillance of activist groups and trade unionists (see Ball, 2013; Lewis and Evans, 2013; *Guardian*, 2013; Whyte, 2015). In other words, there is strong evidence that the police often serve the interests of particular groups in society by concentrating resources and attention on apprehending the perpetrators of certain types of 'crime' and maintaining a particular, dominant, conception of order (Reiner, 2010).

All of that being said, the police also intervene and take control in circumstances in which it is hard to imagine which other group could do so. If we accept that their defining characteristic is their 'right to use coercive force' (Klockars, 1985: 12), we must acknowledge that their particular strength is their ability to take 'decisive action', which may not be opposed by citizens (Bittner, 1970: 40, cited by McLaughlin, 2007: 53). Of course, police can cause considerable harm in the course of behaving decisively, which is precisely why critical studies of the consequences of coercive and violent police action are essential for any consideration of 'democratic policing'. But there are circumstances in which the police's unique authorization to use coercive force (and the knowledge that the public have of this authorization) is essential in providing an effective response to an unfolding emergency. There is, then, still a need to value the public police, and accept that the public police perform some important social functions that few of us would wish to be without.

However, the continued centrality and symbolic importance of the police in discussions of policing serves to promote, make visible and 'dramatize' (cf. Manning, 1977) a particular set of harms (intentionally caused criminal harms) and a particular set of responses to those harms (police use of force, criminalization). As well as failing to reflect what the police actually spend much of their time doing (dealing with calls for service from the public, resolving conflicts, asserting their authority over marginalized groups), this deflects attention away from both the overtly political 'high policing' (cf. Brodeur, 1983) functions of the police and from the harms (including corporate and state violence, exploitation, poverty, environmental degradation) that are not generally considered to be police business (despite being potentially far more fundamental to the wellbeing of society). Thus, the symbolic dominance of the police over discussions of policing makes it difficult to broaden the horizons of these discussions in the ways I have proposed above. In order to pursue democratic policing, then, the activity of policing needs to be reclaimed from the literally and symbolically violent institution of the police.

Conclusion: towards a pro-democratic agenda for policing research

In this chapter I have attempted to sketch the outlines for an ambitious (re)imagining of 'democratic policing'. It clearly goes far beyond the rather limited aspiration to 'democratize' the police via the ballot box, as adopted by the coalition government. It also, while clearly drawing on elements from the existing literature, goes beyond most previous proposals as to how to develop democratic policing: even those provided by the radical commentators of the 1980s who, although they favoured more participative approaches in police governance in order to ensure representation for the views of minority groups, were still rather police-centric (see Jones, Newburn and Smith, 1994). I have attempted to weave together some radical democratic theory with a social harm perspective on crime, with insights from more conventional policing sources. My argument may be perceived as a challenge by those who are more or less content with the current constitution, both institutional and ideological, of policing, police organizations and, indeed, the broad field of police studies in this country. I hope, however, that it has suggested some possible fruitful areas for further research and analysis, which may help to put flesh onto the bones of the ideas outlined here, and may even provide additional momentum to existing campaigns in favour of approaches to policing that promote rather than undermine social justice and democratic self-determination. To my mind there are three empirical research questions that should provide the backbone of any attempts to take this initial, preliminary exercise in (re)imagining further:

1. What are the main threats to safety, social justice and self-determination in today's society?
2. What forms of policing are best suited to addressing these threats?
3. What does the police's 'capacity for decisive action' make them particularly good (and bad) for in society today?

Clearly some of the evidence needed to start to address these questions is already available, but much more remains to be done. The objective here is to shift the analytical gaze away from the police (as fascinating as they are) and on to 'safety' as the ultimate product that we expect *policing* to deliver. The production of 'safety' is clearly a goal that one would hope is shared by police organizations, and therefore the suggested research agenda does not preclude collaboration with the police. Nonetheless, it is an agenda that has the potential to yield some challenging and, potentially, unpalatable findings for police organizations. The question is whether police organizations, and the researchers who stake their careers on researching on, with and for them, are willing to consider whether, as Robert Peel suggested to parliament back in 1828, we now require 'a new mode of protection' (quoted in Critchley, 1967: 48).

Acknowledgement

Many thanks to Barry Goldson and Ian Loader for their very helpful feedback on the first draft of this chapter

Notes

1 Two exceptions to this are Reiner (2013) and Wood (2014).
2 For example, the final report of the Independent Police Commission (Stevens, 2013) used the word 'police' in its title, stated that it was an 'independent inquiry focusing on the future of policing' in its subtitle, and then in further introductory text stated that its 'overarching objective is to examine the roles and responsibilities of the Police Service in England and Wales'.
3 Indeed, if we consider Robert Peel's statement (after the passage of the Metropolitan Police Act 1829) that 'I want to teach people that liberty does not consist in having your house robbed by organized gangs of thieves, and in leaving the principal streets of London in the nightly possession of drunken women and vagabonds' (quoted in Critchley, 1967: 54), then we can see that Peel refers to a very specific and narrow conception of safety, and one that arguably provides only a rather limited amount of 'liberty'.
4 http://independentpolicecommission.org.uk/
5 The Labour party has since pledged to introduce the report's final recommendations (Cooper, 2013), which include proposals for replacing PCCs with governance arrangements incorporating lower-tier local authorities, and possibly directly elected Local Policing Boards and some form of 'participatory budgeting' involving local people.
6 This formulation of their work is, as Manning (1977: 15) has argued, an ironic 'legitimating theme'. It is ironic because the manifest failure of the police either to spend significant proportions of their time dealing with crime, or to make a clearly identifiable impact on the amount of crime means that 'their stock is oversold'.

7 To observe that the police are often concerned with rather trivial offences is certainly not to deny the considerable suffering such offences can cause to individuals and communities, particularly those who experience them on a regular basis.

8 For example, the use of mounted police charges and the controversial containment technique of 'kettling' against students protesting the rise in university tuition fees; the significant use of police resources and abuse of powers of arrest to disrupt protests against 'hydraulic fracturing' test sites in Manchester and Sussex; and the capacity of the police to use the offence of 'aggravated trespass' legislation as a way to criminalize peaceful but disruptive direct action.

9 For example, following a peaceful direct action protest by environmental activists at the gas-fired West Burton power station there were allegations that the police passed papers relating to the case directly onto the owners EDF so that they could pursue civil action against them (Ball, 2013). Similarly, police dealing with protestors against the cull of badgers in Gloucestershire were filmed stating that their details could be passed to the National Farmers Union to enable them to pursue a private prosecution (*Guardian*, 2013).

References

Arblaster, A. (1994) *Democracy*. Buckingham: Open University Press.

Association of Chief Police Officers (ACPO) (2010) *Response to Home Office consultation paper Policing in the 21st Century*. London: Association of Chief Police Officers.

Ball, J. (2013) 'EDF drops lawsuit against environmental activists after backlash', *The Guardian*, 13 March. Available at: www.theguardian.com/environment/2013/mar/13/edf-lawsuit-environmental-activists-backlash.

Banton, M. (1964) *The Policeman in the Community*. London: Tavistock.

Bayley, D. H. (1994) *Police for the Future*. New York: Oxford University Press.

Bayley, D. H. and Shearing, C. D. (1996) 'The future of policing', *Law and Society Review*, 30(3): 585–606.

Berman, G., Coleman, C. and Taylor, M. (2012) 'Police and Crime Commissioner Elections 2012', House of Commons Research Paper 12/73 London: House of Commons.

Bittner, E. (1970) *The Functions of the Police in Modern Society: A Review of Background Factors, Current Practices, and Possible Role Models*. Rockville, MD: National Institute of Mental Health.

Bittner, E. (2005 [1974]) 'Florence Nightingale in Pursuit of Willie Sutton: A Theory of the Police' in Newburn, T. (ed.) *Policing: Key Readings*. Cullompton: Willan.

Brodeur, J.-P. (1983) 'High and low policing: remarks about the policing of political activities', *Social Problems*, 30(5): 507–520.

Brown, J. (ed.) (2014) *The Future of Policing*. London: Routledge.

Chambers, S. (2014) 'Who is policing the Police and Crime Commissioners?', *Safer Communities*, 13(1): 32–39.

Choongh, S. (1998) 'Policing the dross: a social disciplinary model of policing', *British Journal of Criminology*, 38(4): 623–634.

Cooper, Y. (2013) 'Yvette Cooper speech at the launch of the Report of the Independent Police Commission.' Available at: http://press.labour.org.uk/post/68060991512/yvette-cooper-speech-at-the-launch-of-the-report [accessed March 2015].

Crawford, A. (2008) 'The pattern of policing in the UK: policing beyond the police' in T. Newburn (ed.) *Handbook of Policing*. Cullompton: Willan.

Critchley, T. A. (1967) *A History of the Police in England and Wales: 900–1966*. London: Constable and Co.

Crouch, C. (2004) *Post-Democracy*. Cambridge: Polity Press.

Davies, M. (2014) 'The path to Police and Crime Commissioners', *Safer Communities*, 13(1): 3–12.

Dixon, D. (2005) 'Why don't the police stop crime?', *Australian and New Zealand Journal of Criminology*, 38(4): 4–24.

Dryzek, J. (2000) *Deliberative Democracy and Beyond: Liberals, Critics, Contestations*. Oxford: Oxford University Press.

Evans, R. and Lewis, P. (2013) *Undercover: The True Story of Britain's Secret Police*. London: Faber and Faber.

Farthing, S. (2012) 'Public unconvinced by PCCs'. Available at: www.liberty-human-rights. org.uk/news/latest-news/public-unconvinced-pccs [accessed 20 March 2015].

Garland, J. and Terry, C. (2012) *How Not to Run an Election: The Police and Crime Commissioner Elections*. London: Electoral Reform Society.

Gilling, D. (2014) 'Reforming police governance in England and Wales: managerialisation and the politics of organisational regime change', *Policing and Society*, 24(1): 81–101.

The Guardian (2013) 'Badger cull police threaten to pass protestor's details to farmers' union', Available at: www.theguardian.com/environment/video/2013/sep/24/badger-cull-p olice-protester-farmers-union-video [accessed 27 March 2015].

Herbert, N. (2011) 'It's time for you to have a say on policing', *Daily Telegraph*, 28 March. Available at: www.telegraph.co.uk/news/uknews/crime/8410429/Its-time-for-you-to-ha ve-a-say-on-policing.html.

Her Majesty's Inspectorate of Constabulary (HMIC) (2012) *Taking Time for Crime: A Study of How Police Officers Prevent Crime in the Field*. London: Her Majesty's Inspectorate of Constabulary.

Jackson, W. and Monk, H. (2014) 'Police violence at anti-fracking protests: pacifying disruptive subjects', *Criminal Justice Matters*, 98: 12–13.

Jefferson, T. and Grimshaw, R. (1984) *Controlling the Constable: Police Accountability in England and Wales*. London: Muller.

Jones, T. and Newburn, T. (2002) 'The transformation of policing? Understanding current trends in policing systems', *British Journal of Criminology*, 42(1): 129–146.

Jones, T., Newburn, T. and Smith, D. (1994) *Democracy and Policing*. London: Policy Studies Institute.

Jones, T., Newburn, T. and Smith, D. (2012) 'Democracy and Police and Crime Commissioners' in Newburn, T. and Peay, J. (eds) *Policing: Politics, Culture and Control*. Oxford: Hart.

Joyce, P. (2011) 'Police reform: from police authorities to police and crime commissioners', *Safer Communities*, 10(4): 5–13.

Karn, J. (2013) *Policing and Crime Reduction: The Evidence and its Implications for Practice*. London: The Police Foundation.

Kinsey, R., Lea, J. and Young, J. (1986) *Losing the Fight against Crime*. Oxford: Blackwell.

Klockars, C. B. (1985) *The Idea of Police*. London: Sage.

Lewis, P. and Evans, R. (2013) *Undercover: The True Story of Britain's Secret Police*. London: Faber and Faber.

Lister, S. (2013) 'The new politics of the police: Police and Crime Commissioners and the "operational independence" of the police', *Policing*, 7(3): 239–247.

Lister, S. (2014) 'Scrutinising the role of the Police and Crime Panel in the new era of police governance in England and Wales', *Safer Communities*, 13(1): 22–31.

Lister, S. and Rowe, M. (2014) 'Electing Police and Crime Commissioners in England and Wales: prospecting for the democratisation of policing', *Safer Communities*, 14(1): 22–31.

Loader, I. (1997) 'Policing and the social: questions of symbolic power', *British Journal of Sociology*, 48(1): 1–18.

Loader, I. (2000) 'Plural policing and democratic governance', *Social and Legal Studies*, 9(3): 323–345.

Loader, I. (2014) 'Why Do the Police Matter? Beyond the Myth of Crime-fighting' in Brown, J. (ed.) *The Future of Policing*. London: Routledge.

Loader, I. and Muir, R. (2011) 'Why Labour has it wrong on elected police: a manifesto for progressive police and crime commissioners', *New Statesman Politics Blog*. Available at: www.newstatesman.com/blogs/the-staggers/2011/09/crime-commissioners-police [accessed 20 March 2015].

Loftus, B. (2010) 'Police occupational culture: classic themes, altered times', *Policing and Society*, 20(1): 1–20.

McLaughlin, E. (2007) *The New Policing*. London: Sage.

Manning, P. K. (1977) *Police Work: The Social Organization of Policing*. Cambridge, MA: MIT Press.

Manning, P. K. (2005) 'The Study of Policing', *Police Quarterly*, 8(1): 23–43.

Manning, P. K. (2010) *Democratic Policing in a Changing World*. Boulder, CO: Paradigm.

May, T. (2011) 'Police Reform', Home Secretary's speech to ACPO Summer Conference, 4 July. Available at: www.gov.uk/government/speeches/police-reform-home-secretarys-speech-to-acpo-summer-conference.

Millen, F. and Stephens, M. (2012) 'Police authorities, accountability and citizenship', *Policing*, 6(3): 261–271.

Neocleous, M. (2000) *The Fabrication of Social Order: A Critical Theory of Police Power*. London: Pluto Press.

Newburn, T. (2012) 'Police and crime commissioners: the Americanization of policing or a very British reform?', *International Journal of Law, Crime and Justice*, 40(1): 31–46.

Paris, R. (2001) 'Human security: paradigm shift or hot air?', *International Security*, 26(2): 87–102.

Pemberton, S. (2005) 'Deaths in police custody: the "acceptable" consequences of a "law and order" society?', *Outlines*, 7(2): 23–42.

Power, N. (2012) 'Dangerous subjects: UK students and the criminalization of protest', *South Atlantic Quarterly*, 111(2): 412–420.

Raine, J. W. and Keasey, P. (2012) 'From Police Authorities to Police and Crime Commissioners: Might policing become more publicly accountable?', *International Journal of Emergency Services*, 1(2): 122–134.

Rawlings, P. (2002) *Policing: A Short History*. Cullompton: Willan.

Reiner, R. (1992) 'Policing a postmodern society', *Modern Law Review*, 55(6): 761–781.

Reiner, R. (2010) *The Politics of the Police*. Oxford: Oxford University Press.

Reiner, R. (2013) 'Who governs? Democracy, plutocracy, science and prophecy in policing', *Criminology and Criminal Justice*, 13(2): 161–180.

Scraton, P. (1982) 'Policing and Institutionalised Racism on Merseyside' in Cowell, D., Jones, T. and Young, J. (eds) *Policing the Riots*. London: Junction Books.

Simey, M. (1988) *Democracy Rediscovered: A Study in Police Accountability*. London: Pluto Press.

Spencer, S. (1985) 'The weakness of police authorities and the case for reform', *Local Government Studies*, 11(6): 31–34.

Stevens, Lord (2013) *Policing for a Better Britain: Report of the Independent Police Commission*. Available at: http://independentpolicecommission.org.uk/uploads/37d80308-be23-9684-054d-e4958bb9d518.pdf [accessed October 2015].

Storch, R. (1976) 'The policeman as domestic missionary: urban discipline and popular culture in northern England 1850–1880', *Journal of Social History*, 9(4): 481–509.

Tombs, S. (2008) 'Workplace Harms and the Illusions of Law' in *Criminal Obsessions: Why Harm Matters More than Crime*. London: Centre for Crime and Justice Studies.

Tombs, S. and Whyte, D. (2007) *Safety Crimes*. Cullompton: Willan.

UNDP (1994) *Human Development Report 1994*. New York: Oxford University Press.

Westley, W. (2005 [1970]) 'Responsibilities of the Police' in Newburn, T. (ed.) *Policing: Key Readings*. Cullompton: Willan.

White, A. and Gill, M. (2013) 'The transformation of policing: from ratios to rationalities', *British Journal of Criminology*, 53(1): 74–93.

Whyte, D. (2015) 'Policing for whom?', *Howard Journal of Criminal Justice*, 54(1): 73–90.

Winsor, T. (2013) 'Operational Independence and the New Accountability of Policing', John Harris Memorial Lecture to the Police Foundation, 11 July. Available at: www.hmic.gov.uk/media/hmcic-tom-winsor-john-harris-memorial-lecture.pdf [accessed March 2015].

Wood, D. (2014) 'The importance of liberal values within policing: police and crime commissioners, police independence and the spectre of illiberal democracy', *Policing and Society*.

Young, I. M. (2000) *Inclusion and Democracy*. Oxford: Oxford University Press.

10

PARTICIPATORY INNOVATION IN CRIMINAL JUSTICE

Why, how, and how far?

Albert W. Dzur

Criminal justice institutions are both more and less impervious to democratic innovation than they seem at first glance. They are more resistant, despite being legitimated by their service to the public, because of the many ways they repel citizen awareness and involvement: policing, prosecution, adjudication, and imprisonment are largely non-transparent and non-participatory. Nevertheless, the criminal justice system contains different professional cultures, each with access points for innovation as well as normative motivations for reform. Moreover, criminal justice happens in many rooms: alongside the formal courtroom there is the nondescript church hall where a gang truce is settled, the school where a playground conflict is worked on by students themselves, and other quasi-formal settings in which tensions can receive proper hearing and settlement. This chapter describes three such sites of participatory innovation: schools, non-governmental community organizations, and prisons. Drawing from interviews with reformers in each area, it discusses motivations for encouraging citizen participation, barriers to change, and resources available to sustain and expand innovation. While still far from common, these innovative practices help challenge the common normative assumption that criminal justice institutions are inherently undemocratic and must involve coercive power, the systematic imposition of rigid hierarchies, and glaring inequalities throughout the process.

The two faces of institutions

Twenty years ago, Robert Bellah and his colleagues argued that American institutions were marked by serious dysfunction. Their subtle and underappreciated conclusion was that 'democracy means paying attention'. American democracy had not been paying much attention – to the way government, work, and even family structures had become 'corrupt; means have wrongly been turned into ends', in particular the ends of narrow economic success and individual fulfilment (Bellah, 1991: 291). Institutions bring out our best and our worst. They help us form and maintain intimate attachments, produce and deliver goods and services, and enact the very rules we live by. Yet they can also negatively influence how we do these things. If they are saturated by what Marc Stears calls the 'transactional mindset' (2011: 12) of the marketplace, as Bellah et al. believe American institutions are, or by patriarchy and racism, as others argue, the families, jobs and laws we have will be correspondingly affected. Institutions focus our attention, sometimes on the wrong things:

> We live in and through institutions. The nature of the institutions we both inhabit and transform has much to do with our capacity to sustain attention. We could even say that institutions are socially organized forms of paying attention or attending, although they can also, unfortunately, be socially organized forms of distraction.
>
> *(Bellah et al., 1991: 256)*

Bellah et al.'s argument, although rooted in descriptive political sociology, was intended to be normative:

> Because we have let too much of our lives be determined by processes 'going on over our heads,' we have settled for easy measures that have distracted us from what needs to be attended to and cared for. One way of defining democracy would be to call it a political system in which people actively attend to what is significant.
>
> *(Ibid.: 273)*[1]

To see something as an institution is to recognize that it is more than an instrument that serves a fixed purpose but instead is a semiautonomous domain with a history and an organizational density that make it difficult for those outside the domain – or in one corner of it rather than another – to understand. Moreover, an institution works on us even as we work within it and through it; institutions are major forces in our lives.

Sociologists and others who study institutions think of them as stable arrangements that guide action and comport with communal values. 'The function of institutions is always the same,' writes Talcott Parsons, 'the regulation of action in such a way as to keep it in relative conformity with the ultimate common values and value-attitudes of the community' (Parsons, 1990: 331). Institutions emerge to accomplish tasks that would be difficult to manage in a more inchoate or ad hoc fashion, such as to execute and regulate the consequences of norm breaking, but they do so in a way that inevitably reflects the normative commitments of the social order in which they are embedded. 'To institutionalize,' writes Philip Selznick, 'is to infuse with value beyond the technical requirements of the task at hand' (Selznick, 1992: 233). Marriage and family life, the practice of medicine, the meting out of justice, and the education of the next generation, among many other undertakings, are all institutionalized and they all reflect social norms regarding proper relationships, roles and interactions; they exist to make certain actions easier and others harder.

Even though most institutions are public to a degree, in that they are socially embedded, we can differentiate some as *public* institutions when they produce nondivisible common goods such as public safety, are supported by public revenues, and are managed by people held publicly accountable. Private institutions, by contrast, produce private goods – as when a private security force protects only certain individuals, paid for and held accountable primarily to a subgroup, although of course also constrained by the legal system. That an institution is public places a special burden on it to install and heed public procedures of accountability that can determine whether the institution is, in fact, infused with public values.

However, the special burden tends to be rather lightly felt. A persistent theme in the sociology of institutions concerns the way that the rules and offices that impose useful regularity can also conflict with the values intended. Robert Michels' famous study of covert oligarchical tendencies in overtly democratic organizations, for example, pointed to the ways institutional imperatives can lead to delegation of authority and divisions of labour that, in turn, can lead to concentrations of power that violate the values of the groups. 'Who says organization,' Michels wrote, 'says oligarchy' (1962: 365). Michels thought these power-concentrating tendencies of institutions strong enough to call them 'iron laws', although contemporary scholars dispute both their strength and universality (see Blaug, 2010, and Graeber, 2012).[2] Yet even if they are not iron or ever present, the tendencies of institutions to serve internal rather than external purposes are powerful and common enough to pose problems.

Even more troublesome than the chronic potential for institutions to violate their own core values are the barriers institutions place on thought. Because of our own dependence on institutions, it is hard to even see what they are doing. While it is true that institutions are social creations, it is also true that they powerfully shape how we think about them and, indeed, who we are. This is not a matter of nefarious or underhanded or corrupt institutions or power-hungry elites, it is standard operating practice. 'How can we possibly think of ourselves in society,' writes Mary Douglas, 'except by using the classifications established in our institutions?' (1986: 99). 'They fix processes that are essentially dynamic, they hide their influence, and they rouse our emotions to a standardized pitch on standardized issues' (ibid.: 92). This is just what institutions are for: they label, classify and rank order; they think for us. As Douglas puts it, 'The instituted community blocks personal curiosity, organizes public memory, and heroically imposes certainty on uncertainty' (ibid.: 102).

Especially important is how institutions can think for us in ways that extract normative elements and replace them with sheer process, thus deflecting concern for others. They can strip away aspects of human beings that make a person familiar, replacing them with other features that make it harder for those responsible for their welfare inside and outside the institution to recognize and act on that responsibility. Zygmunt Bauman has described the 'management of morality' that can occur in modern institutions through the 'social production of distance, which either annuls or weakens the pressure of moral responsibility', the 'substitution of technical for moral responsibility, which effectively conceals the moral significance of the action', and through 'the technology of segregation and separation, which promotes indifference to the plight of the Other which otherwise would be subject to moral evaluation and morally motivated response' (Bauman, 1989: 199).

What Bauman is concerned about occurs quite straightforwardly in criminal justice institutions. People are distanced from the law-abiding and treated in a technical rather than moral fashion as soon as they are suspects, a process that continues as defendants are given a case number and finally, in some parts of the US, compelled to wear orange jumpsuits and shackles in court. Such management of morality is normal for institutions that handle a large volume of human business: complex men and women turn into *clearances*, *caseloads* and *dockets*. The very 'language in which things happen to them,' writes Bauman, 'safeguards its referents from ethical evaluation' (ibid.: 103). Both linguistic and material forces of separation are even stronger with respect to human beings accused of harming others. By the very accusation they have already become a candidate for expulsion from the warm 'circle of proximity where moral responsibility rules supreme' (ibid.: 195).

Repellent institutions

In addition to doing our thinking for us and shaping how we perceive those they have a hold of, criminal justice institutions repel public examination and participation in three distinct ways. Consider, first, how the work being done is physically removed from both the lay public and the officials not directly involved. Erving Goffman called prisons 'total institutions' because they are separate and complete worlds for those inside; communication and interaction with those outside, indeed even visibility, are all tightly circumscribed and controlled (Goffman, 1962: 4). The work of criminal justice administration, which handles the content of probation orders among other tasks, is normally conducted outside the public by-ways. Courses on 'life skills', 'anger management' and the like are held in mirrored glass or blasé concrete block buildings – sometimes lacking exterior signs communicating what happens inside. The court process leading to prison or probation is decreasingly public and increasingly technocratic. Plea bargaining's dominance means very few public trials: around 1 to 4 per cent of state and federal criminal cases go to trial (Galanter, 2004; Ostrom et al., 2004). Even when there are trials, moreover, a fair number of jurors find them off-putting, convoluted and oddly disempowering (Burnett, 2001).[3]

Criminal justice institutions repel, second, because of their sheer complexity. As Lucia Zedner points out, the common phrase 'criminal justice system' should be resisted 'on the grounds that this label masks its plural, disparate, even chaotic, character' (Zedner, 2010: 71). What is really a 'series of largely independent organizations with differing cultures, professional ethos, and practices' is not easy even for practitioners to come to grips with, much less members of the lay public (ibid.: 72). In his critique of the kind of structured distraction that permitted America's steep rise in incarceration, William Stuntz indicates how the many-handedness of the criminal justice decision-making process thwarted the assessment of responsibility:

> Where state and local officials alike were responsible for rising levels of imprisonment, neither was truly responsible. Prosecutors sent more and more defendants to state prisons in part because state legislators kept building more prison cells ... . For their part, the legislators kept adding to their state's stock of prison beds because local prosecutors kept sending defendants to state prisons: if they're coming, you must build it. Neither set of officials fully controlled the process by which those prison beds were made and filled, so neither was able to slow or reverse that process. And the voters with the lar-gest stake in that process – chiefly African American residents of high-crime city neighborhoods – had the smallest voice in the relevant decisions.
>
> *(Stuntz, 2011: 255)*

Thus, even the officials and professionals involved in specific decisions at one level cannot be said to plan, intend, or even fully comprehend the cumulative institutional consequences of their actions.

Third, and most subtly, criminal justice institutions repel public awareness and involvement because they perform and characterize tasks in ways that neutralize the public's role. It has long been restorative justice doctrine that criminal jus-tice institutions 'steal conflicts' (Christie, 1977: 4) and have 'a monopoly on justice' (Zehr, 1990: 121). These are perhaps only dramatic ways of saying something quite uncontroversial, namely, that institutions take up social problems and grow their budgets and their authority to the extent that they can show that they can do *health care, justice* or *education* better than any alternative mode. Institutions are constantly in competition with non-institutional modes of accomplishing the same goals and thus have a tendency to characterize social problems in the ways that they can manage them. Criminal justice institutions can make it seem that they are the dif-ference between disorder and order, yet they are not. The 'vast majority of crime problems', as Nicola Lacey puts it, are handled through 'social policy and social institutions beyond the criminal process' (2001: 9). Informal social control is far more important than the formal coercive measures criminal justice institutions deliver and yet our public discourse – influenced, of course, by the ways our institutions think for us – construes courts, prisons and probation officers as the active agents and families, neighbourhoods and civil associations as passive recipients of crime control benefits produced by institutions.[4]

Yet perhaps we should just shruggingly acknowledge the ways institutions think and act for us as simply part of modern life. We are surrounded, after all, by complex and quasi-autonomous systems such as financial markets, so why is it surprising or troubling that public institutions are like this as well? Here we must draw a normative distinction between institutions that require greater public scrutiny, challenging and checking and those that do not. Some institutions have clearly defined and uncontroversial objectives, the pursuit of which is easily monitored. Civil engineering agencies that plan and build highways, sewers or airports may not require significant continuous public engagement. Other institutions are charged with tasks that do not have discernible, long-lasting negative effects. The Bureau of Weights and Measures no doubt influences how we count and calculate but does not appear to hold much risk of impairing people's lives. By contrast, it should be obvious that criminal justice institutions lack clearly defined, uncontroversial and easily monitored objectives and at the same time pose enormous risks for impairing human development when operating poorly or unfairly.

Although complex and quasi-autonomous, public institutions cannot function without taxpayer support, operate under the oversight of managers selected by officials elected in free, competitive elections, and purport to deliver non-divisible goods like public safety. Although they are resistant and repellent to public responsibility, they are nevertheless the public's responsibility. To put it plainly, the public needs to be more responsible for the work being done by their institutions not only because of the plural and contested nature of core values pursued by them or because of the potentially severe negative consequences flowing from neglectful or uncaring policies and practices, but also because institutions depend upon the public to function and implicate us in what they do – even if we cannot or will not see it. If we are to have public institutions at all, we must hold ourselves accountable for what they do and for the reasons they do what they do.

My argument for greater citizen participation in criminal justice differs from similar process-orientated arguments that point to the proper groundwork for normative judgements rather than advocating a specific substantive value, in particular those stressing the importance of legitimacy. Legitimacy arguments valorize the normative role of consent: subjects of laws should have a concrete and not abstract or merely symbolic role in authorizing those laws and should understand what they must obey (see Waldron, 2006). Yet behind self-protection stands the broader conception of self-government that I wish to tap: the good of being able to control the powers to which you contribute and which speak and operate in your name. Because of the institutionalization of core dimensions of social action such as criminal justice, citizens are indirect and often unknowing supporters of laws that affect people differently – some well, others poorly; some fairly, others unfairly. Such public ignorance, reinforced by and indeed *produced* by modern institutions, can harm one's own interests to be sure, but what I am pinpointing is the lack of concern for others that it implies. In my view what is problematic is not simply the risk to ourselves of public institutions that we are failing to steer through deliberate choice making, but also the fact that such a diffuse and quasi-autonomous system makes it difficult to hold each other accountable for our laws and the impact of the execution and adjudication of these laws on others not like us.

Institutionally fostered public ignorance makes citizen-beneficiaries collaborationists.

To be clear, my argument is not anti-institution or anti-bureaucracy – 300 million people live in the US after all. It is simply to say that if we have institutions and bureaucracies we must make place for human contact and particularized responsibility. We must learn how to rationally disorganize our way back into our institutions, especially and specifically those most likely to dehumanize and reproduce social inequality. Contemporary penal institutions in particular are characterized by their all too sharply concrete negative effects: shame, degradation, feelings of inferiority, physical suffering, not to mention economic impairment – many of these experienced to some degree too by the spouses and children of the incarcerated. Alongside these negative effects, of course, are the equally troubling racial and socioeconomic biases of the current American system.

Participatory innovations

So, how might we build institutions that help citizens understand a person rather than an offender, and permit a widening of responsibility for tensions and problems rather than letting us rest complacent with standard categories of crime and punishment? Where might we begin to foster this kind of load-bearing participation? One place this could happen is the jury system, which is only barely used today despite constitutional entrenchment and strong public support. The major challenge for reformers in this area is to increase the number of trials by raising the costs of plea bargaining or by otherwise encouraging jury trials. Such changes may deviate from present practice, but they are fully consistent with basic law and the longer span of legal history (for more on this see Dzur, 2012: Chapter 7). I want to focus here, however, on other access points into criminal justice institutions. Indeed, my strategy is to look constructively upon the fragmentation of the system and to suggest the many possibilities for innovation – and invitations to citizen responsibility – it presents.

Criminal justice in many rooms

The photographer Joel Sternfeld travelled the country documenting locations where injustices occurred: murder, vehicular homicide, corporate and political criminality. Here are the camp remains stretched out under the open sky of Cody, Wyoming, where 110,000 Japanese-Americans were imprisoned during World War II; here is the cosy, leafy street in Queens where Kitty Genovese was stabbed to death while 38 bystanders failed to come to her aid or call for help; here is the curve in the Los Angeles highway, winding past a neighbourhood park towards the Angeles National Forest in the distance, a patch of road where Rodney King was pulled over by police officers in 1991 and savagely beaten. Then, at the very end of *On This Site: Landscape in Memoriam*, after the acknowledgements, almost like an afterword and easy to miss, is a simple picture of an unassuming place where justice was made; a flawed place for flawed people.

The room is in a mosque on Central Avenue, in the Watts neighbourhood of Los Angeles, famous for the six-day riot in 1965. A rust-coloured pile carpet covers the floor, two mismatched couches and an overstuffed upholstered chair cluster along one corner in violation of feng shui, an ancient wall heater that looks like a cheese grater runs up one wall, fluorescent lights hum in a stained white sponge-board ceiling – one can almost see divots where bored people have tossed pencils up into it. Three feet below the ceiling, a cord with a dividing cloth wrapped loosely around it is stretched diagonally across the room. The picture, taken at seated eye-level from the far end, draws your eye into the warm barren expanse of rust carpet in the central picture frame. It is an ugly room, a room you want to get out of as soon as possible. But it was here, Sternfeld notes, that the deadly gang rivalry between the Crips and Bloods came to a halt. The deliberation gang leaders held, seated in those grungy couches, eyeing that carpet, listening to the fluorescent lights, saved hundreds of lives in a truce lasting more than a decade.

Rooms like these help us open up a different future. We sit together side by side, we talk, we drink bad coffee, we wait, we listen, we talk some more. It is common to use the words 'meeting' and 'dialogue', but we make things when we meet in rooms like these and talk. We make safer neighbourhoods, we make parents of teenage boys less restless at night, we make emergency rooms and morgues and funeral homes less populated. These dingy rooms are where we find and express our democratic agency, even if we want to linger not on their dusty lumpy furniture gazing out over the rust-coloured carpet. 'Let's do this', I can hear the participants say, together, before eagerly releasing themselves out of the room into the streets made instantly more peaceful.

Community justice

An important site of lay public action is found within restorative justice programmes. Of particular significance are robustly public programmes such as Community Reparative Boards in Vermont, which are staffed by citizen volunteers and hold their meetings in public places like libraries, community centres and town halls. They conduct dialogues with offenders convicted but not sentenced for nonviolent offences like underage drinking, impaired driving and shoplifting. They seek to communicate the meaning of the harm for the victims involved, to determine how to repair damages and how to avoid such action in the future.[5] Other explicitly public programmes in places like Oakland, Baltimore and Brooklyn conduct neighbourhood dialogues heading off conflicts before they become formal offences (Abramson and Moore, 2001; Dzur, 2013).

Lauren Abramson is the founder of the Community Conferencing Center in Baltimore, an organization that aims to divert people from the criminal justice system before they enter it by providing 'a highly participatory community-based process for people to transform their conflicts into cooperation, take collective and personal responsibility for action, and improve their quality of life' (Abramson interviewed in Dzur, 2013). Abramson's centre has helped thousands of people address problems in their communities before they become formally designated as crimes to be handled by the justice system.

Not long ago, Abramson's centre was called on to handle a typical neighbourhood problem. All was not well on Streeper Street in Southeast Baltimore. Kids played football in the road late into the night, bumping into cars, setting off alarms, even breaking mirrors and windows. Why couldn't they play in the park just two blocks away? Were they selling drugs in the street rather than just playing football? Tensions between adult residents and the players escalated into arguments, into hundreds of calls to the police and into petty retaliations such as putting sugar in gas tanks. Finally, when police interventions didn't succeed and the conflict threatened to get more serious than minor property damage, a neighbourhood organization contacted the Community Conferencing Center to arrange a meeting with those affected.

One of the centre's facilitators, Misty, canvassed the neighbourhood for three weeks, going door to door inviting everyone to participate in a conference where they could articulate concerns and contribute to a desirable and workable solution. Remaining neutral, she encouraged attendance by showing them a list of those who had already agreed to participate. In all, 44 people attended, with a mix of adults and youth.

The conference began with angry comments. Parents defended their children against what they felt was unfair treatment by neighbours. In turn, the adult residents expressed their frustration over the late-night noise created by the football games: was this really the best place to play football at night? The children explained that the park two blocks away that the adults thought was much safer than the street was actually fouled by dog waste at one end and inhabited by drug dealers and older bullies at the other; problems that the adults had not heard before. From that point on, the neighbours started brainstorming possible solutions. They shifted focus from what to do about a bunch of noisy young people to how to find a safe place for the neighbourhood children to play. Misty asked people how they might put their solutions into practice and in less than half an hour the group had come to an agreement on a list of actions, such as adults volunteering to chaperone kids in the park and kids helping clean up the neighbourhood.

The next day, in fact, Don Ferges chaperoned 22 kids in the park. By the end of three weeks, the number had grown to 64, and by the end of the summer there was a thriving football league. What started out as a public nuisance warranting police action developed into neighbourhood-wide recognition of common interests and action to improve the space they shared. The residents had the power to make these changes, but it took a well-structured and facilitated conference to deliberate and act together.

As Abramson puts it,

We've defined 'community' as the community of people who have been affected by and involved in the conflict or the crime. Everybody who's involved in or affected by the situation, and their respective supporters, is included. We really widen the circle. Thus, conferences usually include between ten and forty people. The Streeper Street neighbourhood conflict had been going on for two years and 44 people attended. Conferences are always about engaging the entire community of people affected by whatever's going on and giving them the power to try to fix it.

(Ibid.)

Participatory conflict resolution in schools

Another site of participatory innovation is found in schools. Consider a story I call 'Basketball Blowup', which took place in Forest Grove Community School, a public charter school located in a coastal agricultural community in Oregon.[6] During recess some months ago, a group of seventh-grade students were playing basketball. Tensions from inside the classroom were coming out in the game. Two boys were closely guarding another boy, trying to steal the ball by reaching in aggressively. Angered, the boy lashed out and punched one of his opponents.

When the victim's father heard what had happened, he came to Principal Vanessa Gray with an ultimatum: 'Either that boy gets suspended or I am going to call the police and ask them to charge him with assault.' Principal Gray had a different plan. After reassuring the parent, she sought out the basketball players and a group of students who were on the playground and pulled them into her office one by one. As she asked each individually to tell her about what had happened on the court, they all said the same thing. The facts surrounding the basketball blowup were not in dispute.

Principal Gray allowed the victim to go home, sent his teammate back to class and kept the perpetrator in her office for a while to talk. Over the course of their conversation she came to realize that communication was something he needed to work on. Being able to use his voice when problems were mounting and he felt stressed and frustrated was an underdeveloped skill. Telling him she understood his frustration, she also made it clear that it was not acceptable to communicate with his fists. Moreover, Gray took responsibility for her own role in the conflict, acknowledging to the perpetrator that he had come to her earlier in the year to say that basketball games could get overly aggressive.

This is really helpful for me to do a better job of trying to understand what a kid is communicating to me and for you, kid, to learn a little more about how to use your voice. The way you expressed the tensions on the basketball court earlier this school year was in the same tone you use when you tell me that school is boring or you are going skiing this weekend. What you said did not make me concerned that you were angry. And I'm wondering if your way of expressing your frustration with your classmates has also been similarly flat and that you need to work on feeling more comfortable with saying 'Hey I'm upset!', 'I'm mad!', 'I want someone to do something about it!', 'I want someone to work with me on this'.

(Gray interviewed in Dzur, 2014b)

Before sending him home for the day, Gray told him that there were going to be further conversations when he came back to school.

The next day the conferencing began and Principal Gray told the three students that they could not play basketball until they had had a congress with all the basketball players about what the rules were going to be and how they were going to go forward with the game.

I really wanted these three to understand they messed up the basketball game. And I wanted the other basketball players to understand they were bystanders. They knew these tensions were going on a long time before it erupted and before I knew about it. I wanted them to understand they had a responsibility to right a wrong and there are lots of ways for them to do it.

(Ibid.)

Rather than sealing off a problem, attributing blame to a specific central actor and taking ownership of it as a simple disciplinary matter for the administration to take care of, Principal Gray did four things: she made the problem public; she had conversations with everyone involved; she spread out responsibility for the conflict, herself included; and she empowered everyone involved – including bystanders and others in the school – to figure out ways of creating more peaceful basketball games at recess. Yes, there was an offence that happened that should not have, and yes there was an offender and a victim. But the participatory process Gray used focused on the relationships that were causing tension, and that focus allowed her to help students themselves play a bigger role in solving the problem by working on the skills that would help them to have better relationships in the future.

Just like the citizens involved with Lauren Abramson's community justice centre, Forest Grove Community School students are learning – by doing – important lessons in how to work and live together. Like Abramson, Gray is introducing people as far as they are capable into an institutional field of self-government. Her school is fostering a more deliberative and more collaborative mode of being together through *everyday* routines performed by students, teachers and administrators who refuse to let themselves be captured by conventional assumptions about disciplinary order being dependent on institutional hierarchies. Civic engagement is not a free-standing class or a subject area in this school, nor is it an extracurricular activity; it pervades the culture of the playground, the library, the hallways, the assembly rooms, the school garden and the principal's office.

Prisons as sites of public awareness

Another place of participatory innovation is the prison. While there are obviously severe limits placed on the kind of lay citizen involvement permitted, there are also many ways in to these restrictive environments. Prison education programmes like Inside-Out, which links college and university teachers and students with groups of current prisoners, do more than provide educational opportunities for prisoners. They create spaces of public dialogue about prison life and, more generally, about the reality of punishment. Over fifty Inside-Out programmes exist across the US, in 60 prisons, in 25 states. More than 10,000 people have taken these credit-bearing courses, which bring 15 to 18 college students together with the same number of prisoners for a few hours every week for one semester. They participate as fellow members of the same class, usually focused on issues of criminal justice, and work together on a class project. Other arrangements between universities and prisons have emerged organically, using the Inside-Out model as just a starting point.

Lisa Guenther, a philosopher at Vanderbilt University, has held reading groups in a maximum security prison in Nashville with six graduate student 'outsiders' and ten 'insiders' who are prisoners, including some on death row.[7] The small size of the group and its meeting schedule were established through negotiation with the prison administration. Guenther's group engages in wide-ranging discussions driven largely by prisoners' interests. Last year they read Plato's dialogues concerning the trial and punishment of Socrates, which became a way of talking about the prison experience that otherwise would have been difficult.

> They were really good and interesting discussions, and it also helped to mediate the situation so we weren't talking about prison in some kind of stark direct way. That can turn into a kind of voyeuristic situation where the insiders are expected to be experts on suffering in prison and the outsiders, who know little or nothing about prison, go to them to be educated. Weird power dynamics can unfold in a situation where you bring together people who often have very different economic, racial, gender social positions and also different levels of formal education. Everything we do is about negotiating that terrain and trying to create and recreate the space for meaningful conversation through and across these chasms of social inequality. You cannot undo inequality by just having the best intentions to treat everyone as a singular human being. You really have to work at creating the situation in which a conversation can happen and keep happening. Plato helped in ways I had not anticipated to open up a situation where we have a third term in the room. We all had the character of Socrates to look at and to talk about and we could bring different insights or different perspectives to bear on that third term.
>
> *(Guenther interviewed in Dzur, 2015)*

Connections made between the reading group and the prison catalysed further outside work, such as an art show held on campus exhibiting work done by the prisoners in the group, campus workshops and conferences related to mass incarceration, as well as community organizing on the death penalty. Here, too, prisoners have helped shape an agenda.

We develop a kind of activist practice within the group focused on issues that have been identified by the insiders as of central importance to them.

> One of the extraordinary things to me is that abolishing the death penalty was definitely not first on their list. The issues that everyone agrees are the most important are medical care – or lack thereof – and the school-to-prison pipeline, so broad-based social transformations such that kids would not be funneled into the prison system, and not end up in a place like they are.
>
> *(Ibid.)*

It is a slow, long-term strategy, aiming not at electoral politics but 'the level of the demos understood as people, socially situated, with broad, intersectional concerns' (ibid.).

William DiMascio, as head of the Pennsylvania Prison Society, has experimented with a different kind of participatory innovation. DiMascio has organized deliberative forums involving visitors and prisoners in every prison in the state. These forums involve moderated small-group dialogue about possible choices on current issues such as social security, health care policy and school violence, which are laid out in nonpartisan booklets published by the National Issues Forums Institute.

> In Spring 2013 we held a deliberative forum training session at the State Correctional Institute at Huntingdon, Pennsylvania. We trained eight life sentenced prisoners and eight outside guests – a professor and students from Juniata College and four members of the Prison Society chapter of prison visitors. Our intention was manifold: first, we wanted to get forums going in the prison; second, we wanted to have our chapter trained so they could help reluctant prison administrators to see the interest and value in permitting the forums to take place; and third, to stimulate interest in public deliberation on the campus.
>
> *(DiMascio interviewed in Dzur, 2014a)*

As with Guenther's reading group, one purpose of DiMascio's deliberative forum is empowerment. Here, within the space of a moderated group discussion, you have the freedom to form your own opinion on something, to express it to others, and shape an ongoing group discussion. After a first round of forums, which DiMascio spearheaded, prisoners in a number of prisons requested further sessions.

> There is a thirst, if you will, to be heard, to be relevant, to feel like people can engage with them, people are interested in hearing what their opinions are. And this is something they are deprived of, for the most part, while they are in prison. You know the steel bars and the big fences and all really cannot

prevent that quite natural human desire. So I think that is why they requested them. My goal is to begin to bring marginalized men and women back into a society where their thoughts and feelings are heard.

(Ibid.)

Prison life is 'day in and day out, a pretty dismal and boring existence – one that really reinforces the lack of humanity in everybody who is there', notes DiMascio. 'I have always been taken by the fact that in visiting with different inmates I met some positively brilliant minds. And yet they live in this intellectual wasteland' (ibid.).

While only contingently achieved because of prison administration reluctance, DiMascio's deliberative forums show the possibility of creating a platform for discussion that can regularly bring lay citizens in to local prisons to share experiences and engage in dialogue with prisoners. Such circulation of people and ideas serves the simple but also very difficult goal of responsibilization: placing one in the position of taking responsibility for what one thinks and does. By becoming involved, lay citizens can learn indirectly about the causes and consequences of crime and punishment and achieve sobriety about incarceration.

I believe that people would see what they do not seem to want to see if they would begin to accept responsibility for what our criminal justice system is doing. The failed system has cost untold millions of dollars. I do not think people realize generally that the system operates the way it does.

(Ibid.)

Participatory innovation is thus something that has both the exceedingly long-term goal of public awareness but also the concrete, short-term objective of improving well-being one participant at a time. Prisoners coming to make choices about what to read, how to focus their thinking, and how to argue are active citizens in the republic of ideas even as their civic agency is otherwise severely hampered. This is a democratic education in one of the least democratic places imaginable.

Conclusion: barriers and openings

Now the sobering point: community justice organizations, democratic schools, prison-college programmes and deliberative forums in prison are the exception rather than the rule in the current American institutional environment. They fly in the face of counter-democratic pressures: bureaucratic demands for efficiency, cost-control and clear chains of command; legal constraints that carve out specific zones of authority and responsibility; and economic incentives to assert what sociologist Andrew Abbott (1988) calls 'jurisdictional control' over certain problems, issues and tasks. All of these elements, displayed in the left-hand columns of Table 10.1, operate as powerful barriers to democratic agency.

TABLE 10.1 Barriers and openings for participatory institutions

Barriers	Openings
Jurisdictional claims of professions	Wicked cross-profession problems
Authority/responsibility/obligation	Division of labour/shared responsibility
Expertise	Local/social knowledge
Hierarchy/efficiency	Release of individual and group capacity

Yet my research indicates that practitioners find opportunities for change, and necessary resources and allies as well. Wicked problems such as crime and punishment, which admit no unidimensional expert response, can prompt otherwise risk-averse professionals to collaborate with community members.[8] Abramson's community justice centre is recognized by many in the Baltimore police and the Maryland judiciary as a practical and economically efficient alternative to the traditional process. Fixed and centralized government authority is given a reason to relax when participatory processes yield results by using local problem-solving knowledge. Hierarchy in schools, when counterproductive in nurturing the love of inquiry, as many democratic teachers and principals have discovered, can also loosen its organizational hold. More generally, widespread resentment of invasive, autonomy-threatening managerialism among skilled professionals motivates strategically useful allies in democratic culture change.[9]

Worth noting, too, as a strategic advantage, is how the participatory democracy these practitioners are enacting at the local and institutional level can improve lives immediately because it does not depend on the lengthy grinding of legal or political machinery. Children in more participatory schools, neighbours taking part in inclusionary community justice efforts and prisoners enabled by deliberative forums to interact as citizens can improve their well-being at the very moment they conduct their work. Their collaborative, reflective and, at times, load-bearing work can be, itself, a valuable end result.

Participatory innovation does not just happen naturally; it is part of a quiet struggle going on inside fairly closed institutions. In American education, for example, student participation in norm setting and adjudication is 'counter-normative'.[10] Much more common is the top-down approach of the principal applying the rule and meting out a sanction. The ongoing struggle between these modes comes to the surface in debates over the hardening of school disciplinary sanctions against student norm-breakers and in discussions of alternative procedures such as restorative justice. Seemingly microscopic, trivial, and all too local from the perspective of grand theory, these are the small battles, I think, that will define future institutions as fields of self-government or will continue to reproduce the repellent status quo. Thus, I think more attention should be paid to what might sustain and encourage people like Vanessa Gray, Lisa Guenther, William DiMascio and other innovators who are on the inside of institutions making them more reflective and participatory.

It is commonplace to assert against arguments like mine that widespread lay participation is somehow too 'pure' or 'utopian' for the real world of hetero-geneous publics and complex policy problems. I think this is exactly wrong. In fact, I have found that appeals to collaboration and efforts to substantively deploy public forums frequently occur when the going gets tough for city managers, school district leaders and police chiefs. They find, in times of crisis, that rationally disorganized institutions are the way to regain public trust after a budget shortfall, police shooting, or school performance failure. It is the expert institution, sealed off from the public it is meant to serve, that is too pure for this modern world. Partici-patory innovators may be utopian, but they are also realists; they know the huma-nizing practices they seek to bring into currently closed and repellent institutional spaces are desperately needed in the real world.

Notes

1 Ironically, but also in keeping with their thesis that contemporary institutions distract, Bellah et al. do not discuss criminal justice institutions even though at the time of writing America had begun its steep mass imprisonment trajectory.
2 Blaug convincingly argues that conventional treatments of organizations in Michels and elsewhere have mistakenly naturalized hierarchy and have failed to capture its destabi-lizing and nonfunctional characteristics. Graeber provides a similar argument about Weberian bureaucracy's feet of clay.
3 Burnett's experience was bureaucratic and disempowering, but note that the large-scale survey research of Gastil et al. (2010) found jurors more likely to have a positive civic experience when they deliberate more, when the case they are adjudicating is complex – the more of a load they are expected to bear, and when they are treated well by the court.
4 As Zedner puts it, 'to assume that crime control is the prerogative of criminal justice agents and institutions obscures the role played in controlling crime by informal sources and institutions of social order – not least the family, the school, religious institutions, and the community. Such ability as criminal justice institutions have to tackle crime relies heavily upon these informal sources of order and their interdependent relationship with them' (2010: 73).
5 For more on the Vermont programme, see Karp, 2001, and also Dzur, 2008, especially Chapter 6.
6 This story is based on an interview with Vanessa Gray. See Dzur, 2014a.
7 Guenther's discussion group is strictly voluntary and is not a credit-bearing course affiliated with a university.
8 On the pressures contemporary wicked problems place on professionals to open up their practices to citizen participation, see Levine, 2013: 4–10.
9 See Stears, 2011, for more on increasing resentment of managerialism.
10 This is Dana Mitra's assertion, after studying the ways schools routinely and pervasively suppress what she calls 'student voice'. See, e.g., Mitra, 2008.

References

Abbott, A. (1988) *The System of Professions: An Essay on the Division of Expert Labor*. Chicago, IL: University of Chicago Press.

Abramson, L. and Moore, D. B. (2001) 'Transforming Conflict in the Inner City: Community Conferencing in Baltimore', *Contemporary Justice Review*, 4(3/4): 321–340.

Bauman, Z. (1989) *Modernity and the Holocaust.* London: Polity.

Bellah, R., Madsen, R., Sullivan, W. M., Swidler, A. and Tipton, S. M. (1991) *The Good Society.* New York: Knopf.

Blaug, R. (2010) *How Power Corrupts: Cognition and Democracy in Organisations.* London: Macmillan.

Burnett, D. G. (2001) *A Trial by Jury.* New York: Vintage.

Christie, N. (1977) 'Conflicts as Property', *British Journal of Criminology*, 17(1): 1–15.

Douglas, M. (1986) *How Institutions Think.* Syracuse, NY: Syracuse University Press.

Dzur, A. (2008) *Democratic Professionalism: Citizen Participation and the Reconstruction of Professional Ethics, Identity, and Practice.* University Park, PA: Penn State University Press.

Dzur, A. (2012) *Punishment, Participatory Democracy, and the Jury.* New York: Oxford University Press.

Dzur, A. (2013) 'Trench Democracy in Criminal Justice #1: An Interview with Lauren Abramson', *Boston Review*, 13 December. Available at: www.bostonreview.net/blog/a lbert-w-dzur-trench-democracy-criminal-justice-interview-lauren-abramson.

Dzur, A. (2014a) 'Trench Democracy in Criminal Justice #2: An Interview with William DiMascio', *Boston Review*, 16 May. Available at: www.bostonreview.net/blog/albert-w-d zur-trench-democracy-criminal-justice-2-interview-william-dimascio.

Dzur, A. (2014b) 'Trench Democracy in Schools #3: An Interview with Vanessa Gray', *Boston Review*, 11 July. Available at: www.bostonreview.net/blog/albert-w-dzur-trench-democracy-schools-3-vanessa-gray.

Dzur, A. (2015) 'Teaching Philosophy on Death Row: An Interview with Lisa Guenther', *Boston Review*, 26 June. Available at: http://bostonreview.net/blog/albert-dzur-trench-democracy-philosophy-death-row-lisa-guenther.

Galanter, M. (2004) 'The Vanishing Trial: An Examination of Trials and Related Matters in Federal and State Courts', *Journal of Empirical Legal Studies*, 1(3): 459–570.

Gastil, J. E., Deess, P., Weiser, P. J. and Simmons, C. (2010) *The Jury and Democracy: How Jury Deliberation Promotes Civic Engagement and Political Participation.* New York: Oxford University Press.

Goffman, E. (1962) *Asylums: Essays on the Social Situation of Mental Patients and Other Inmates.* Chicago, IL: Aldine.

Graeber, D. (2012) 'Dead Zones of the Imagination: On Violence, Bureaucracy, and Interpretive Labor', *HAU: Journal of Ethnographic Theory*, 2(2): 105–128.

Karp, D. (2001) 'Harm and Repair: Observing Restorative Justice in Vermont', *Justice Quarterly*, 18: 727–757.

Lacey, N. (2001) 'Social Policy, Civil Society and the Institutions of Criminal Justice', *Australian Journal of Legal Philosophy*, 26(4): 7–25.

Levine, P. (2013) *We Are the Ones We Have Been Waiting For: The Promise of Civic Renewal in America.* New York: Oxford University Press.

Michels, R. (1962) *Political Parties: A Sociological Study of the Oligarchical Tendencies of Modern Democracy.* Glencoe: Free Press.

Mitra, D. (2008) *Student Voice in School Reform: Building Youth-Adult Partnerships that Strengthen Schools and Empower Youth.* Albany, NY: SUNY Press.

Ostrom, B. J., Strickland, S. M. and Hannaford-Agor, P. L. (2004) 'Examining Trial Trends in State Courts: 1976–2002', *Journal of Empirical Legal Studies*, 1(3): 764–770.

Parsons, T. (1990) 'Prolegomena to a Theory of Social Institutions', *American Sociological Review*, 55(3): 319–333.

Selznick, P. (1992) *The Moral Commonwealth: Social Theory and the Promise of Community.* Berkeley: University of California Press.

Stears, M. (2011) *Everyday Democracy: Taking Centre-Left Politics beyond State and Market.* London: Institute for Public Policy Research.

Stuntz, W. J. (2011) *The Collapse of American Criminal Justice.* Cambridge MA: Harvard University Press.

Waldron, J. (2006) 'The Core of the Case against Judicial Review', *Yale Law Journal*, 115: 1345–1406.

Zedner, L. (2010) 'Reflections on Criminal Justice as a Social Institution', in *The Eternal Recurrence of Crime and Control: Essays in Honour of Paul Rock*, ed. D. Downes, D. Hobbs, and T. Newburn. London: Oxford University Press.

Zehr, H. (1990) *Changing Lenses: A New Focus for Criminal Justice.* Scottdale, PA: Herald Press.

AFTERWORD

Justice in modernity

Nils Christie

FIGURE A.1 Lady Justice

Here she is: Lady Justice. We can find her at the entrances of many courts and she can also be found in sculptures and paintings. She carries the scales of justice and, being blindfolded, she is free from any undue influence or distraction. She communicates important symbolic messages. And, once inside the court, more is to follow. With some luck we might find the room for the proceedings and also a seat. We may even feel able to relax for a while in this 'foreign territory' until the door in front of us opens and the judge(s) enter(s), often in colourful gowns. We all stand up. When the judge(s) are seated, we too can sit down again. A ceremony of grandeur: they, above us all.

Once upon a time much of this was highly needed. And it still is, in some settings. When *The Emperor* and those close to him were almighty, Lady Justice was essential to settle any conflicts that might emerge between them. This was also the case when the bourgeoisie gained influence. But now?

Welfare states have emerged and consolidated in large parts of Europe. Such states claim they are there to satisfy the needs of *all* citizens and especially those in need of welfare in all situations. But, and this is the simple question I wish to raise here, has Lady Justice seen to it that similar universal welfare ideals prevail within penal institutions? Maybe it is time to move Lady Justice for a while, from the entrances of the courts to the gates of some of our major prisons.

New equipment for Lady Justice

But if Lady Justice were to be moved to the gates of prisons, we would have to equip her differently. In particular, we would need to remove her blindfold so that she could see what sort of people were entering the prisons. She would soon observe that those arriving as prisoners were nearly all from the same social class, and enduring poverty at the bottom of society.

Study after study of prison populations in modern western societies persistently produce similar results and conclusions, aptly communicated in the title of a recent postgraduate thesis: 'Too much of nothing' (Thorsen, 2004). Too much of unemployment, too much of divorce and absent family ties, too much of miserable housing conditions. And, we might add, too much of minority ethnic status. Loïc Wacquant (2009) captures such phenomena succinctly with the title of his book: *Punishing the Poor*.

This has, of course, always characterized modern penal practices. The rich and powerful operate with relative impunity while the poor and miserable are routinely held to account. Paradoxically this is especially accentuated in societies that claim to be 'welfare' states: 'more pain to the poor!' Not the most attractive banner for the penal systems of welfare states!

As noted, such states are supposed to provide welfare for all, but their penal systems represent an anachronism in paying insufficient attention to the primary significance of social class. In particular, poverty is typically overlooked in any deliberations concerning mitigating factors when punishment is dispensed. The notion that you don't hit a person who is already down is deeply embedded in our moral sensibilities. But such thinking, and welfare discourse more broadly, has been excluded from the courts and penal institutions.

Standing at the prison gates Lady Justice might also have to lay down another piece of equipment. Surrounded by prison guards she would have no need for the sword in her right hand. Instead she might take hold of a microphone to report on her findings: 'They are poor and miserable and this ought to form a major consideration if they are sentenced to receive even more pain.'

Given this, how might penal policy and practice be reformulated in welfare states worth the name?

My basic response to this question is: let us invite welfare into the court when punishment is to be decided upon. Many among those awaiting sentence have had a miserable life from the very beginning and 'witnesses' might be invited to submit 'evidence': school friends and teachers, family members of all sorts, not least favourite aunts. Furthermore, functionaries from the range of welfare agencies might be expected to explain their negligence. If the 'offender' lived on the street and was without work, for example, why was his/her housing situation and unemployment not put right? How could she/he have been left behind in this misery? What sort of help had she/he received? Court practice such as this might function as a constant reminder to the system of pressing and enduring unmet needs. Instead of functioning in a way that legitimizes the system of social service, removes 'troublemakers' and conceals deficiencies through the imprisonment of unsolved needs, this alternative court practice would serve to expose weaknesses in the welfare system. In doing so, the exposure might function as a driving force for progressive reform of the welfare system itself.

This line of reasoning does not necessarily lead to a total rejection of all forms of punishment. But, and this is the major point, in welfare states utmost care is required when the extent and nature of punishment is to be decided. People who, by circumstances in life, have suffered more than most others, must be offered compassion and understanding when they encounter those vested with the power to deliver pain.

'They could have been my children'

At the same time, a thorough examination of the biographical circumstances of the person to be punished might also serve to convert the simple image of a 'criminal' to a picture of 'a full human being'.

We know, from personal life experiences in addition to scientific research, that the closer we come to people who have broken the law, the less attractive the delivery of pain becomes as an appropriate response.

We had an interesting illustration of this phenomenon in Norway some time back. A relatively high-profile politician was well known for his stern attitudes and lack of lenient sentiments. But then he was to function as a lay judge and he was confronted with a case involving three young 'delinquents'. The newspapers had reported that their behaviour was particularly problematic and a stern sentence was expected, but, in actual fact, the three youngsters received the most lenient sentences imaginable in the circumstances. Bewildered journalists flocked around the politician and asked if he had changed his views on penal policy. Oh no, absolutely not. 'Delinquent' youngsters deserve stern punishments he maintained. But these three – who were completely unknown to him before he met them in court – were not of that 'sort'. Deep down these were 'good boys': 'they could have been my children!'

Here lies a central challenge for penal reform in welfare states. We have to resist the anonymity created by modernity. We have to create social systems where we see each other as full human beings and where we can evaluate human acts in full social context. But this is a complex task to accomplish and it appears to be at odds with the prevailing mood of our time.

The fruits of modernity

We have a tradition in my country, Norway. Each New Year evening our prime minister appears on radio and TV with wishes for a happy new year, followed by some political reflections. A central topic of these short speeches has regularly been the need for further development of the country. No stagnation, we have to move on! It is as if we are on a train in a beautiful landscape – a good country, well run – but nonetheless, we have to see to it that we do not stand still, we must always move on, develop the land, the districts, the towns and, not least, ourselves.

But such developmental progress has a twin sister. Her name is mobility. And mobility serves to dissolve social networks and human interactions. We 'develop' and 'progress' from living in tight-knit, stable communities to looser and more fluid ones. Poets might write about the blessings of open landscapes. Sociologists are, rightly so, more concerned about empty social landscapes, societies without cohesion or, even worse, societies where we don't know one another. Neighbours, fellow students, colleagues, potential friends or wrongdoers – they are, in many ways, foreign to us in some forms of modernity. Classical accounts are provided by George Homans (1951) and Robert Putnam (2000). Trains and cars have changed social life, you can move in and out of your community, you belong everywhere, and nowhere. Or you can retreat into privacy,[1] away from neighbours and they from you. Virtual communication prevails. Sherry Turkle (2011) analyses this in her book *Alone Together*. And then, what has become so clearly brought into focus by Richard Wilkinson and Kate Pickett (2010) and by Thomas Piketty (2014), economic distance between social classes widens and it increasingly becomes more and more difficult to 'feel', know and understand those who are either far above or far below us.

Centralized ignorance

Modernity is also increasingly characterized by large centralized bureaucracies, organizations and institutions. Modern medicine, for example, has spawned a flora of specialities claiming they need to be based together in the same institution and under a monolithic administration. This, it is claimed, will provide more effective, more efficient and more economical services to the population. The small, local hospital disappears as a consequence, eaten by the mastodons.

The same trend can be found in all public services. Increasing centralization is to be found in social services and policing. The old sheriff – the 'lensmann' we called him in Norway – who was obliged to live in the district in which he functioned is soon gone. He knew those he lived among, and they knew him. But he is now little more than a functionary among a multitude of other functionaries in a huge centralized police station, far removed from his original district. Local knowledge disappears, those who would have known the story of that strange, drunk, threatening man are no longer consulted. Instead, a police officer in a car arrives and takes him away and the man receives his standardized punishment according to the tariff.

This trend toward centralization is also evident in the courts. In Norway, we have at present 66 courts in the country. The goal is to reduce this to 20. Small districts are to be merged with other small districts or else absorbed within larger cities. Large courts create a community of judges, colleagues who can help each other, learn from each other and meet as equals in and out of court. This, it is claimed, will create competence at a high level. But there are costs involved. In this situation, judges will become more insular and distant; living most of their professional and social lives with other judges or, as a minimum, they will associate with other highly educated professionals. But they will lose time and interest for social interactions with a myriad of other people in the districts.

The story of Per and Ole is illustrative. The two men had always quarrelled – as had their fathers – about a wooden fence that separated their two farms. According to Per, the father of Ole had one dark night moved the fence several feet to his advantage. But, according to Ole, this was because Per owed him money that he had never repaid. At a funeral attended by both men, Per struck Ole, knocking out two of his teeth. The new police chief in the modernized, reorganized and enlarged police district did not know either Per or Ole, nor the tradition behind their quarrels. He imposed a severe fine on Per for assaulting Ole. Of course, Per refused to pay. Accordingly, the new judge in the equally modernized, reorganized and enlarged court district was also unfamiliar with the longstanding quarrel and sentenced Per to 30 days in the new centralized prison in Oslo!

Against progress

Progressive penal policy strategies seem to me to contain elements of regression. It appears to be necessary to re-establish forms of social organization so that people will relearn to see and know each other as full social beings and to exercise reciprocal forms of socialization and social control.

In Germany I once came across a postcard with a central message. An image of two strict-looking women meeting in a street appeared over the text: 'The good Lord sees everything, but the neighbours see much more'.

With crime prevention in mind, neighbourhoods ought to be strengthened and democratized to become places where local people engage and participate. We currently have 428 municipalities in Norway. The authorities are planning to reduce this number to 98. Conversely, I want the number of municipalities to increase and, in particular, to split our few large cities into several independent communes, enabling ordinary people to participate with their neighbours to create functioning and sustainable social systems.

And of course, local courts ought to be preserved and, if necessary, increased in number in order that they might serve their local neighbourhoods. The same with police services and stations.

For these tasks, we need the assistance of Lady Justice. After her observations at the prison gates, she ought to move inside the doors of the city halls and say:

Der liebe Gott sieht alles -
und die Nachbarn noch viel mehr.

FIGURE A.2 'The good Lord sees everything, but the neighbours see much more'
Source: © Jürgen Siegmann.

It seems to me that the basic ideas of welfare states have not penetrated our institutions of penal law. Most of the people I observe moving in and out of prisons are miserable people living under exactly the conditions our welfare state was created to prevent. Their failure in life is a reflection of our failure in realizing our ideals of welfare for all.

★ ★ ★

Broken windows are not the best indicators of a neighbourhood in need of crime prevention. Locked doors everywhere, between apartments as well as humans, tell more about the urgent need for progressive change.

Acknowledgement

Thanks to Hedda Giertsen (Oslo) for inspiration and useful comments, and also to Sebastian Scheerer (Bremen) for important clarifications.

Note

1 The concept 'privacy' has its root in 'priver', the Latin word for 'deprived', one who has lost the benefits of participating in the important arenas; the public life.

References

Homans, G. C. (1951) *The Human Group*. London: Routledge & Kegan Paul.

Picketty, T. (2014) *Capital in the Twenty-First Century*. Cambridge, MA: Harvard University Press.

Putnam, R. D. (2000) *Bowling Alone: The Collapse and Revival of American Community*. New York: Simon & Schuster.

Thorsen, L. R. (2004) *For mye av ingenting (Too much of nothing)*. Unpublished thesis. Oslo: University of Oslo.

Turkle, S. (2011) *Alone Together: Why We Expect More from Technology and Less from Each Other*. New York: Basic Books.

Wacquant, L. (2009) *Punishing the Poor: The Neoliberal Government of Social Insecurity*. Durham, NC: Duke University Press.

Wilkinson, R. and Pickett, K. (2010) *The Spirit Level: Why Equality is Better for Everyone*. London: Penguin Books.

ABOUT THE HOWARD LEAGUE FOR PENAL REFORM

The Howard League for Penal Reform is a national charity working for less crime, safer communities and fewer people in prison. It is the oldest penal reform charity in the world. It was established in 1866 and is named after John Howard, the first prison reformer.

We work with parliament and the media, with criminal justice professionals, researchers and members of the public, influencing debate and forcing through meaningful change to create safer communities.

The Howard League for Penal Reform has a strong and long history of working alongside the academic and research communities. A guiding principle of our work has been to develop new ideas and understanding of the consequences of changes and innovations in the penal system.

We campaign on a wide range of issues including short-term prison sentences, real work in prison, community sentences and youth justice.

Our legal team provides free, independent and confidential advice, assistance and representation on a wide range of issues to young people under 21 who are in prisons or secure children's homes and centres.

By becoming a member you will give us a bigger voice and give vital financial support to our work. We cannot achieve real and lasting change without your help.

Please visit www.howardleague.org and join today.

INDEX